Navigating Choppy Waters

Navigating Choppy Waters

Key Legal Issues College Faculty Need to Know

Kent Kauffman

ROWMAN & LITTLEFIELD
Lanham • Boulder • New York • London

Published by Rowman & Littlefield
An imprint of The Rowman & Littlefield Publishing Group, Inc.
4501 Forbes Boulevard, Suite 200, Lanham, Maryland 20706
www.rowman.com

86-90 Paul Street, London EC2A 4NE

This book is not intended to be the giving of legal advice or as a substitute for seeking legal counsel.

British Library Cataloguing in Publication Information available

Library of Congress Cataloging-in-Publication Data on File

ISBN 978-1-5381-9728-8 (cloth : alk. Paper)
ISBN 978-1-5381-9729-5 (pbk. : alk. Paper)
ISBN 978-1-5381-9730-1 (electronic)

♾™ The paper used in this publication meets the minimum requirements of American National Standard for Information Sciences—Permanence of Paper for Printed Library Materials, ANSI/NISO Z39.48-1992.

Dedication

One special privilege of having a book published is that you get to write a dedication. So, once again, I want to tell my wife, Karen, and our son, Reagan, how forever blessed I am to be in the ambit of your remarkable lives. To paraphrase the words of the apostle Paul, I give thanks whenever I think of you.

Contents

Acknowledgments

This book would not have been possible without the insight and effort from the following persons, whose contributions should be recognized.

John Bond, of Riverwinds Consulting, offered the pivotal expertise that helped take my idea and working paper for a manuscript like this and develop it into a fully realized book proposal. His forthright and astute counsel was integral to launching this project.

Purdue University Fort Wayne awarded me the sabbatical that allowed me to write a significant portion of this book. My former dean, Melissa Gruys, and my current dean, Nodir Adilov, have always provided encouraging and thoughtful leadership for which I am especially grateful, professionally and personally.

Nathan Davidson, Executive Acquisitions Editor at Rowman & Littlefield, read my book proposal and reached out to me with enthusiasm. Our conversations and his vision for this book were crucial to my choice of publisher. Working with Nathan has been a pleasure. My gratitude extends to Assistant Acquisitions Editor Hollis Peterson, for doing what was needed to make a book out of my manuscript. And thank you to those who consented to review my book proposal and chapters for Rowman & Littlefield. Thank you also to Crystal Branson, Associate Production Editor, and her team, including Alison Browdie, Copyeditor, for their outstanding efforts.

I am very thankful for the insights and commentary provided by those who participated in manuscript reviews:

Naomi Gurevich, PhD, Associate Professor of Communication Sciences & Disorders, Purdue University Fort Wayne

Deborah Hoffman, JD, Visiting Assistant Professor of Law, Cleveland State University
Christine Marcuccilli, JD, Title IX Director and Coordinator of Compliance, Purdue University Fort Wayne
Kimberly O'Connor, JD, Professor of Law and Associate Vice Chancellor of Teaching and Learning, Purdue University Fort Wayne
Brad Oliver, EdD, Clinical Associate Professor of Educational Leadership, Purdue University Fort Wayne
Danielle Osmelak, EdD, Assistant Professor of Communication Disorders, Governors State University
Carolyn Stumph, PhD, Clinical Assistant Professor of Economics, Purdue University Fort Wayne
Heather Tierney, PhD, Associate Professor of Economics, Purdue University Fort Wayne
Georgia Wralstad Ulmschneider, JD, Associate Professor of Political Science (retired), Purdue University Fort Wayne
Lesa Rae Vartanian, PhD, Associate Professor of Psychology, Purdue University Fort Wayne
Yvonne Zubovic, PhD, Associate Professor of Mathematical Science, Purdue University Fort Wayne

Their careful attention to content, clarity, and tone served as a refiner's fire and a polishing tumbler.

Rachel Ramsey, PhD, Assistant Director of Faculty Teaching Development at the Purdue University Fort Wayne Center for the Enhancement of Learning and Teaching (CELT) deserves a special note of appreciation. From the beginning of this project, she performed many valuable roles, including sounding board, researcher, editor, coordinator, and all-around gap-filler. Thankfully, Adam Dircksen, the Purdue University Fort Wayne CELT Executive Director, who has graciously supported my efforts through the years at acquainting faculty with many of the book's topics, said yes to my request to rely on Rachel's unique talents in bringing this book to bear.

Finally, I owe a debt of gratitude to the faculty who for many years have given their valuable time to attend my workshops and presentations on various subjects in this book. Their willingness to explore the benefits of viewing their teaching and scholarship through a legal lens, and their responses to the post-presentation surveys, were motivating.

Introduction

Who—beside yourself—really cares about you, professionally? Is there someone you believe is on your side, whom you can turn to for help when you need it at work? Someone who understands enough about what it means to be a college or graduate faculty member that you have confidence in his or her advice? One who will keep those discussions confidential? If so, I hope that person is also a lawyer, because navigating legal issues in higher education may be outside the wheelhouse of even the most seasoned mentor. And if you don't have any legal questions about what you've faced in your teaching and scholarship, then you might be in your first semester or have lived quite a charmed life.

Why, you might be thinking, would one need a book on legal issues faculty are likely to face? If you experience something related to your teaching or scholarship that requires legal expertise, couldn't you just take those legal questions or concerns to your human resources (HR) department or its lawyer, if it has one? Yes, but I'd point you to a 2021 study discussed in the *Harvard Business Review*, showing employees would rather reach out to anyone other than their HR departments when they have concerns about their jobs.[1] Until now, the literature has offered little help to faculty with legal questions. Much has been written for decades on the scholarship of teaching and learning (SoTL), including how college faculty can be more impactful in their teaching or increase their students' success. There are education-law textbooks that focus principally on teaching legal concepts for those who want to be primary- or secondary-school administrators. But there are few (if any) resources for faculty that address their concerns or help them think about their professional endeavors from a legal perspective.

This book is written for you—whether you're a part-time instructor at a two-year college (like I was); whether you're a tenure-track professor at a university (like I was) or whether you're tenured (as I am); whether you work at a public university (as I do) or a private college (as I've done), including an Ivy League institution (I have not). According to the National Center for Education Statistics, whose statistics include data through 2021, there were 3,931 degree-granting post-secondary institutions in the 2020–2021 academic year: 1,587 were public institutions and 2,344 were private institutions.[2] And, as of 2022, the number of college faculty or instructors was over 1.5 million, with 842,400 classified as full-time and 665,200 classified as part-time.[3] Whether part-time or full-time, all faculty everywhere and in all disciplines work in a world that has become ever more fraught with legal pitfalls and the potential for litigation.

While full- and part-time college faculty and lecturers go about their jobs—doing all that is seen (teaching) and unseen (preparing and grading, researching and writing, engaging in service)—little time, if any, may be given to the uncomfortable thought that those acts have legal ramifications. *Navigating Choppy Waters* addresses questions like the following: "Can I be liable for my professional decisions that have negative consequences?"; "What happens if a student were to sue me over a bad grade?"; "Is my syllabus really a contract, and what does that mean if it is?"; "Who owns the intellectual property rights in my teaching materials, especially those that are online?"; "What would happen if I violated FERPA?"; "What is the legal risk for me if a student gets angry at a reference letter I wrote?"; "What are my legal rights if students or others get offended at something I say in my class or post on my own social media?"; and "Could I fight a tenure denial in court?" From outside the university, questions like the following abound: "Are they socialists or communists?"; "Are they teaching the right thing?"; and "Are they indoctrinating their students?" And, from within campus, professors increasingly wonder about questions, like "Can I alter my semester plans after distributing a syllabus?"; "Do students have intellectual property rights in their coursework or does it belong to the instructor or perhaps to the university?"; "Can I take my work products with me if I leave my job?"; and "Will I get in trouble if I express my opinions in class?" Unfortunately, well-meaning nonlegal scholars and writers are occasionally wrong in their conclusions about some of these questions.

Another matter is how sturdy the guard rails are for contingent faculty when they are the object of student, or even colleague, discontent. The proportion of part-time and contingent full-time faculty appointments continues to increase across America's colleges and universities. As the American Association of University Professors (AAUP) found, 68 percent of faculty in US colleges and universities held contingent appointments in fall 2021, compared with about 47 percent in fall 1987.[4] In that same time frame, the percentage of American full-time faculty members who had tenure dropped from 39 percent to 24 percent.

As self-centered as it may seem, it is incumbent on faculty of all kinds to find ways to protect themselves at work.

This book is also written for those with administrative roles. You likely came out of faculty ranks and did the kinds of work you now evaluate and within the constraints of the budgets you now manage. As you may realize, faculty seem to be leaving their jobs at an alarming rate. A 2022 Inside Higher Ed "Survey of College and University Chief Academic Officers" showed 19 percent of provosts reported that faculty members were leaving at significantly higher rates than in the past, and 60 percent said they were leaving at somewhat higher rates.[5] Two years later, the 2024 "Survey of College and University Chief Academic Officers" revealed ongoing difficulty in recruiting or retaining faculty members, notably after the COVID-19 pandemic.[6] Provosts from the South region expressed the highest acknowledgment of faculty turnover (45 percent) and faculty recruitment challenges (71 percent). These findings may reflect the distinct dissatisfaction many faculty experience in their jobs.[7] Perhaps this book will increase your legal knowledge and, consequently, help you lead your unit or institution in an evenhanded way that reduces tensions between faculty and students, and faculty and administration, all while keeping legal risks as low as possible.

Just How Choppy Are the Waters?

During my inaugural semester decades ago, where I taught everything from English composition to intro to government at one college, I was hired to teach a criminal-law course at another college. As a recent law-school graduate, I instituted what I had experienced as a student—anonymous grading of exams. Before taking the first exam, my students went to the department secretary to get a number to put on each of their exams instead of their names. When I finished the grading of my very first essay-heavy exam—and it took forever—I asked for the list that matched the names with the numbers so I could enter the test grades. The grades were not good, which could have been chalked up to this being my first attempt at creating an exam. Or maybe I was difficult to listen to in class, hard to follow, grasping at straws when answering questions, or all of the above. Regardless, all my efforts at impartiality compounded my shock when the department chair called to tell me that some of my students had accused me of personal unfairness in how I graded their exams. Had I possessed anything resembling a career, it would have flashed before me in an instant. Part of my consuming humiliation was my bewilderment about how this ship, which I'd been so thrilled to captain in August, was in mutiny within a month. Anonymous grading—which I've long since given up—may have helped me defend myself against the accusations, but it didn't prevent them. However, had

I known then what I know now about the law on faculty grading, I could have approached that controversy with confidence rather than dread.

Fortunately for me, no student sued or threatened to sue. In fact, at the end of the semester, I got a few sheepish apologies from some of those students about how they had treated me. (Perhaps they smelled the fear at that first class and acted accordingly.) Such is not the case for others. A student at my university sued her professor, the department chair, the dean, and the university after being dismissed from the nursing program for unprofessionalism, which was a violation of the student code of conduct. Even a New York college instructor's refusal to round up a final grade of 69.713 to a passing 70.00 resulted in a lawsuit, and that's not the only litigation example from the shadowy world of grade-rounding. If you're thinking, "but this will never happen to me," so thought the above-mentioned instructors. So thought the graduate assistant teaching a master's-level counseling class in Pennsylvania; this instructor was sued by a student who got a zero in the participation-points portion of her final grade, lowering her total grade to the point that she was ineligible to stay in the counseling program. The student, who sued for millions in damages, claimed she fully participated in class, but the instructor said the student's participation was counterproductive to class discussion. (In case you're wondering, yes, the university was also sued. That's where the money is, to borrow the line from bank robber Willie Sutton.) The outcome of that lawsuit depended on the application of the "arbitrary and capricious" standard, a legal doctrine that will be discussed in the first chapter.

Students in graduate and professional programs have so much at stake that, if you presume those students would be inclined to sue, you're right. Of course, law students come to mind. They have sued their professors for everything from breach of contract (after a low final grade in . . . wait for it . . . a contract-law class) to negligence (alleging the professor injured her during a demonstration in a tort-law class). PhD students have sued dissertation advisors. In one case from Illinois, the student sought punitive damages on the grounds that the advisor stole the student's research. In another case, an economics PhD student in Indiana sued his advisor and the university for, among other things, negligence and defamation after being dismissed from the doctoral program. Medical-school students sue for a range of issues, too, including disciplinary actions for missing too many clinicals and accusations of cheating. In fact, two of the landmark Supreme Court cases in education law, *University of Missouri v. Horowitz*[8] and *University of Michigan v. Ewing*,[9] concerned litigious medical-school students.

As will be discussed in more detail, investigations into or allegations of cheating require that the level of student protection be raised to protect the student's due-process rights. In 2022, a student at a state university in Ohio brought a lawsuit against his university, alleging it violated his Fourth Amendment rights against a warrantless search by requiring that he, along with other students, use their webcams to visually inspect their rooms for any cheating paraphernalia before taking a remote exam given during the COVID-19 lockdown semester. And, in 2023, an instructor at a state university in Texas earnestly—but wrongly—accused his class of using ChatGPT to cheat, after copying and pasting students' final assignments into ChatGPT, which concluded that some of the assignments weren't authentic. ChatGPT isn't intended to catch AI-generated work, so no student was penalized, but some called for the instructor to be disciplined for his rashness. AI and its serious legal implications for plagiarism, as well as copyright and authorship, and even FERPA and student privacy, will be covered in *Navigating Choppy Waters*. For now, suffice it to say that, when using AI to decide whether a student's work or performance is inadequate, faculty need to pump the brakes and make legal considerations before concluding a student has cheated.

But, if you work at a private college, where, consequently, legal standards for student rights generally differ from those at a public institution, are you required to provide your students with such due process, which is a term from the Bill of Rights and the Fourteenth Amendment? Do your students have free speech rights in your classes? Equally important, is your employer required to grant you due process or First Amendment rights? If academic freedom is connected to the First Amendment, and if the First Amendment doesn't apply to faculty at private institutions, then is academic freedom an illusion for thousands of faculty? These questions will be addressed.

Speaking of academic freedom, does it exist for any faculty in Florida, or will it exist in Ohio, where, as of this writing, Senate Bill 83 would, if passed, ban the presentation of "controversial beliefs or policies," according to the American Civil Liberties Union of Ohio.[10] The bill defines controversial beliefs or policies as "any belief or policy that is the subject of political controversy, including issues such as climate change, electoral politics, foreign policy, diversity, equity, and inclusion programs, immigration policy, marriage, or abortion."[11] Even the Ohio State University Board of Trustees issued a formal opposition to the bill, including an assertion that, if passed, the bill would impact the university's ability to attract the best faculty and researchers.[12] As if this isn't disheartening enough, consider the 2022 passage of Florida's "Stop Woke Act," as it is so risibly called. This infringement on academic freedom is not even a thinly veiled attempt at prohibiting any whiff of critical race theory; its leading advocate (and signer of the bill) called the legislation necessary to stop the "state-sanctioned racism that is critical-race theory."[13] As will be discussed in a later chapter, legal opponents to the Stop Woke Act include professors and students from various Florida colleges and universities.[14]

Indiana, the state where I work, passed a bill in 2024, SB 202, that takes aim at the "perception that higher education discourages conservative views"[15] by, among other things, making more state university board of trustee seats subject to partisanship and by requiring faculty to show—including for tenure and a newly created post-tenure review system—how they meet yet-to-be-determined "intellectual diversity" standards. A law professor from Indiana University said about the bill, "It is nakedly about censoring speech, it is nakedly about punishing."[16] Even the president of Indiana University expressed concern that the bill would put academic freedom at risk.[17]

At a more granular level, you might have wondered if a teaching tactic, activity, or even topic in which you engage is protected by academic freedom or the First Amendment. Is an anodyne approach the only way to teach, for fear of the repercussions that might ensue if you try something different or even risky? There is an answer, and it involves courts applying what is known as the "germaneness standard." Before getting to that chapter, consider a few examples from across the country: Are jokes about sex off limits?; Can a professor use the F-word in class?; Can one say b—ch or f—t in class?; and, to turn the tables, can a syllabus prohibit students from saying "God bless you" in class? Can professors prohibit students from saying in class what they consider to be hate speech? We will turn to the Supreme Court for help, once again, but the resolution depends in part on whether the college is a public institution and whether there has been a "substantial disruption" of the learning environment.

Beyond the general risks associated with grading or other similar decisions involving your professional judgment, there are other, more specific legal issues that impact the work that a college faculty member does.

Intellectual Property Concerns

The AAUP has for decades been sounding the alarm about the tensions percolating between faculty and their employers regarding the intellectual property that faculty create.[18] Whether it involves patents or copyrights, the AAUP has produced policy statements and fact sheets that help faculty come to grips with the monetization of faculty work, some of which faculty may reflexively think is their property. Often, contract and employment law, as expressed in university intellectual property policies, is controlling. But not always. College intellectual property policies generally distinguish between what are often termed "patentable works," "traditional works of scholarship," "university works," "instructional works," "course modules," or other similar terms. And, as it concerns ownership or licensing that universities claim to teaching materials, particularly online teaching materials, one needs to make the distinction between what is a "commissioned work," what is a "work for hire," and what is the "teacher exception" to the work for hire doctrine—if the teacher exception still exists at all.

If you leave your employer, can it continue to use your teaching materials without paying you, the original creator of that which is being reused? Can the content in your online classes be repopulated in other sections (or even other divisions or schools owned by your employer) without your agreement? Can joint authors do whatever they individually want with scholarly papers, regardless of their coauthors' consent or knowledge? Can your students sell their class notes, or are those your property? Could you sue if you found your own test questions on an educational-support/tutoring website, where students pay to access study materials and, of course, practice tests? Professors have sued in all these instances, giving the rest of us insights as to what makes something worthy of copyright and who has the rightful ownership claim.

FERPA: A Great Example of Why You Shouldn't Go to Law School

At the outset, let's agree to this about the Family Educational Rights and Privacy Act (FERPA): it is a nearly inscrutable concept tied to a ridiculously long statute.[19] Did you know there are federal regulations that interpret and, therefore, augment the FERPA statute?[20] Then there is the case law, including that promulgated by the Supreme Court,[21] which applies the statute and the regulations to actual situations. Even if you've attended an employer-mandated FERPA seminar or taken the obligatory FERPA quiz that concludes your HR-provided self-study training course, one question you may hope you'll never be asked while strapped to a polygraph is if you understand FERPA—unless a shoulder shrug is an acceptable response.

Despite that its official name starts with "Family," FERPA's application to college is meant to protect student privacy. In fact, parents lose their rights to access their children's education records when their children either turn eighteen or begin college, whichever occurs first.[22] Because faculty need to protect student privacy, a starting point for FERPA demystification is the need to understand what qualifies as an "education record." That includes realizing what does not qualify as an education record and what "directory information" is and how all of these terms provide a sense of FERPA cohesion. An urgent question to consider, which will also be answered in *Navigating Choppy Waters*, is whether you risk creating liability for your institution, or even yourself, if you happen to violate your students' FERPA rights.

As well as the documents or information that traditionally fall under FERPA's ambit, faculty often write reference or recommendation letters. Occasionally, faculty discuss their students' bona fides with prospective employers or administrators of graduate schools. Have you considered if those communications are covered by FERPA? Have you ever thought that being honest in a reference or recommendation letter could result in you receiving a summons and a civil complaint for defamation because the student about whom you wrote lost a job opportunity and believed your evaluation was the reason? Sadly, those cases exist and their resolution turns on something older than FERPA, namely, the tort concepts of "privilege," or "immunity," or other defamation defenses.

Speaking of Defamation . . .

If, like Howard Beal from the Oscar-nominated 1976 film *Network*, you've had your own "I'm mad as hell and I'm not going to take this anymore!" moment, you may have contemplated becoming a plaintiff. Every now and then, the news promo is "Man Bites Dog: News at 11:00," and there are instances where faculty have sued their colleagues or even sued their students. Consider the partial quote of a certain nineteenth-century lawyer, Abraham Lincoln, to other lawyers[23]: "Discourage Litigation . . . the nominal winner is often a real loser—in fees, expenses, and waste of time." Despite Lincoln's sage advice, one may believe there is no other choice, particularly in a world where social media and professor-rating websites can put you one click away from lasting reputation damage. For a professor to make the decision to sue a student (it happens) or a colleague (of course it happens), the outcome can depend on whether the plaintiff qualifies as a "public figure" or a "public official." In those instances, the plaintiff bears the higher defamation burden of proving "actual malice." There are court cases that help us understand when academics qualify as public figures in lawsuits by professors against each other, against members of Congress, and even against students.

Then there is the nature of what was said about the plaintiff and if it qualifies as "defamation per se." When a statement is defamatory per se (and, often, state statutes categorize what defamatory statements fall in that category), the plaintiff has a more certain path to winning the case. In a lawsuit by a former regional-university chancellor against a member of the board of trustees, the outcome turned on the question of whether the board member's letter about the chancellor, written to the university president, was defamation per se.

Professors have sued student-run publications over allegations of defamatory pieces, and professors have sued students because of what the students posted online. For example, a professor at a Catholic university sued a student newspaper over an alleged mischaracterization of her abortion-rights work, which she said led to harassment and threats. Professors have sued students for various statements made online about their teaching and treatment of students. A university even sued a student blogger over what the student attempted to post anonymously, which were various criticisms of the administration and their recent actions, including the demotion of a department chair—who was the blogger's stepmother.

Tenure

As discussed earlier in this introduction, the ranks of tenured faculty have decreased in recent decades, while the hiring of contingent faculty has noticeably increased. Is it a coincidence that clarion calls to eliminate tenure, along with increasing use of post-tenure review, have gone hand in hand with full-throated attempts to limit what faculty can teach or discuss in class or even research? Decades ago, the AAUP expressed caution about post-tenure review and how it might impact academic freedom.[24] And, over eighty years ago, the AAUP issued its "Statement of Principles on Academic Freedom and Tenure,"[25] which, among other things, spoke to the need for tenure and provided a mechanism for faculty to move through tenure-track status during a probationary period. One might say the AAUP's creation in 1915 was impelled by key instances of university intrusions of academic freedom (which included dismissal of professors) and a resulting need to create a judicial body–like entity to investigate future allegations, as well as a desire to formulate a tenure definition and structure.[26]

Despite the misunderstanding of academic tenure (it's a job for life) and the more recent maligning of it (it keeps the deadwood faculty around when they're not earning their pay), tenure systems still exist for thousands of faculty. Because of all that is involved in seeking tenure (which is different from promotion) and the implications for it being granted or denied, tenure decisions are monumental. Consequently, legal issues accompany the tenure process, as well as the suspension or firing of tenured faculty. The Supreme Court has spoken to what it means to be an assistant professor and has stated, in a case where a first-year assistant professor was told he would not be back for his second year, there is no property interest protected by the Fourteenth Amendment in a nontenured position.[27] Generally, standards of and judgments reached in the tenure process are outside the scope of judicial review. But does a professor have any legal grounds on which to stand if he or she believes that there was bias in a tenure denial decision or that the tenure process was structurally unfair? *Navigating Choppy Waters* will address those serious questions.

Capsizing Isn't Inevitable

Sometimes, a ship captain's best decision is to stay in port. Or in bed. But that's rarely an advisable way to get through a semester. Ships don't travel in a straight line, and one who heads out to sea believing the only storm is a predicted one proves the aphorism that one who fails to prepare, prepares to fail. By looking at your teaching and research through a legal lens, you will anticipate the "what ifs" in a way that will best protect you if you ever need protection. Being law-literate about grading decisions, academic-dishonesty allegations, syllabi statements, academic freedom, intellectual property, and more shouldn't make you jaded or add to any sense of ennui you might have about being a college faculty member. *Navigating Choppy Waters* will add to your knowledge base and, hopefully, increase your confidence, allowing you to do better what you do best—whether you're a part-time instructor or an endowed chair.

On a final introductory note, I need to provide the boilerplate that *Navigating Choppy Waters* is not intended to be the giving of legal advice or a substitute for seeking legal counsel. Generally, a lawyer (or a nonlawyer unlawfully practicing law) gives legal advice when providing a specific legal opinion, advice, or conclusion to a fact pattern or individual situation. If you believe you need legal help, by all means get it. I have, and I am a lawyer. As British clergyman and academic Henry Kett wrote in a book of poems two centuries ago, "[E]very man who represent himself has a fool for a client."[28]

Notes

1. Joseph Grenny and Derek Cullimore, "How HR Lost Employees' Trust—and How to Get It Back," *Harvard Business Review*, October 2022, https://hbr.org/2022/10/how-hr-lost-employees-trust-and-how-to-get-it-back.
2. National Center for Education Statistics, "Fast Facts: Degrees Conferred by Race and Sex," U.S. Department of Education, https://nces.ed.gov/fastfacts/display.asp?id=1122.
3. National Center for Education Statistics, "Characteristics of Postsecondary Faculty," U.S. Department of Education, 2023, https://nces.ed.gov/programs/coe/indicator/csc/postsecondary-faculty.
4. Glenn Colby, "Data Snapshot: Tenure and Contingency in US Higher Education," *Academe*, 2023, https://www.aaup.org/article/data-snapshot-tenure-and-contingency-us-higher-education#.ZCxtQnbMI2w.
5. Scott Jaschik and Doug Lederman, "2022 Survey of College and University Chief Academic Officers: A Survey by Inside Higher Ed and Hanover Research," 2022, https://www.insidehighered.com/sites/default/files/media/2022-IHE-Provost-Survey.pdf.
6. Colleen Flaherty and Doug Lederman, "2024 Survey of College and University Chief Academic Officers: A Survey by Inside Higher Ed and Hanover Research," April 15, 2024, https://acue.org/wp-content/uploads/2024/05/2024-IHE-Provost-Survey.pdf.
7. Maria LaMonaca Wisdom, "Faculty Job Dissatisfaction Isn't about 'Burnout,'" *The Chronicle of Higher Education*, January 6, 2023, https://www.chronicle.com/article/faculty-job-dissatisfaction-isnt-about-burnout.
8. 435 U.S. 78 (1978).
9. 474 U.S. 214 (1985).
10. Celina Coming, "Senate Bill 83's Four Biggest Problems: An ACLU of Ohio Perspective," April 13, 2023, https://www.acluohio.org/en/news/senate-bill-83s-four-biggest-problems-aclu-ohio-perspective.

11. Ohio General Assembly, Senate Bill 83, 135th General Assembly, introduced February 9, 2023, https://search-prod.lis.state.oh.us/solarapi/v1/general_assembly_135/bills/sb83/PS/02/sb83_02_PS?format=pdf.

12. Ohio State University Board of Trustees, "A Statement from the Ohio State University Board of Trustees," May 16, 2023, https://news.osu.edu/a-statement-from-the-ohio-state-university-board-of-trustees/.

13. WUSF Public Media, "Florida Professors and Students Are among Those Battling for Speech Rights and Academic Freedom," June 21, 2023, https://wusfnews.wusf.usf.edu/education/2023-06-21/florida-professors-students-battling-speech-rights-academic-freedom.

14. WUSF Public Media, "Florida Professors and Students Are among Those Battling for Speech Rights and Academic Freedom," June 21, 2023, https://wusfnews.wusf.usf.edu/education/2023-06-21/florida-professors-students-battling-speech-rights-academic-freedom.

15. Colleen Flaherty, "Bill Threatens Profs Who Don't Give Intellectual Freedom Disclaimer," *Inside Higher Ed*, February 21, 2024, https://www.insidehighered.com/news/faculty-issues/academic-freedom/2024/02/21/bill-threatens-profs-who-dont-give-intellectual.

16. Ibid.

17. Indiana Public Media, "IU President Whitten Comes Out against Controversial Tenure Bill," February 21, 2024, https://indianapublicmedia.org/news/iu-president-whitten-comes-out-against-controversial-tenure-bill.php.

18. AAUP, "Statement on Intellectual Property," June 2014, https://www.aaup.org/report/statement-intellectual-property; AAUP, "AAUP Policy Work on Intellectual Property," https://www.aaup.org/get-involved/issue-campaigns/intellectual-property-risk/aaup-policy-work-intellectual-property.

19. 20 U.S.C. § 1232g.

20. U.S. Department of Education, "34 CFR Part 99—Family Educational Rights and Privacy," Electronic Code of Federal Regulations, https://www.ecfr.gov/current/title-34/subtitle-A/part-99.

21. *Owasso Independent School District v. Falvo*, 534 U.S. 426 (2002); *Gonzaga University v. Doe*, 536 U.S. 273 (2002).

22. 20 U.S.C. § 1232g(d).

23. "Notes for a Law Lecture," dated July 1, 1850.

24. AAUP, "Post-Tenure Review: An AAUP Response," *AAUP Reports and Publications*, https://www.aaup.org/report/post-tenure-review-aaup-response.

25. AAUP, "1940 Statement of Principles on Academic Freedom and Tenure," *AAUP Reports and Publications*, https://www.aaup.org/report/1940-statement-principles-academic-freedom-and-tenure.

26. https://www.aaup.org/report/1915-declaration-principles-academic-freedom-and-academic-tenure.

27. *Board of Regents of State Colleges v. Roth*, 408 U.S. 564 (1972).

28. Henry Kett, *The Flowers of Wit, or a Choice Collection of Bon Mots* (1814).

CHAPTER 1

Liability Risks for Professional Decisions

STARTING WITH THE GOOD NEWS

You Make the Call

- **The Case of the Doubly Correct Corporations-Law Exam Answer**

A good portion of law-school transcripts consists of grades that are directly reposted from cumulative, final exams; in law school, fifteen weeks of briefing case law and waiting to be called on to be the object of the professor's Socratic gifts results in varying degrees of terror and, in the sixteenth week, an essay exam. One grade for one course. It can be difficult to stand out among your classmates when the odds are high that most of the other students are furiously writing the same paragraphs in response to labyrinthian hypotheticals put on those exams. So, when a law student taking a corporations final in a New York law school saw the question that asked her to analyze and apply Delaware corporate law, she decided to go the extra mile and, perhaps, earn some extra credit. It would make sense to ask students to apply Delaware corporate law; it is the corporate king of American law. Over 60 percent of the Fortune 500 corporations are incorporated in Delaware, and the state has its own, specialized corporate-law court, the Court of Chancery. But the law student answered the essay question by applying Delaware and also New York law. Her essay responses were correct—in both Delaware and New York. The professor, however, gave her a zero on that question, which was worth 30 percent of the total exam grade, because he did not ask students to discuss New York law. In the professor's view, the student didn't follow his directions and that was a fatal error because, to him, it showed she didn't know which was the correct answer. Losing all possible points for that question caused the student to get a D for the course, contributing to her being on academic probation due to having a GPA that was below the school's requirement, placing her status as a law student at risk. So, she sued, alleging the professor's grading was arbitrary and capricious and not accurately reflective of the knowledge she demonstrated on that exam.

Did the student win? Or does a professor have the right to mark as incorrect an answer that is, technically, correct but fails to follow the instructions?

(The answer will be given at the end of the chapter. Consider how the principles in this chapter affect your decision and reasoning.)

As I wrote in the introduction, my first semester as an adjunct instructor was more difficult than I had thought possible. Preparing for classes and teaching and grading took more time than I could have realized. And having a few students who let it be known they thought I was not up to the task made me question if my desire to enter the academic profession showed what horrible judgment I possessed. But I stayed. David Sedaris did not. The uniquely self-deprecating humorist and author of eighteen books or collections of essays, many of them best sellers, once taught a college course. Once. As he describes in *Me Talk Pretty One Day*,[1] a year after graduating from the Art Institute of Chicago, his alma mater hired him to teach a writing course two weeks before the semester started—because the slated instructor quit to take a higher-paying job delivering pizzas. Sedaris's performance as a brand-new instructor made me seem like Aristotle by comparison. His preparation for class consisted of cutting oak-leaf name tags out of cardboard paper for his nine students. Because Sedaris wrote best when he smoked, he encouraged everyone to join along, which resulted in an asthmatic student dropping the course. Because he didn't want to miss the broadcast of his favorite soap opera, "One Life to Live," during his class, he brought in a TV and, after a few complaints about how class time was being used, made students write "guessays" that predicted the next day's episode. Eventually, one student reached her limit and yelled at him in class, "Just who in the stinking hell do you think you are?" He paused and replied, "I'm the only one who is paid to be in this room." Unfortunately, the student demanded to know what he was being paid. Sedaris wrote that, after he told the class, the laughter was loud, violent, and prolonged.

Can an Instructor or a Professor Commit Educational Malpractice?

Even without having a law degree, one could make a relatively sturdy argument that David Sedaris's performance as a creative-writing instructor was negligent. As much enjoyment as I got out of reading about Sedaris's made-for-a-short-story performance, college students paid money to sit in a room while the instructor smoked cigarettes as he watched his "stories," as they used to be called. Negligence is the failure to act with reasonable care, resulting in some legal harm to the plaintiff. Negligence has four elements that need to be proved: 1) a legal duty of care owed by the defendant to the plaintiff; 2) breach of the duty to the plaintiff by the failure of the defendant to exercise reasonable care; 3) damages (an injury recognized as compensable by the legal system) suffered by the plaintiff; and 4) causation between the defendant's conduct and the plaintiff's injuries.

Many of the lawyer advertisements on television involve lawyers seeking clients who may have been injured through someone's or some company's negligence. Most of us carry some form of insurance, be it automobile or homeowner's insurance, to protect us against our own negligence. And so it is with doctors and lawyers and other professionals who maintain liability insurance in the event they are sued for malpractice, which is the tort of professional negligence, or a failure to provide one's services at the prevailing professional standard. Mistakes happen, and, because of that fact, one might wonder if professors, like other professionals, should be mindful of how their actions put them at risk for a malpractice claim. Fortunately, the news on educational malpractice is very good—for instructors and educational institutions.

One can find educational malpractice claims brought as far back as the 1970s. In an often-cited case from that era, the claim was brought against a high school, not a college.[2] And, in that case, the court refused to accept educational malpractice as a theory of liability, and that view has long since migrated to colleges and universities. Logically, one could find that an instructor or a college could commit educational malpractice by providing negligent instruction in a class or even an inadequate education. In a case from Kansas involving such a claim against a college, its supreme court noted a federal court's statement that educational malpractice "has a seductive ring to it; after all, if doctors, lawyers, accountants and other professionals can be held liable for failing to exercise due care, why can't teachers?"[3] And yet, the court determined—as do many, many other federal and state courts—that educational malpractice is not a legally accepted claim.[4] Setting out the reasons, the court answered its own question this way:

> [T]he answer is that the nature of education radically differs from other professions. Education is an intensely collaborative process, requiring the interaction of student with teacher. A good student can learn from a poor teacher; a poor student can close his mind to a good teacher. Without effort by a student, he cannot be educated. Good teaching method may vary with the needs of the individual student. In other professions, by contrast, client cooperation is far less important; given a modicum of cooperation, a competent professional in other fields can control the results obtained. But in education, the ultimate responsibility for success remains always with the student. Both the process and the result are subjective, and proof or disproof extremely difficult.[5]

In another much-cited case from the 1970s, a New York court considered the efficacy of educational malpractice, deciding that public policy prevented courts from having the prerogative to evaluate educational policies or their implementations.[6] Courts across the country continue their refusal to recognize lawsuits that are labeled as or implied to be educational malpractice. In a case brought by a law student in Oklahoma, the student's allegations against his constitutional-law professor were that he often arrived late for class, ended class early, and cancelled classes without scheduling makeup sessions. The student's suit, which wasn't even filed against the offending professor, included breach of contract, fraud, and negligence. But the court ruled against the student on all his claims that related to being provided with an inadequate education.[7]

There seems to be no distinction between public and private universities in the rejection of the doctrine of educational malpractice. In a 2021 federal case against Yale University, a student sued over Yale's refusal to partially refund tuition and fees after the COVID-19 lockdown required a transition from in-person to online classes. Yale sought to have the case dismissed on the grounds that the student was suing for what was, essentially, educational malpractice. Even though the court dismissed the suit, it made sure to note that Yale's argument was incorrect that the student was bringing an educational malpractice claim.[8] In another 2021 case involving Northwestern University students and alumnae who were displeased with the University's transition to online classes during the COVID-19 lockdown, the court acknowledged that Illinois doesn't recognize educational malpractice but viewed the class-action suit as alleging breach of contract instead.[9] Faculty should breathe a sigh of relief in the realization that courts have historically refused to countenance lawsuits alleging negligent instruction. However, as will be discussed later in the chapter, there is a consequential difference for faculty between doing something that might be considered negligent and doing something reckless or intentionally harmful to a student.

THE TAKEAWAY

Educational-malpractice lawsuits are generally not accepted by American courts, because of the continued respect for the original view expressed when those lawsuits were first brought, that courts should not evaluate how well or poorly educational institutions or their faculty do what they do. College faculty might be disciplined or dismissed for negligence in their teaching actions or failures to act reasonably, but such negligence does not give rise to legal liability.

The Nature of the Relationship between Students and Professors

When students enroll in a college or university, they agree to pay tuition, administrative costs, lab fees, and room and board, and they purchase or rent books or e-books. All of those transactions are governed by contract law. (More attention and explanation on what makes something a contract will be provided in the next chapter on syllabi.) For example, if students fail to pay tuition, or fail to pay back a school loan, they will be sued for breach of contract. However, if a student fails to get the education he or she was promised, is that a breach of contract if it can't be educational malpractice? In a loose sense, it is. The law has historically concluded that the relationship between students and their universities is contractual in nature.[10] When students claim to have received an inadequate education in contravention to what they were promised, courts often conclude that those students must point to a specific contractual promise that was made but not delivered by the institution.[11]

In recent years, many of the breach-of-contract lawsuits filed by college students were not related to the quality of instruction but concerned the mode of instruction, due to institutions moving to all online (or even off-campus) courses because of COVID-19–necessitated restrictions. Students from across the country, including at Temple University, the University of Pennsylvania, Loyola University of Chicago, and Indiana University, sued their institutions, alleging breach of contract; namely, they alleged that they didn't get the in-class educations they were promised or did not receive partial refunds related to not being on campus. In a case brought against Indiana University (a companion case was also brought by a Purdue University student against Purdue), the court didn't accept the universities' argument that these were really educational-malpractice suits but instead pointed to housing and meal contracts in ruling that the students could go forward with their breach-of-contract suits.[12]

But, in some of the above-mentioned cases and in others, courts discussed a different kind of contract that students and universities have made: an implied contract.[13] Usually, one thinks of a contract as being an exchange of terms, where each side expressly knows what the other is giving in order to get something in return. But a contract can also be implied, where the behavior of the parties shows the existence of a contractual relationship. For instance, in 2023, a student brought a COVID-19–related class-action suit against the Illinois Institute of Technology for failing to provide partial refunds to students who paid for on-campus and in-person courses. After the suit was originally dismissed, the United States Court of Appeals for the Seventh Circuit (a federal appellate court with jurisdiction over lower federal courts in Illinois, Indiana, and Wisconsin), interpreting Illinois law, concluded that the student had sufficiently shown the existence of an implied contract for in-person education and access to campus facilities, based on that institution's custom and traditions of offering in-person education.[14] These recent cases involving the COVID-19 lockdown and related refund and breach-of-contract claims do not alter the historical view that courts are strict in determining if students have valid breach-of-contract claims related to their educational experiences, whether the contract in question is thought to be express or implied.

Before the contractual relationship took its place as the primary lens through which these conflicts were viewed, courts saw colleges as being in a parental-like relationship with their students, something known as "in loco parentis."[15] The doctrine of in loco parentis also applied to more than academic matters and included the university's prerogative to regulate the social behavior of students, but courts did not apply the doctrine in a way that imposed a formal duty on colleges to protect students from harm. But, as universities began to recognize their students were adults who had been given more rights in the 1960s and 1970s (voting rights at younger ages, drinking rights, etc.), the primacy of the in loco parentis doctrine began to recede.[16] Contributing to this erosion was a judicial acceptance of the notion that, because public colleges and universities are state actors, students at those institutions had free speech and due-process rights and could not be summarily expelled.[17] Even in cases where minors are college students and engage in considerable amounts of consequential, adult-only activities on campus, courts reject the argument that the college stands in place of a student's parents or guardians.[18]

THE TAKEAWAY

Colleges and universities, but not faculty, are in contractual relationships with their students. In order to bring a successful breach-of-contract claim against an institution, a student needs to demonstrate that specific promises made by the institution created either an express or implied contract. The doctrine of in loco parentis is generally no longer applicable at colleges or universities.

The Guiding Star for Faculty Decisions about Grades: The Arbitrary and Capricious Standard

You Make the Call

- **The Case of the Too-Talkative Therapy Student**

A doctoral student teaching a master's-degree-level therapy internship course at a private research university in Pennsylvania included a participation portion of twenty-five possible points that students could earn toward their final course grade. One of the students in the class received zero points for her participation grade, despite much evidence she talked in class. Due to a lack of any participation points, the student earned a C+ in the course, whereupon she filed a grade appeal and grievance. After the student lost her appeal, she transferred to the human development program because her GPA prevented her from remaining in the counseling program. Then she sued—for $1.3 million, alleging that such an amount is the difference between what she would have earned in her career as a therapist, compared to what she would earn as a drug-and-alcohol counselor. Making such a calculation requires the services of a finance specialist, and the student had two: her hired expert and her father, a finance professor at the same university. The instructor's reasoning for granting the student no participation points was that the student's participation was disruptive and revealed a lack of the self-reflection needed for a licensed therapist. The student said she was being discriminated against for being in favor of gay marriage and for criticizing the department, which the instructor and other faculty called a baseless claim. A four-day, non-jury trial was held. Among the witnesses, various faculty agreed with the instructor's view that the student lacked professionalism and responded poorly to criticism. The judge (who would render the verdict and was himself a parent and an adjunct professor at another college) suggested the parties should settle the case and said he could not understand how professors at the university could award a participating student zero participation points.

Did the student win? Does an instructor have the discretion to award no participation points for student participation the instructor considers to be unsuitable or disruptive?

(The answer will be given at the end of the chapter. Consider how the principles in this chapter affect your decision and reasoning.)

Statistically speaking, the odds are low that a grade you give a student on a project, a presentation, or an exam—or for participation, if you do that—will result in that student being so resentful that he or she would file a lawsuit over it. But, even though the odds are great you won't get struck by lightning in a given year (1/1,222,000)[19] or attacked and killed by a shark over your lifetime (1/4,332,817),[20] I would bet you stay inside during thunderstorms and don't swim in the ocean at night or when schools of baitfish are swimming by. Practicing preventative care is better than practicing curative care, much less, emergency care. This is not to say that faculty should give all students As to avoid conflict, but that one should engage in grading and other similar activities requiring professional judgment with an understanding of what the state of the law is in a worst-case scenario. Thankfully, in this area, the law is on the side of faculty. There's no guarantee you'll never be on the receiving end of a grade appeal, a grievance, or even a lawsuit, but, with this knowledge, you'll be less likely to unwittingly find yourself in those unfortunate situations.

Courts do not want to get involved in grade disputes. It's not just a reservation; it's a general unwillingness to entertain student lawsuits about negative academic decisions. One of the earlier, influential cases, and one cited many times, involved a law student who sued his professor and the law-school administration in federal court over an F the professor gave the student in a tax-law course. Finding first that no federal right or claim was at stake in the suit, the court then turned to the essential claim, which was that the student was the victim of unfair grading. In choosing to dismiss the suit by abstaining from it, the judge provided a template for what many courts would later follow:

> *The assignment of grades to a particular examination must be left to the discretion of the instructor. He should be given the unfettered opportunity to assess a student's performance and determine if it attains a standard of scholarship required by that professor for a satisfactory grade. The federal judiciary should not adjudicate the soundness of a professor's grading system, nor make a factual determination of the fairness of the individual grades* [emphasis added]. Such an inquiry would necessarily entail the complete substitution of a court evaluation of a complainant's level of achievement in the subject under review, and the standard by which such achievement should be measured, for that of the professor. *It would be difficult to prove by reason, logic or common sense that the federal judiciary is either competent, or more competent, to make such an assessment*[21] [emphasis added].

One could ask the reverse question: who, more so than judges, is qualified to evaluate faculty grading? They are highly educated, they hear arguments in oral and written form and then issue reference-laden, written, analytical conclusions about those arguments by applying standards to fact patterns. And they don't like lateness. But there is an inherent, long-game logic to judges abstaining from grade disputes. A Pandora's box would be opened if eighteen million college and graduate students would have the option of taking grade disputes to court. In that world, high-achieving students (with the money for lawyers or the moxie to represent themselves) who didn't think they deserved a B would be as inclined to litigate as students who got an F or a D. One court acknowledged this in a case where a nursing student sued her professor and college after failing a course with a 73.7-percent grade, rather than being given a passing (and rounded) grade. In dismissing the suit, the court said, in part, as follows: "From the judiciary's point of view, there is an interest in the economy of litigation. In today's society, there is a universal desire to prevent overburdening an already severely taxed system with additional causes of action."[22]

THE US SUPREME COURT'S VIEW ON THE JUDICIAL REVIEW OF ACADEMIC EVALUATION

The US Supreme Court has issued two decisions that are on point in this area. They both involve disputes over academic decisions made by university faculty, and they both build on the precedent that faculty (or, in a larger sense, institutional) evaluations of students are generally not fit for judicial review.

UNIVERSITY OF MISSOURI V. HOROWITZ (1978)

In *Missouri v. Horowitz*,[23] a medical-school student who received poor evaluations, including less-than-satisfactory clinical evaluations of a pediatrics rotation, was, nevertheless, advanced to her next year but was put on probation, as determined by a faculty-student panel, the Council on Evaluation. During that year, her faculty advisor continued to be dissatisfied with her performance, rating it as "unsatisfactory." The Council on Evaluation met again and recommended she be dismissed from the school, "absent radical improvement." The student then took oral and practical exams as part of her internal appeal and spent time with seven practicing physicians, five of whom would eventually recommend she not be allowed to graduate. The Council met again and recommended the student be dismissed, and all administrative personnel later concurred, whereupon the student filed a federal lawsuit.

A major aspect of the case concerned a topic that will be discussed later in the chapter: the level of due-process requirements owed to students at public universities on the receiving end of negative academic performance evaluations or misconduct accusations. But part of the case involved the court having to grapple with whether it, or other courts, should evaluate the performance of academicians in their role as evaluators of students. Speaking to that issue, the court noted the subjective nature of academic evaluations, including the decision to dismiss a student for unsatisfactory performance, and it wrote that such expert evaluation is not "readily adaptable to the procedural tools of judicial or administrative decisionmaking."[24] And, as it concerned more specifically whether courts should, as it were, re-grade faculty grades, the court majority followed a standard from a few earlier federal cases. It stated that, because "courts are ill-equipped to evaluate academic performance," judicial involvement in academic decisions should be limited to where there has been a showing of "arbitrariness or capriciousness."[25] By requiring a showing that an academic decision was arbitrary or capricious (in many court cases, it is also titled "arbitrary and capricious"), a high hurdle was established for students to overcome.

UNIVERSITY OF MICHIGAN V. EWING (1985)

The student in *Michigan v. Ewing*[26] was enrolled in a dual academic program, known as Inteflex, where, after six years of successful study, students would receive an undergraduate and a medical degree. In order to qualify for the final two years of the program, these students had to pass part 1 of a medical licensing exam. The student in question received the lowest test score in the Inteflex program history. After being denied the opportunity to retake that exam and after exhausting all internal appeals, the student was dismissed from school and brought a federal lawsuit. And, as in *Missouri v. Horowitz*, a key part of the case's resolution involved whether the student was provided sufficient due process. That part of the case will also be discussed later in this chapter.

The student argued at his university-level appeal that his exam grade didn't accurately reflect his academic progress or potential "because his mother had suffered a heart attack 18 months before the examination; his girlfriend broke up with him about six months before the examination; his work on an essay for a contest had taken too much time; his makeup examination in pharmacology was administered just before the NBME Part I; and his inadequate preparation caused him to panic during the examination."[27] Furthermore, the student alleged that other medical students who also flunked the same exam were given retake opportunities.

Building on its decision in *Missouri v. Horowitz*, which was cited in *Ewing*, the court was unanimous. Noting that the faculty decisions about the student's academic performance were made with careful deliberation, the court provided two, valuable, follow-up sentences: "When judges are asked to review the substance of a genuinely academic decision, such as this one, they should show great respect for the faculty's professional judgment. Plainly, they may not override it unless it is such *a substantial departure from accepted academic norms as to demonstrate that the person or committee responsible did not actually exercise professional judgment*"[28] [emphasis added]. In those sentences, the court provided a footnote that quoted from another part of the earlier *Horowitz* decision: "University faculties must have the widest range of discretion in making judgments as to the academic performance of students and their entitlement to promotion or graduation."[29]

Take comfort in *Michigan v. Ewing*. It greatly limits your litigation risk when making traditional academic evaluations. Not only have the key sentences from the *Ewing* decision's main portion been repeatedly quoted by lower courts but also that footnote's quotation from the *Horowitz* case (and that quotation wasn't in the court's majority opinion) has also been cited by courts when faced with lawsuits over negative academic decisions made by faculty.[30]

THE TAKEAWAY

The US Supreme Court has endorsed the view that faculty should be granted wide latitude when making professional judgments about a student's academic performance. Other federal and state courts follow this standard. In the absence of evidence that a faculty's decision was "arbitrary or capricious," courts will not get involved, and those cases, if filed on express or implied grounds of unfair grading or similar academic evaluation, should be dismissed.

What Makes a Faculty Decision "Arbitrary and/or Capricious"?

You Make the Call

- **The Case of the Unrounded Grade**

A college student at a public university in Ohio sued his instructor because the student received a B in the instructor's course. (Sometimes lightning does strike.) According to the student, the B was due, in part, because the instructor scheduled a mandatory field trip that was not during class time, and the student was unable to attend. But the impetus for the lawsuit was that the instructor failed to round up the student's final grade, which was a 95.28 percent, to the 96 percent needed to earn an A. Adding insult to injury, the instructor rounded up two other students' final grades to an A, where one student's grade was a 95.8 percent and the other student's grade was a 95.3 percent—just .02 percent higher than the suing student's percentage, which, unrounded, resulted in a final grade of a B.

Does this pass or fail the arbitrary and capricious test?

(The answer will be given at the end of the chapter. Consider how the principles in this chapter affect your decision and reasoning.)

Because educational malpractice is not really a thing, legally speaking, and due to the wide latitude and discretion courts grant professors in their professional decision-making, faculty should teach and grade with confidence. But courts will grant students the right to sue when there has been a showing that a professor's actions are arbitrary or capricious. That standard requires some explanation.

At the outset, it is important to realize that analyzing for arbitrariness and capriciousness does not involve or allow judges to act as super-graders, asking themselves if they would have done what the faculty in question did. That would be unworkable. Even faculty colleagues in the same department disagree with each other's professional decisions. You might not allow for lateness, while others have a punctuality sliding scale; you might permit students to use notes or more when taking exams, while others don't; you might use rubrics for grading written work and deduct considerably for typos, while others find that to be unnecessary or too time-consuming; you might give a cumulative, final exam, while others think that's brutal and anachronistic. In the case earlier quoted in the chapter involving the nursing student who sued because she received a failing grade of 73.7 percent and sought judicial relief for what she believed was unfair grading, that judge also spoke to the impracticality of courts imposing their views in such matters: "Like the appraisal of artwork or the appreciation of music, grading determinations are essentially subjective and evaluative, lacking firm rules or guidelines or purely empirical data."[31]

As the Supreme Court said in *Michigan v. Ewing*, courts are not to override the academic evaluation of an instructor unless the decision or action is "*a substantial departure from accepted academic norms as to demonstrate that the person or committee responsible did not actually exercise professional judgment.*"[32] That is a generous standard. Grade-rounding, or the refusal to do it, as shown in the prior "You Make the Call" case, can lead to litigation and, for us, the need to contextualize what is meant by that standard. In a grade-rounding case from New York, a nursing professor refused to round up a final and failing grade of 69.713 to a passing 70.00 and, per school policy, the student was expelled because she had already failed the course once. The student sued, and a lower court involved in the case concluded the professor's failure to help out a last-semester senior, thereby making her no longer eligible to graduate, was "arbitrary and capricious." You might agree with that. But, on appeal, a higher court disagreed. In ruling against the student, the court acknowledged the general imperative that courts stay out of grading fights and said, "we do not take it upon ourselves to 'round off' the petitioner's failing mark since the College has no policy to support such action."[33] There is even a case from New York where a math professor's decision to deny a dyslexic student a calculator for a final exam was upheld. Despite the claim that the student was discriminated against because of a disability, the court noted that the professor operated within the bounds of the college's ADA policies and had provided the student with numerous accommodations in the course, including allowing a calculator on an earlier test. Most importantly, for our purposes, the court agreed with the professor's claim that, for the final exam, calculator usage would defeat the objectives and purpose of the exam.[34]

The essence of acting in a way that is either arbitrary and/or capricious is a lack of rationality with respect to the decision or evaluation. As tedious as grading can be, if it becomes random and one would actually throw piles of projects in the air to see where they land, or flip a coin to determine a B from a C, then those actions would not withstand the arbitrariness standard. Thankfully, no case law with these examples has been found. But there are more difficult fact patterns courts must reconcile with the arbitrary and capricious standard. A speech-and-learning-pathology PhD student at a private university in Illinois brought a lawsuit against the university and her faculty advisor. She alleged that he sexually harassed her but lost on the grounds that the professor's asking her out for drinks and suggesting they spend time together didn't constitute quid pro quo (this for that) harassment.[35] She also sued him for stealing her research and using it to his advantage, but the court said that claim was barred by the statute of limitations, meaning she hadn't filed that suit within the required time frame.[36] And she also sued for having been dismissed from the PhD program for failure to complete her degree. This last claim was based on the allegations that her advisor had usurped a key research idea of hers for his own work and that she had been treated unfairly. Once again, she lost, although, at the trial, the court agreed with her that she was treated arbitrarily by her advisor and the other faculty who reviewed her work. But the appellate court disagreed, concluding that there was an independent, rational basis for the cumulative faculty evaluations, none of which violated any graduate policies.[37] One of the many cases the court cited in its first of two opinions on this matter was the US Supreme Court case, *University of Missouri v. Horowitz.*

THE TAKEAWAY

The arbitrary and/or capricious standard is the North Star that guides judicial analysis when students attempt to sue over an unsatisfactory grade or academic dismissal. It protects faculty whose actions can be classified as rational or tied to professional judgment. Under this standard, courts will not substitute their views on the correctness of a grading decision.

Capriciousness involves rashness in evaluating a student. This can be shown, at least enough to allow a lawsuit to proceed, when a student presents evidence that the professor may have been biased in some way, including racially, against the student. In one example, where a PhD student was expelled for plagiarism in a course, the student, who was Korean, was able to show that other students in the same course who were not Asian had also been caught committing more plagiarism than he had, but they were not sanctioned.[38] The student also alleged the professor told the student's family to "go back to Korea." In a similar case, in a master's-level course, a nurse-practitioner student of Haitian descent who was dismissed for poor grades was able to overcome the arbitrary and capricious standard because she was able to show that the professor who gave her a consequential and low final grade treated her discriminatorily when his behavior toward her was compared with his behavior toward white students in the class. Part of her evidence included the affidavits (sworn, written statements made under penalty of perjury) of three students in the class who stated that the classroom seating was divided by race and that the professor seemed to lecture to the white side of the room and even gave white students answers during exams but did not provide answers during exams to students on the other side of the room.[39]

But a student's allegation, without evidence, that a professor discriminated against him or her does not by itself overcome the arbitrary and capricious hurdle. Believing that one was the victim of racial or national origin discrimination is a conclusion, and such a conclusion needs to connect to a factual allegation. In a case where an Ethiopian American student was dismissed from a state university's pharmacy program for academic reasons, the student sued, claiming he was the victim of racial discrimination by a number of university officials. The student's pro se (self-representing) federal lawsuit used the term "arbitrary and capricious" with respect to how he was graded. However, the court dismissed most of the suit because, with respect to how the student was graded, the court stated "bare, conclusory allegations are insufficient to show racial, discriminatory animus."[40]

A case involving class-attendance grades should be considered carefully. A student got an F in a programming controller case (preventing him from receiving his degree) because he got a zero for his attendance grade, due to the professor's policy that no attendance points would be awarded if students missed more than six classes. The attendance grade was one third of the total course grade. In the lawsuit, the student claimed that he was never absent but that the professor was chronically so late to class the student would leave after waiting, even up to sixty minutes, for the class to start. Furthermore, a classmate submitted an affidavit stating he received no deduction on his attendance grade even though he also repeatedly left class for the same reason that the failed student did. This opened the door to allowing the student's suit to go forward because the appellate court said the evidence presented sufficiently raised the issue whether the professor applied his attendance policy in an arbitrary and capricious way.[41]

Courts also use other terms in place of arbitrariness or capriciousness. Some courts, instead, require a showing that an instructor's evaluation was the result of "bad faith." As a legal term, "good faith" tends to mean sincerity or honesty in one's actions. Consequently, actions showing bad faith are duplicitous or contrived. One appellate court in Indiana discussed this standard in a case where a public-university dental student who was expelled for poor clinical evaluations and missed classes sought an injunction (a court order requiring someone to do or stop doing something) to be reinstated.[42] In denying the student's request, the court said the student failed the evidentiary bar of showing that he was the victim of arbitrariness or capriciousness, or "bad faith." A few decades later, the same court defined bad faith in a case where an economics doctoral student at a public, Indiana university sued his professor and the university after the professor concluded that the student's doctoral thesis work was unsatisfactory.[43] There, the court said, while ruling against the student, "bad faith is not simply bad judgment or negligence. Rather, it implies the conscious doing of a wrong because of dishonest purpose or moral obliquity."[44] (I'm not sure "moral obliquity" clarifies our understanding of this.) Other courts, when dealing with student suits over grades, have added bad faith to their lexicon, even making it a variable for consideration along with arbitrariness and capriciousness.[45]

GRADING AT PUBLIC INSTITUTIONS SHOULDN'T INTERFERE WITH STUDENTS' FIRST AMENDMENT RIGHTS

Although there is a later chapter on the free-speech rights of faculty and students in teaching settings, it is important to note that faculty at public colleges and universities may not figuratively or literally downgrade students whose speech or views faculty don't like. It is a bedrock principle of American life that the First Amendment protects unpopular speech,[46] and faculty at public institutions are state actors who should protect their students' essential free-speech rights—not just because it is a constitutional prerogative but also because it is the right and moral thing to do.

A case from California is instructive and cautionary. At a speech class in a community college, the professor asked students to give an informative speech on any topic of their choosing. One of the students chose God and his Christian faith as his topic, and part of his speech included talking about his belief that marriage should be between a man and a woman. (This class was held during the time that California's Proposition 8, on gay marriage, was on the ballot.) After the student recited a dictionary definition of marriage and quoted two Bible verses, the professor interrupted the student's speech, called him a "fascist bastard," refused to let the student finish the speech, and then dismissed the class. When the student asked about his speech grade, the professor wrote on the grade evaluation form, "[a]sk God what your grade is" and "pros[elytizing] is inappropriate in public school."[47] Among the lawsuits the student eventually filed, one was against the professor for violating the student's First Amendment rights. The professor defaulted (failed or refused to respond to the lawsuit, thereby losing it automatically), and the college disciplined the professor for his actions against the student, actions that an appellate court referred to as aggressively abusive. After the professor defaulted, the trial court awarded the student $5,000 in damages (an award of money), and, in a follow-up claim, the court ordered the professor to pay the student's legal fees of $7,697.50.[48]

THE TAKEAWAY

A student could overcome the arbitrary and capricious standard if it can be shown that a faculty member acted without any rational basis, or acted with rashness, class-wide inconsistency, or malevolence toward the student or the student's course-related views or constitutionally protected beliefs.

Due-Process Requirements for Public Colleges and Universities

You Make the Call

- **The Case of the Cheating Med Student Who Would Have Been "Due-Processed" Differently Had She Been a Law Student**

At a public medical school, two professors coteaching a course believed one of the students was acting surreptitiously during a final exam. Their suspicions were based on the student holding her test paper up in the air, looking around the room, and writing her exam on her left thigh, positioning herself in such a way that she was turned toward another student seated just two seats away. When this other student got up midway through the exam to ask one of the professors a question, the professors advised this other student to cover her exam document more carefully. When this second student left the exam room, the first student's odd test behaviors ended. The professors had a combined experience of over thirty-five years, and that experience gnawed at them. So, when they checked both exams for consistency, they discovered that the student who caught their attention had the exact same answers as the student whom they had warned to be more careful—for seven pages in a row—until the time during the exam when the other student was cautioned to be more circumspect in how she displayed her own test. The professors then asked a statistician to evaluate the likelihood of both exams having the exact same wrong multiple-choice answers on those seven pages of the exam, and the conclusion was 1 in 200,000. The professors gave the suspiciously acting student an F in the course for cheating on the final, explaining to her their reasoning and statistical analysis. The student appealed the F to the professors directly and presented her own statistical analysis, which then caused the professors to do a second analysis, whereby they reduced the chance of cheating to a range from 1 in 500 to 1 in 5,000. The student then appealed the F to the department chair of the two professors, who ruled against her. She then appealed to the medical school's student promotion committee, where she was represented by legal counsel. The professors chose not to attend this hearing, but the transcripts of their meeting with the student, and other related documents, were presented to the committee. Finally, the dean adopted the committee's recommendation, and the student was dismissed.

In her lawsuit against her professors and various administrators, the student argued she was denied her due-process rights because 1) the professors were not required to be at the student promotion committee hearing and, therefore, she couldn't cross-examine them; 2) the rule under which she was charged prohibited the "appearance of cheating," which she said was vague and overbroad; and 3) she was judged under the "substantial evidence" standard. Notably, had she been an undergraduate or a law-school student at the same institution, then—thanks to those schools' student-conduct and appeals policies—she would have been able to cross-examine the accusing professors at a hearing, she wouldn't have been subject to an appearance-of-cheating standard, and she would have been found guilty only of cheating under a higher standard of proof—clear and convincing evidence.

Did the student win on the grounds that she was denied due process?

(The answer will be given at the end of the chapter. Consider how the principles in this chapter affect your decision and reasoning.)

Because public college and universities are governmental entities, they—through their employees—must abide by the US Constitution's (and their own state's constitution's) provisions on protected rights. Due process, which is mentioned in both the Fifth and Fourteenth Amendments, is one of those rights. Private institutions, however, generally owe no civil liberties or civil rights to their students, unless an exception can be made when a statute applies universally what the Constitution cannot. For example, as will be discussed in a later chapter, a California statute, called the Leonard Law, requires that students at private educational institutions be given the same speech rights as students at public institutions have.[49] As it concerns due process, which is no easy constitutional subject to understand, it does not apply to college students at private colleges or universities, including religious institutions. Therefore, whatever process rights those students have are granted to them by university policy (which is another example of contract law) or by the standard about which this chapter is primarily concerned: the arbitrary and capricious standard. In a case discussed earlier in the chapter, where a PhD student at a private university in Illinois sued her professor and the university after being dismissed, no mention in either appellate court decision was made of "due process." There was simply an analysis of arbitrariness and capriciousness.[50] In a case involving a private nursing college in West Virginia, a student was expelled for having a low cumulative GPA, because the college increased its graduation-eligible GPA requirement after the student was enrolled and, according to the student, after she was assured by the faculty that the graduation-eligibility requirements wouldn't be changed. While ruling against her, the Supreme Court of West Virginia applied only the arbitrary and capricious standard.[51] And, in a Mississippi case, a student was expelled from a private osteopathic-medicine college for a variety of discipline-worthy behaviors. After multiple university appeals, the student sued and lost. In upholding the expulsion, the court made sure to acknowledge that, because the college involved was private, no due-process analysis would be done.[52] All that was left was to determine whether there had been any breach of contract or arbitrary and capricious action, and the student's case was dispatched forthrightly.

THE TAKEAWAY

Students at private colleges and universities do not have due-process rights with respect to how they are graded or disciplined. Faculty are required to follow only the arbitrary and capricious standard or contractual obligations established by college policies.

Due-Process Requirements for Academic Decisions and Academic Discipline: There Is a Difference

Due process is bifurcated, in that there is "substantive" due process and also "procedural" due process. Substantive due process concerns an elementary fairness in the substance of an underlying action. Courts often reference substantive due process by discussing whether the government deprived a person of a life, liberty, or property interest and, if so, for a sufficient reason. Procedural due process is about whether the government followed the necessary steps before taking away one's life, liberty, or property. And the higher or more sacred the interest at risk is (the substantive due-process right), the more extensive the procedural due process is to be provided. For faculty and their decision-making concerning student performance or behavior, procedural due process is the more relevant issue, and the two US Supreme Court cases earlier discussed are a starting point again.

UNIVERSITY OF MISSOURI V. HOROWITZ (1978)[53]

In this case, a medical student was dismissed for poor attendance and clinical evaluations (including personal hygiene), not because her grades were failing. She had many conversations with faculty members prior to her dismissal, but she was never given an informal or formal hearing, even though a review committee met and recommended her dismissal. Because the university dismissed her based on a purely academic decision made by her faculty about her worthiness, the Supreme Court concluded no hearing was required. Procedural due process had been satisfied by applying the arbitrary and capricious standard. And the court did not find that the student was denied a life, liberty, or property interest protected by the Fourteenth Amendment in being dismissed from medical school for academic reasons. But the court recognized a higher standard existed for the review of academic discipline of students. Referencing one of its earlier cases involving the discipline of a high-school student, *Goss v. Lopez*, the court said that all that was required for due process in a disciplinary review was some form of an "informal give-and-take" between the student and the decision-maker about the student's conduct.[54] Here, though, the barest of procedures needed had been provided.

UNIVERSITY OF MICHIGAN V. EWING (1985)[55]

This student was dismissed from a dual undergraduate-medical degree program for failing an exam on which a passing grade was required for earning the degree. The student was given multiple appeals of the dismissal decision, including an in-person hearing. In upholding the university's decision, the court assumed the student had a substantive property interest at stake but nevertheless concluded that any due-process requirements had been satisfied. This was because the court already concluded that the decision was not arbitrary or capricious but, rather, was made with careful deliberation.[56] Because the student was not being disciplined (i.e., for acting unethically or violating a behavior policy), the due-process requirement was minimal.

THE TAKEAWAY

The US Supreme Court's decisions on public-university students' rights to due process show that less is required for the review of a faculty's decision that is purely academic, because of the arbitrary and capricious standard. However, for a faculty's disciplinary action against a student, some opportunity—not necessarily a formal hearing—is required for the student to provide his or her own version of events.

As courts grappled with due-process claims made by students at public colleges and universities, they followed the US Supreme Court precedent and continued to distinguish between the due process required in making a final decision on a professor's academic judgment about a student and that required in making a final decision about whether a student cheated or engaged in any other discipline-worthy conduct. In a case decided a few years after *Horowitz*, a dental student at a public institution went to court, seeking an injunction ordering the dental school to accept him back in good standing after he had been dismissed for various academic shortfalls, including missing too many classes and having too low a GPA.[57] During one clinical course, the student was expected to perform five root canals throughout the semester, but he cancelled all five, of which three cancellations were made on the day of the appointments. By the time of his dismissal, he had earned twenty-one clinical points, whereas the class average was seventy-five (rounded up). The student's suit included claims of breach of contract and a denial of due process, in part on the grounds that the written university policy on student dismissal wasn't followed in his case. In ruling against the student, the court noted that the university policy that the student referenced was a policy on the process of dismissing a student for "disciplinary" reasons; there was no written policy on dismissing a student for academic insufficiency.[58]

Even in cases where universities fail to follow their own written policy on academic dismissal entirely, that is no guarantee the student will win. In a case where a psychology PhD student was dismissed for academic reasons—and where she sued for breach of contract, infliction of emotional distress, and sex- and disability-based discrimination—the student argued that her due-process rights were violated because the faculty who initially found her work lacking were also part of the review process and because the university policy on appeals was not properly followed.[59] In finding for the university, the court agreed with a lower court's conclusion that no facts were presented that showed anyone acted arbitrarily or capriciously toward the student and that, even if the upper-level appeal process wasn't correctly followed, the department-level review the student received passed the constitutional due-process requirement for academic dismissal.[60] In other words, she may not have received perfect or ideal due process, but it was good enough.

Decisions to discipline a student for wrongful academic behavior invoke a higher due-process standard because the stakes are higher for the student. (It is worse to be considered a cheat rather than a dolt.) And, in those instances where disciplined students sue, courts often inquire for due-process purposes about the opportunity the charged student had to counter the allegations or to offer his or her own story. For example, a student in a community college was flunked in a nursing course for having cheated on a homework assignment in that course. The decision to flunk the student was made by the professor in consultation with other nursing faculty, and the consequence for the F was dismissal from the nursing program.[61] The student asked his school for a hearing to appeal the sanctions against him, but his request was denied on the grounds that his sanctions were academic decisions. In the legal case, the court ruled in favor of the student, concluding that flunking him in a course for an alleged plagiarism on an assignment was an academic disciplinary decision that warranted more due process for him than he received, which was almost none.[62] Furthermore, and importantly, nothing in the school's disciplinary policies granted faculty the unilateral right to decide to flunk a student in a course as punishment for cheating on an assignment. Even though courts don't require a university to follow a "literal adherence" to its stated policies,[63] when it comes to professors meting out academic discipline, the due-process bar is still set higher.

THE TAKEAWAY

Disciplining a public-university student for cheating or a similar improper course-related action should be done with careful deliberation and with attention to your institution's policies on students' rights. Compared to the lower due-process expectations attendant to a purely academic decision, when faculty take disciplinary action against a student, more "process" is required. Some basic appeal mechanism is required for students to provide their own version of events. While that does not necessarily mean that a formal hearing or a cross-examination opportunity is mandated, disciplinary due process involves more than satisfying the arbitrary and capricious standard.

The Possibility of Immunity for Faculty Decisions at Public Institutions

Having a valid defense to a lawsuit is, of course, a good thing. For example, truth is a defense to a defamation claim, because an essential element of defamation (which will be discussed in a later chapter) is that the defendant's harmful statement made to a third party about the plaintiff was false. But there is something better than having a good defense or defense lawyer, and that is having immunity against being sued in the first place. Qualified immunity for government actors is not a controversy-free subject; however, creation of such immunity is an attempt to balance the need to hold government actors accountable for reckless or malicious actions while also protecting them against being sued for their every unpopular action or even unpopular opinion.[64] Many states have statutes that provide qualified immunity in some form. Because faculty at public colleges and universities are state actors, it is possible that, if their state law has an immunity provision for government actors, it will help the faculty to be released from the suit, even if it continues against the institution.

By way of example, Indiana has such a statute related to limited instances of immunity from tort liability.[65] It states, "A governmental entity or an employee acting within the scope of the employee's employment is not liable if a loss results from the following:"[66] and then lists various situations or actions against which a government employee is immunized. One of those listings says a state employee will not be liable for "[t]he performance of a discretionary function."[67] If you're thinking that grading or similar judgments are discretionary functions and that grading is an act an instructor does during the course of his or her employment, you would be right. The discretionary aspect of grading is, perhaps, the primary reason why courts are so resistant to getting involved in grade fights, choosing instead to apply the arbitrary and capricious standard. In a case from Indiana, earlier referenced in this chapter, an economics doctoral student sued his professor and Purdue University after the professor concluded that the student's doctoral thesis work was unsatisfactory. The lawsuit was for breach of contract, negligence, and defamation. Yet, before ruling for Purdue on all counts, the appellate court acknowledged approvingly that the trial court granted the professor's motion to be removed from the suit because he was "a public employee acting in the course of his employment."[68] Similar cases in Indiana resulted in public-university professors being excused from student suits related to academic decisions or academic discipline because they were immune, due to the fact that they were acting in the course of their employment and engaged in a discretionary function.[69] And a later statute requires that the state provide and pay for legal counsel when a state employee is defending themself under this immunity umbrella.[70] That qualifies as very good news.

Not all faculty actions are covered by state-granted immunity, however. Continuing the Indiana example, a student could keep a professor in a lawsuit by showing that the professor's actions were, according to another statute, "clearly outside the scope of the employee's employment; malicious; willful and wanton."[71] That reads as an alternate description of the arbitrary and capricious standard. But, in a case that proves the adage, once again, that no good deed goes unpunished, a professor at a state college in Indiana was required to stay as a defendant in a student lawsuit, where a student was injured in the last class of the semester. Why would a student sue a professor for getting injured while in class? Well, the professor invited everyone to his house for the last class to discuss the final exam and enjoy some social time together, and the student broke her ankle when she tripped and fell on the professor's porch steps as she left for the evening.[72] In responding to the negligence suit, the professor argued that holding his class at home was covered by Indiana's Tort Immunity Statute, because he was acting as a professor of a state college at the time of her injury. But the court disagreed, believing that the professor's employment was incidental to the injuries the student sustained, which she said were due to poor lighting and the absence of a handrail. Hence, the court concluded that there was no "causal connection" between the student's injuries and the professor's status as a state employee and, consequentially, no tort immunity.[73]

THE TAKEAWAY

If you teach at a state college or university, your state may have a statute that provides legal immunity for your actions when you are acting in the scope of your employment (which means doing a job-related task) and the action for which you have been sued is a discretionary function. The professional judgment involved in grading decisions entails using the kind of discretion for which immunity should apply. But be careful about off-campus actions with students that could result in injury. Holding class in alternate locations, including at your home or in a public place, is a great way to build rapport with your students and make the semester more meaningful and fun. But . . . when engaged in those semi-unofficial, off-campus activities, make sure you are covered by an insurance policy.

Cheating Detection, Online Courses, and AI/ChatGPT

You Make the Call

- **The Case of the Remote Room Scan**

Because of the COVID-19 pandemic, during the spring 2021 semester at a state college in Ohio, the college required students to pass a "daily health assessment" in order to attend classes in-person. Otherwise, they attended remotely. A student in a Chemistry II course was unable to pass the assessment because of various health and immunity issues he lived with, so he attended all his courses remotely. Early in the course, the student disputed a syllabus policy that said, "The proctors and I reserve the right to ask any student, before, during, or after an exam to show their surroundings, screen, and/or work area. We will send you a private chat to ask you to do this. If you do not see the chat message, I will use the microphone to ask you to check the chat." That policy was removed a few days later. The university's policy on remote exams was that students had to take them where they would be alone and uninterrupted. Because the student in question lived at his mother's home, that private place was his bedroom. Part of the remote anticheating devices the university used included built-in software in Blackboard, as well as proctoring tools in Respondus and Honorlock, both of which use some form of AI to flag suspicious activity. A few hours before a remote test was to be given, the university testing service emailed the student to tell him that it would be conducting an electronic room scan to check for the presence of any unauthorized test-aid materials. The student responded that he had various confidential materials (including tax forms) in his room and that he had no time to clean up his room before the test. Before the test started, the testing services proctor conducted a room scan by using the student's computer camera. The visual search took place in less than a minute, and the scan was video recorded and retained, per university policy. Other students taking the remote test can see the room scans of the other students. The testing services has no policy on what to do if a student refuses a room scan. Sometime after taking the exam, the student sued the university in federal court, alleging the room scan violated his Fourth Amendment right against an unreasonable search of his property.

Is the room scan a search, for Fourth Amendment purposes? If so, is this an unreasonable search? (Did the student win?)

(The answer will be given at the end of the chapter. Consider how the principles in this chapter affect your decision and reasoning.)

Attempts at preventing or catching cheating or plagiarism might be akin to having Sisyphus play the arcade game Whac-A-Mole. When Harvard suspected in 2012 that over half the class in an introduction-to-Congress course had cheated on a take-home final exam, it investigated over 120 students whose answers were more than coincidentally similar and ended up requiring the withdrawal of around seventy of them.[74] The rules for this infamous exam might lead one to think cheating wouldn't have been considered, since the instructions said, in part, "The exam is completely open book, open note, open internet, etc. However, in all other regards, this should fall under similar guidelines that apply to in-class exams." Students were also told not to discuss the exam with others.[75] Two upshots of the scandal were the eventual creation of a Harvard undergraduates honor code[76] and Yale encouraging its faculty to keep all exams in-class.[77] Yet, a 2013 *Harvard Crimson* survey of graduating seniors showed that over 30 percent of respondents acknowledged cheating on papers or take-home exams.[78] And this was before the COVID-19 pandemic caused almost all courses to be online, triggering its own cheating pandemic.[79] Proctor U, an online test-monitoring service, reported that, before the COVID-19 pandemic, the cheating rate for the tests it proctored was less than one percent, while, during the spring 2020 lockdown semester, the cheating rate increased to above eight percent (from a sample size of 1.3 million exams).[80] And back at Harvard, during the 2020–2021 academic year, twenty-seven students, representing a six-year high, were forced to withdraw because of academic dishonesty.[81]

AI DETECTION AND CHEATING ACCUSATIONS NEED TO BE JUDICIOUSLY CONSIDERED

The ramifications of AI are countless. Some of the possibilities are life-changing, and some of them are, possibly, life-extinguishing, according to the US State Department. A 2024 US State Department–commissioned report on the national security risks of advanced AI discusses in its executive summary the worst-case scenario, "catastrophic" risks posed by AI, defining catastrophic risk to include human extinction.[82] On a much lighter note, Chapter 4 discusses the intellectual-property controversies posed by AI and whether students or faculty can claim copyright ownership to AI-generative and AI-collaborative work.

The ease of access to AI and its ability to live up to stated and feared capabilities has created conditions on campus where, perhaps, the oral exam and the "blue book" essay might come back into fashion. There are a host of technologies, including Turnitin, GPTZero, ZeroGPT, and Copyleaks, that claim they can assist in finding work that was generated by AI. Thinking about this issue from a course-planning perspective, an economics colleague of mine created an equation-based "vulnerability index" to help business faculty determine how at risk their courses are to ChatGPT-generated cheating. In his research study, he used this vulnerability index across disciplines and teaching modalities, and this index provides a way for instructors to assess the vulnerability of their courses to various language-based predictive models.[83]

AI-assisted cheating isn't just for students. Two lawyers were caught in 2023 using ChatGPT to write a legal brief, which cited six cases that never existed outside a predictive language algorithm. Because judges and their clerks look up case law, the lawyers (who failed to do that themselves) were fined $5,000.[84] Yet, it could be asked how could anyone consistently catch AI-created student work when, in 2023, three British lecturers used ChatGPT to write a paper on the dangers of students using ChatGPT, which they were able to get published in a peer-reviewed journal.[85] The putative authors, who notified the journal after the paper was accepted, titled it, "Chatting and Cheating: Ensuring Academic Integrity in the Era of ChatGPT."[86] Getting the paper published was intended to be an urgent plea on the urgency for colleges to come to grips with AI-generated plagiarism, a need crystalized in the realization that the paper sailed through the journal's online plagiarism detector and was read by four peer-reviewers who raised no red flags.

As mentioned in the Introduction, in 2023 an instructor at a state university in Texas errantly accused many students in his class of using ChatGPT, putting their completion of the course (and college degrees for some) at risk. After copying and pasting their final assignments into ChatGPT, the instructor asked it to determine whether the submissions were authentic. According to the *Washington Post*, he even wrote on one student's paper: "I will not grade chat Gpt s***."[87] But ChatGPT is not intended to catch AI-generated plagiarism, and, ultimately, no student was penalized. This highlights that faculty should not put the cart before the horse when it comes to declaring students' work to be plagiarized, including when using software that claims to be capable of catching AI-generated work.

It is a serious thing to accuse a student of cheating, and, as discussed earlier, students who are so accused at public universities are entitled to a higher standard of due process than if the F they got was the result of a purely academic decision. Faculty at public and private colleges risk appearing to be rash or even arbitrary if they are content to let AI be the sole determinant for accusing a student of cheating. Recent research shows an alarming rate at which AI detectors incorrectly conclude whether work is AI-generated.[88] One study on AI-detection sites claimed their accuracy to be around 28 percent, with the best tool achieving only 50 percent accuracy.[89] Even the US Constitution was flagged by an AI-detector as being AI-generated.[90] This is because the Constitution has been fed so many times into large language models (LLM) like ChatGPT for its training and fine-tuning, that the Constitution has what is known as low perplexity, which to AI detectors indicates a higher chance that it was written by AI. (As of July, 2023, OpenAi.com removed its AI Classifier, due to its low rate of accuracy.) As many colleges have done, your institution may caution against using AI detection, or it may advise against its use, or, perhaps it may have made certain AI detection technology unavailable.[91] But other research also brings into question whether the studies, themselves, on AI detectors are accurate.[92] Then there is the care faculty need to take against jumping to conclusions with respect to foreign students, because some evidence indicates that GPT detectors have a detection bias against those for whom English is not their primary language.[93]

Furthermore, one can sincerely ask whether the use of AI-generated work is plagiarism at all. Notwithstanding the extreme examples of asking OpenAI to write you a novel like *The Great Gatsby*, for instance, if a traditional definition of plagiarism is the unattributed work or written ideas of other people, then, without a clear policy about unauthorized use of AI, students could make a sound argument that their use of ChatGPT, for instance, broke no rule. As well, students might use AI to help them generate solutions or find answers to questions that haven't been formally asked, but which could lead to the answers, calculations, or other work students will personally generate. AI might be thought of as a student's administrative assistant, rather than a cheating pathway. Therefore, faculty concerned about avoiding unnecessary entanglements, legal or otherwise, should include an AI policy in their syllabi, one that at the very least details what is prohibited conduct, particularly if there is no existing institutional policy. A sample below on prohibited AI use comes from my university's Center for the Enhancement of Learning and Teaching (CELT).[94]

- [This course] assumes that work submitted by students—all process work, drafts, low-stakes writing, final versions, and all other submissions—will be produced by the students themselves, working individually or in groups. This means that the following would be considered violations of academic integrity: a student has another person/entity/artificial intelligence (e.g., ChatGPT) do the writing of any substantive portion of an assignment for them.
- Developing writing, analytical, and critical thinking skills are integral learning outcomes of this course. Thus, all writing assignments should be the product

of the student's efforts. Developing strong competencies in this area will prepare you for a competitive workplace. Therefore, any work produced with the assistance of AI or other automated tools is not permitted and will be considered a violation of academic integrity.
- In the event of suspicion regarding the use of AI or other automated tools to complete coursework, the instructor reserves the right to assign a grade of 0 for the work in question. Furthermore, the instructor will schedule a meeting with the student to discuss the matter and determine if it constitutes a case of academic misconduct. Maintaining academic integrity is crucial for your growth and preparation for a competitive future in the professional realm.

Where student use of AI is permitted, syllabi statements should also be included that provide clarity on how or when it may be used, including if instructor permission is required.

THE TAKEAWAY

Faculty at public universities should consider if their use of remote testing, anti-cheating mechanisms unreasonably interfere with students' Fourth Amendment rights against unreasonable search and seizure. If possible, do not go beyond your institution's rules, so at the very least you can show you've done nothing arbitrary or capricious. No faculty should make a formal decision on whether a student has plagiarized or cheated simply by relying on AI-detection software. Include in your syllabus an AI policy on prohibited and any allowed AI use, and provide students with the opportunity to present their side of the story upon letting them know you suspect the submission of prohibited, AI-generated work.

Final Takeaways

- Don't worry about committing educational malpractice. That type of tort lawsuit hasn't been accepted in American courts due to the judicial view that courts shouldn't evaluate how well or inadequately students believe they have been taught.
- Colleges, but not faculty, are in contractual relationships with their students.
- The US Supreme Court and other federal and state courts grant faculty wide latitude when making professional judgments about a student's academic performance. A student suing a faculty member would have to provide some evidence early in the case that a faculty's action was arbitrary or capricious.
- The arbitrary and/or capricious standard is the North Star that guides judicial analysis when students attempt to sue over an unsatisfactory grade or aca-

demic dismissal. It protects faculty whose actions can be classified as rational or tied to professional judgment. Under this standard, courts will not substitute their views on the correctness of a grading decision.

- A student could overcome the arbitrary and capricious standard if it can be shown that a faculty member acted without any rational basis, or acted with rashness, class-wide inconsistency, or malevolence toward the student or the student's course-related views or constitutionally protected beliefs.
- Students at private colleges and universities do not have due-process rights with respect to how they are graded or disciplined. Faculty are required to follow only the arbitrary and capricious standard or contractual obligations established by college policies.
- Less due process is owed to public-university students when they contest a negative academic decision. The arbitrary and capricious standard and existing university policy is what must be satisfied.
- Disciplining a public-university student for cheating or a similar improper course-related action should be done with careful deliberation and with attention to your institution's policies on students' rights. Some basic appeal mechanism is required for students to have an opportunity to provide their own version of events, but that does not require a formal hearing or a cross-examination opportunity.
- If you teach at a state college or university and are sued over a grade or a cheating determination, your state may have a statute that provides limited immunity against tort liability for those discretionary actions because they were committed in the scope of your employment.
- Add policy statements to your syllabi on what constitutes prohibited or accepted use of ChatGPT and other forms of AI. Be careful about accusing a student of unlawfully using AI-generated work in your course, based solely on AI-detection software. Provide students with a chance to respond to your accusation.

How Did You Make the Calls?

1 – The Case of the Doubly Correct Corporations-Law Exam Answer

In this case, a law student at New York Law School received zero points on a corporations-law exam answer for answering an essay question twice: once by applying Delaware law, as was asked in the question; and a second time by applying New York law, which was the state where the law school was located. Because of the zero, her grade on the exam was a D, which caused her GPA to sink low enough to put her at risk for academic expulsion because she had already been on academic probation. When she disputed the grade with her professor, he told her that her answer on Delaware law was correct and, had she stopped there, she would have received full credit for that answer. But, by not following his instructions and providing an extra answer, the implication was that she didn't know which answer was correct, but hoped he would make the choice. Her attempts at internally appealing the grade failed, and then she sued.

Did the student win? Or does a professor have the right to mark as incorrect an answer that is, technically, correct but fails to follow the instructions?

Decision: The New York Supreme Court, Appellate Division (which is the mid-level appellate court in New York) ruled in her favor.[95] It remanded the case back to the trial court that dismissed the case, because it found that the law school presented no evidence to the student that the decision of the professor was rational and not arbitrary and capricious (beyond the professor's theory of his grade decision), in light of the impact the D had on her law-school future. In the same case, however, she also lost an argument that her low grade in a constitutional-law final exam that same semester was due to the professor misleading some of the class, including her, to believe they couldn't use the text or other reference material on the exam, when in fact they could. Here, the court agreed with the school that, even if it was the professor's fault on the miscommunication, having those test aids would have provided only marginal help. The court concluded that how hard a test would be with or without the use of extra materials is not something it should evaluate.

Decision 2: But . . . there's more. The law school appealed, and the highest New York appellate court reversed, deciding in favor of the school.[96] The court cited the US Supreme Court decision in *Michigan v. Ewing*, among others, and ruled that this corporations-law exam kerfuffle was a substantive grading dispute and that courts are not supposed to get involved in those conflicts unless there's evidence of bad faith, arbitrariness, capriciousness, or irrationality. Otherwise, it added, court intervention would promote countless instances of litigation.

2 – The Case of the Too-Talkative Therapy Student

In this case, a graduate assistant teaching a master's-level therapy internship course at Lehigh University gave a student a zero for her class-participation grade, because the instructor thought the student's participation was disruptive and counterproductive to the experience of everyone in the class. That resulted in the student getting a C+, which necessitated her changing her degree program to social work. She then sued the instructor and the university for $1.3 million, which was what her lawyer said she would lose over the course of her career, since she wouldn't be a therapist—due to that C+. Her father was a finance professor at the university and testified at the trial about the unfairness of his daughter's grade. The student argued that she was discriminated against because she was in favor of gay marriage, while claiming the instructor was not, an accusation the instructor vehemently denied. At the non-jury trial, other faculty also testified about the lack of professionalism of the student in their classes. During the trial, the judge implored the parties to settle but also stated that he didn't understand how a student who attended every class and did participate was given no class-participation points.

Did the student win? Does an instructor have the discretion to award no participation points for student participation the instructor considers to be unsuitable or disruptive?

Decision: The trial judge ruled in favor of Lehigh University and the instructor. Acknowledging that neither he nor any attorney in the case could find any case where a court overturned a course grade, the judge concluded that he was bound by existing case law and that no sufficient evidence was presented that the C+ was given for anything other than purely academic reasons. The student appealed, and the Pennsylvania Court of Appeals affirmed the decision.[97] The court found the university's evidence of the student's unprofessionalism in class plausible and concluded that, even though another instructor might not have given the student zero participation points, it had no authority to change the grade. Summarily, that type of grading is too subjective and not amenable to judicial review.

3 – The Case of the Unrounded Grade

A college student at the University of Cincinnati sued his instructor because the instructor wouldn't round up the student's 95.28-percent final grade, resulting in a B, to a 96-percent final grade, which would have resulted in an A. The student believed he was owed the rounding for two reasons: 1) he lost points for missing a mandatory field trip that was scheduled for an out-of-class time when the student couldn't attend; and 2) he came to learn that two other students' grades were rounded up to an A, including that of one student who had his 95.30-percent grade bumped up to an A.

Does this pass or fail the arbitrary and capricious test?

Decision: The instructor won. The Ohio Court of Appeals ruled that courts should stay out of these kinds of fights and called the student's field trip complaint "patently feckless."[98] As to the student's argument that he was discriminated against because those two other students got grade-rounded As, the court said, in more formal language, too bad so sad. They got higher grades to start with than he did, and that's the kind of call instructors are entitled to make.

(This case will be discussed again in the next chapter on whether a syllabus is a contract, because the student also argued that the instructor's failure to round up his grade breached the contract created by the course syllabus.)

4 – The Case of the Cheating Medical Student Who Would Have Been "Due-Processed" Differently Had She Been a Law Student

In this long and winding road of a case, a medical student at Indiana University was caught cheating on a final exam, after two professors thought her in-exam behavior was suspicious. Statistical analysis, while varying, convinced the professors that the student copied copious amounts of an unwitting student's exam answers. The professors gave the student an F in the course for cheating, which the student appealed internally multiple times, but she was ultimately expelled by the dean, who followed the recommendation of the student promotion committee. In the lawsuit, the student argued she was denied her due-process rights because 1) the professors were not required to be at the student promotion committee hearing and, therefore, she couldn't cross-examine them; 2) the rule under which she was charged prohibited the "appearance of cheating," which she said was vague and overbroad; and 3) she was judged under the "substantial evidence" standard. Notably, had she been an undergraduate or law-school student at the same university, then—thanks to those schools' student-conduct and appeals policies—she would have been able to cross-examine the accusing professors at a hearing, she wouldn't have been subject to an appearance-of-cheating rule, and she would only have been found guilty of cheating under a higher standard of proof—clear and convincing evidence.

Did the student win on the grounds that she was denied due process?

Decision: The student lost. The Indiana Court of Appeals concluded that nothing the decision-makers did in the investigation and disciplinary process was arbitrary or capricious; nor was she denied her due-process rights. [99] As to the professors' belief that the student had cheated, the court found nothing arbitrary or capricious in their suspicions or beliefs (based on their statistical analysis). And, regarding her due-process claim, the court acknowledged that due-process expectations are higher in academic discipline cases, but the standard is met when the student is given the opportunity to respond to and defend against the charges, which she was. There's no requirement of a formal tribunal before a neutral party or a right to cross-examine witnesses. Nothing required that every student in all colleges or schools at Indiana University be judged by a singular standard when accused of cheating. And, even though she was charged with the appearance of cheating (admittedly, a vague concept), she was found to have actually cheated. Finally, considering the student had been caught cheating on an earlier exam and was suspended despite the student promotions committee's recommendation that she be expelled, the court concluded that her expulsion this time—and the manner in which she was dismissed—passed the due-process test.

5 – The Case of the Remote Room Scan

A Cleveland State University student with health issues that prevented him from taking in-person classes during the COVID-19–affected spring 2021 semester was subject to a pre-exam, remote visual scan of his home bedroom before he took an online exam. Per university rules on students taking online exams, students were subject to having their computer camera accessed by the testing services personnel, who would scan their location for any unauthorized test aids. When testing services contacted him for the room scan two hours before a scheduled exam, the student asked that the scan not be done because he had no time to put away various confidential items in his room. The scan took place, nevertheless, and it lasted less than a minute. The student then brought a federal lawsuit, alleging a violation of his Fourth Amendment's search and seizure rights.

Is the room scan a search, for Fourth Amendment purposes? If so, is this an unreasonable search? (Did the student win?)

Decision: In a lengthy and case law–laden decision, a federal district court agreed with the student.[100] It first concluded that the student had a reasonable expectation of privacy in his room and that the scan qualified as a "search" for Fourth Amendment purposes. It then ruled the search to be constitutionally unreasonable. Despite the quickness of the room scan, the court noted that other students could see it and that other, less intrusive means for combatting remote exam honesty were available and in use. In weighing the student's privacy interest against the university's interest in scanning the student's room, the court ruled that the search was unreasonable, but . . . only issued an injunction that the university no longer remotely scan that student's room. It refused to apply its ruling to any other Cleveland State student because no other student legally opposed the room scan.

Decision 1.5: Cleveland State University appealed the court's ruling but, in 2023, the student passed away. Consequently, because no other student was involved in this case, all appeals in this matter were considered moot and the original court decision was vacated (rescinded; annulled).[101]

Notes

1. David Sedaris, *Me Talk Pretty One Day* (United Kingdom: Abacus, 2002).
2. *Peter W. v. San Francisco Unified School District*, 60 Cal.App.3d 814 (Cal. Ct. App. 1976).
3. *Finstad v. Washington University of Topeka*, 845. P.2d 645 (Kan. 1993).
4. Id.

5. Id., at 692.
6. *Donohue v. Copiague Union Free School District*, 47 N.Y.2d 440 (N.Y. 1979).
7. *Bittle v. Oklahoma City University*, 6 P.3d 509 (Okla. Civ. App. 2000).
8. *Michel v. Yale University*, 547 F.Supp.3d 179 (D. Conn. 2021).
9. *Polley v. Northwestern University*, 560 F.Supp.3d 1197 (N.D. Ill 2021).
10. *Zumbrum v. University of Southern California*, 25 Cal.App.3d 1 (Cal. 2d Dist. 1972).
11. *Gordon v. Purdue University*, 862 N.E.2d 1244 (Ind. App. Ct. 2007).
12. *Indiana University v. Spiegel*, 186 N.E.3d 1151 (Ind. Ct. App. 2022).
13. Id.; *Neel v. Indiana University*, 435 N.E.2d 607 (Ind. Ct. App. 1982).
14. *Hernandez v. Illinois Institute of Technology*, 63 F4th 661 (7th Cir. 2023).
15. K. B. Melear, "The Contractual Relationship between Student and Institutions: Disciplinary, Academic, and Consumer Contexts," *Journal of College and University Law* 30, no. 1 (2003): 175–208.
16. *Bradshaw v. Rawlings*, 612 F.2d 135 (3rd Cir. 1979).
17. *Dixon v. Alabama State Board of Education*, 294 F.2d 150 (5th Cir. 1961).
18. *Benefield v. University of Alabama at Birmingham*, 214 F.Supp.2d 1212 (N.D. Ala. 2002).
19. https://www.weather.gov/safety/lightning-odds.
20. https://www.floridamuseum.ufl.edu/shark-attacks/odds/compare-risk/death/.
21. *Keys v. Sawyer*, 353 F.Supp. 936, at 939–40 (S.D. Tex. 1973).
22. *Johnson v. Cuyahoga County Community College*, 489 N.E2d 1088, at 1090 (Ct. Common Pleas, 1985).
23. 435 U.S. 78.
24. Id., at 90.
25. Id., at 91.
26. 474 U.S. 214.
27. Id., footnote 2.
28. Id., at 225.
29. Id., footnote 11.
30. *Rollins v. University of Alabama*, 885 F.Supp.2d 1239 (S.D. Ala. 2018).
31. *Johnson v. Cuyahoga County Community College*, 489 N.E2d 1088, at 1090 (Ct. Common Pleas, 1985).
32. 474 U.S 214, at 225.
33. *McIntosh v. Borough of Manhattan Community College*, 78 A.D.2d 839 (N.Y. App. Div. 1980).
34. *Hamilton v. City College of New York*, 173 F.Supp.2d 181 (S.D.N.Y. 2001).
35. *Bilut v. Northwestern University*, 645 N.E.2d 536 (Ill. App. Ct. 1994).
36. *Bilut v. Northwestern University*, 692 N.E.2d 1327 (Ill. App. Ct. 1998).
37. Id.
38. *Park v. Purdue University*, 2011 WL 1361409 (N.D. Ind. 2011).
39. *Jacques v. Adelphi University*, 2011 WL 6709443 (E.D.N.Y. 2011).
40. *Jemaneh v. University of Wyoming*, 82 F.Supp.3d 1281 (D. Colo. 2015).
41. *Ochsner v. Washington Community College, District No. 17*, 811 P.2d 985 (Wash. Ct. App. 1991).

42. *Neel v. Indiana University*, 435 N.E2d 607 (Ind. Ct. App. 1982).
43. *Gordon v. Purdue University*, 862 N.E.2d 1244 (Ind. Ct. App. 2007).
44. Id., at 1251.
45. *Zimmeck v. Marshall University*, 2014 WL 108668 (S.D. W.Va 2014).
46. *Texas v. Johnson*, 491 U.S. 397 (1989).
47. *Lopez v. Candale*, 630 F.3d 775, at 783 (9th Cir. 2010).
48. *Lopez v. Candale*, 2011 WL 13268830 (C.D. Cal. 2011).
49. Cal. Educ. Code § 94367(a) (1992, amended in 2006).
50. *Bilut v. Northwestern University*, 645 N.E.2d 536 (Ill. App. Ct. 1994); *Bilut v. Northwestern University*, 692 N.E.2d 1327 (Ill. App. Ct. 1998).
51. *Bender v. Alderson Broaddus College*, 575 S.E.2d 112 (W. Va. 2002).
52. *Mahaffey v. William Carey University*, 180 S.3d 186 (Miss. Ct. App. 2015).
53. 435 U.S. 78.
54. Id., at 86.
55. 474 U.S. 214.
56. Id., at 225.
57. *Neel v. I.U. Board of Trustees*, 435 N.E.2d 607 (Ind. Ct. App. 1982).
58. Id., at 611.
59. *Schuler v. University of Minnesota*, 788 F.2d 510.
60. Id., at 515.
61. *Nelson v. Spokane Community College*, 469 P.3d 317 (Wash. Ct. App. 2020).
62. Id., at 320.
63. *Amaya v. Brater*, 981 N.E.2d 1235 (Ind. Ct. App. 2013).
64. *Pearson v. Callahan*, 555 U.S. 223 (2009).
65. Immunity of Governmental Employee, Ind. Code § 34-13-3-3 (1998).
66. Ind. Code § 34-13-3-3(a).
67. Ind. Code § 34-13-3-3(a)(7).
68. *Gordon v. Purdue University*, 862 N.E.2d 1244, at 1247 (Ind. App. Ct. 2007).
69. *Klene v. Indiana University Purdue University-Indianapolis*, 2009 WL 10681243 (S.D. Ind. 2009).
70. Ind. Code § 34-13-3-5(e).
71. Ind. Code § 34-13-3-5(c).
72. *VanValkenburg v. Warner*, 602 N.E.2d 1046 (Ind. Ct. App. 1992).
73. Id., at 1050.
74. https://www.nytimes.com/2013/02/02/education/harvard-forced-dozens-to-leave-in-cheating-scandal.html.
75. https://www.thecrimson.com/article/2012/8/30/academic-dishonesty-ad-board/.
76. https://www.harvardmagazine.com/2014/05/harvard-college-adopts-honor-code.
77. https://yaledailynews.com/blog/2012/11/28/miller-discourages-take-home-finals/.
78. https://www.harvardmagazine.com/2014/05/harvard-college-adopts-honor-code.
79. https://www.insidehighered.com/news/2022/04/28/study-online-exam-cheating.

80. https://www.washingtonpost.com/local/education/another-problem-with-shifting-education-online-a-rise-in-cheating/2020/08/07/1284c9f6-d762-11ea-aff6-220dd3a14741_story.html.

81. https://www.thecrimson.com/article/2022/11/8/honor-council-withdrawals/.

82. https://www.cnn.com/2024/03/12/business/artificial-intelligence-ai-report-extinction/index.html; https://assets-global.website-files.com/62c4cf7322be8ea59c904399/65e7779f72417554f7958260_Gladstone%20Action%20Plan%20Executive%20Summary.pdf.

83. N. Adilov, et al., "ChatGPT and the Course Vulnerability Index," *Journal of Education for Business*, https://doi.org/10.1080/08832323.2023.2260929.

84. https://www.reuters.com/legal/new-york-lawyers-sanctioned-using-fake-chatgpt-cases-legal-brief-2023-06-22/.

85. https://www.theguardian.com/technology/2023/mar/19/ai-makes-plagiarism-harder-to-detect-argue-academics-in-paper-written-by-chatbot.

86. D. Cotton, P. Cotton, and J. Shipway, "Chatting and Cheating: Ensuring Academic Integrity in the Era of ChatGPT, *Innovations in Education and Teaching International*, DOI: 10.1080/14703297.2023.2190148.

87. https://www.washingtonpost.com/technology/2023/05/18/texas-professor-threatened-fail-class-chatgpt-cheating/.

88. https://www.searchenginejournal.com/should-you-trust-an-ai-detector/491949/#close.

89. https://communities.surf.nl/en/ai-in-education/article/ai-generated-text-detectors-do-they-work.

90. https://arstechnica.com/information-technology/2023/07/why-ai-detectors-think-the-us-constitution-was-written-by-ai/.

91. https://www.rumidocs.com/blog/top-20-us-schools-recommend-against-ai-detectors; https://www.vanderbilt.edu/brightspace/2023/08/16/guidance-on-ai-detection-and-why-were-disabling-turnitins-ai-detector/.

92. W. Walters, "The Effectiveness of Software Designed to Detect AI-Generated Writing: A Comparison of 16 AI Text Detectors," *Open Information Science* 7, no. 1 (2023): 20220158. https://doi.org/10.1515/opis-2022-0158; https://www.searchenginejournal.com/should-you-trust-an-ai-detector/491949/#close.

93. https://arxiv.org/abs/2304.02819v3, https://doi.org/10.48550/arXiv.2304.02819.

94. https://www.pfw.edu/offices/enhancement-learning-teaching/pedagogical-resources/Teaching%20in%20the%20Age%20of%20AI.

95. *Susan M. v. New York Law School*, 149 A.D.2d 69 (N.Y. App. Div. 1989).

96. *Susan M v. New York Law School*, 556 N.E.2d 1104 (N.Y. 1990).

97. *Thode v. Ladany*, 2014 WL 10795057 (Pa. Super. Ct. 2014).

98. *Collins v. Grier*, 1983 WL 5148 (Ohio Ct. App. 1983).

99. *Reilly v. Daly*, 666 N.E.2d 439 (Ind. Ct. App. 1996).

100. *Ogletree v. Cleveland State University*, 2022 WL 17826730 (N.D. Ohio).

101. *Ogletree v. Bloomberg*, 2023 WL 8468654 (6th Cir. 2023).

CHAPTER 2

Your Syllabus and Contract Law

BE CAREFUL ABOUT PLAYING LAWYER IN YOUR COURSE

You Make the Call

- **The Case of the Individually Graded Group Project**

A student was enrolled in an undergraduate nursing course, "Health Promotion in a Multicultural Society," which was a prerequisite for all upper-level courses, at a university in New Jersey. The university's course catalog stated on the front page that it was, "informational only and does not constitute a contract between [the university] and any student." The syllabus for the student's course was nine pages and included information on course assignments and exams and how they would be graded and weighted. This student was part of a six-member group working on a project that involved a written paper and a class presentation, and, at this group's presentation, the professor thought the student's portion had nothing to do with the written paper of the project at all or with the other parts of the presentation. In fact, his part of the presentation questioned the validity of the project assignment. When the other five group members told the professor about the difficulties they had with their sixth member throughout this project, imploring her not to have their presentation effort lumped in with his, the professor disregarded her syllabus's policy on this project and gave those five students a group grade but gave this student a zero for his presentation grade. She also told this student to submit his portion of the written project separately. He did so and received an 81 on it. The average of his zero and the 81 resulted in a D for the course—which wasn't a passing grade. The student appealed his grade and was granted a do-over for the project. But the professor never received the second project because, during the same time and without the professor's knowledge, the student's lawyer succeeded in getting the university to agree to an alternate project that would be submitted to and graded by someone else. This time, he submitted a new project to an associate dean, but that alternative assignment was judged insufficient, putting his original grade back on his transcript. The student retook the course with the same professor and with the kind of conflict one might have predicted. Suffice it to say that, after getting an F the second time and losing his internal appeals, the student sued the professor (and the university) for breach of contract, based on the professor's actions in deviating from her syllabus when she bifurcated the grades in that group project.

Did the student win his breach-of-contract claim? May the professor deviate from the grading method described in her syllabus?

(The answer will be given at the end of the chapter. Consider how the principles in this chapter affect your decision and reasoning.)

What parents first told their children they couldn't swim for a half hour after eating? My mom adhered to that maxim, and I'm still sour over missing valuable, childhood swim time. While there's no harm in beginning digestion on dry land, no one has ever drowned because a full stomach obstructed the mechanics of swimming, and neither pediatricians nor the Red Cross endorse this long-held conviction.[1] Ducks even swim while eating. Such is the case with folklore: it sounds true and it gets passed down. And so it is with the belief that a syllabus is a contract. Determining whether a syllabus is a contract necessitates that one first learn what a contract is (and isn't) and then apply those principles to syllabi, because the answer really does matter.

Who Says a Syllabus Is a Contract?

For decades, the academic world has stated in some form that a syllabus is a contract, and one would suppose that is to be expected. Undoubtedly, a syllabus's formality and extensive detail on course policies, points' accumulation, grade distribution, classroom behavior, and consequences for student failure to adhere to the syllabus's rules give the typical syllabus a contract-like appearance. Furthermore, advocating that a syllabus is a contract may help inculcate the notion that course expectations and objectives are to be clearly set and respected. And it also may contribute to the perception that a syllabus based on scholarly, accepted, best practices is a learning tool fit for documenting teaching effectiveness.

ACADEMIC LITERATURE HAS SAID A SYLLABUS IS A CONTRACT

As far back as the 1990s, an article in a peer-reviewed education journal claimed that a student signature on the last page of a syllabus made it a "binding agreement," as long as that signatory page included language that students have read and understood its implications.[2] Understanding the implications of a syllabus is a lot to ask of college students during the first class of the semester, is it not? A 2002 article from the same journal has been repeatedly cited for the proposition that a syllabus is a contract.[3] Two authors in a later article referred to a syllabus as a "paper contract" between faculty and students.[4] One author referred to syllabi as "complex legal contracts."[5] Other academics have suggested that instructors should present their syllabi to their students as contracts, to emphasize the gravity of course expectations.[6] My research on the academic literature and the syllabus-as-contract theory shows that, while many authors cite earlier authors,[7] I have yet to find a journal article that cites supporting legal authority for the view that a syllabus is a contract.[8] A blog post from the *Chronicle of Higher Education* on the syllabus-as-contract theory stated, "So sure, your syllabus is a contract—but a fluid one, which gets updated and amended regularly. When students find a loophole, all you can do is honor it, and then make sure it is eliminated."[9] Notably, however, more recent academic literature has taken the opposite view, concluding that syllabi are not contracts.[10]

COLLEGES HAVE SAID A SYLLABUS IS A CONTRACT

Many colleges and universities have put on their web pages an assortment of statements indicating a syllabus is a contract or has contract-like aspects.[11] Often, these web pages are part of the information offered by university centers or offices on teaching and learning,[12] which do valuable work in helping faculty of all stages and titles improve their student learning efforts. One graduate school web page declared a syllabus to be a social contract, a constitution, and also a contract that "binds both you and your students,"[13] which is quite a tall order for a syllabus. One university's Center for Teaching and Learning web page said, "[a]t one level, a course syllabus is a *contract* between the instructor and the student."[14] Another university's online PDF on syllabi said in its first line that a syllabus is a contract between the instructor and student.[15] Other universities' web pages that relate to teaching reference a journal article (cited earlier in this chapter) when discussing the purposes of a syllabus, including stating that a syllabus "serves as a contract between the instructor and the student."[16] Even an Ivy League university's publishing house website had an article on course planning that included this loose description of a syllabus: "It's also *a kind of contract* [emphasis added]—an agreement on shared expectations between students and the instructor."[17]

A Primer in Contract Law

You Make the Call

- **The Case of the Unrequited Accommodations Assurance**

A young woman entered a college in Maryland at the age of seventeen and stayed for thirteen years. Along the way, she earned an undergraduate degree in psychology, a master's degree in leadership and teaching, a "masters plus 30 certificate" in education, and she was working toward a PhD in the school of education. From the beginning, the college was aware of the student's attention deficit disorder (now generally called ADHD) and provided her with learning accommodations. The PhD program of which she was a part had a two-time fail policy, meaning that a student is dismissed from the program if the student fails an exam and then fails the same exam a second time. Throughout the student's time in the PhD program, she was provided other students' class notes, extra time to complete exams, and extended deadlines on certain assignments. In May of the year in question, the student paid her summer and fall tuition. During October, the student emailed the disability services coordinator (who was also a college vice president), asking for various accommodations for her upcoming exams, including extra time to take them and a "solitary environment" in which to take them. The coordinator emailed the student back and, in that response, promised a "solitary environment," which was an accommodation not required by law. The student took the first four of her six exams in a large computer lab where another student was also present, hand writing her own exams due to a disability. The student took her remaining exams in a solitary environment. Upon learning she failed three of the first four exams, she said it was due to the noise caused by the second student's hand writing. In January of the following year, the student sought more accommodations for those retakes, including having a third retake opportunity if needed (due to not having a solitary environment the first time) and also asked to be allowed to take them open book. She was allowed to take the exams with books and notes but was not allowed to take them a third time, and, upon flunking them a second time, she was ultimately dismissed from the PhD program. Among the allegations in her lawsuit was breach of contract. She alleged that the disability services coordinator made a binding promise to her in the email response from October, allowing her to have her requested "solitary environment," which she did not receive on the day when she failed the three exams.

Did the college's affirmative email response to the student's request for a solitary exam environment create a contract with the student?

(The answer will be given at the end of the chapter. Consider how the principles in this chapter affect your decision and reasoning.)

While a syllabus has some contract-like attributes, those similarities would not, on their own, make a syllabus a contract. Likewise, just because a document represents what might be thought of as an agreement, an agreement by itself doesn't make a contract. That may seem counterintuitive, but a contract is a *legally enforceable agreement*, not just any agreement.[18] To say that a contract is an agreement is to be half right. Every contract is an agreement, but not every agreement is a contract. In the same way, every baseball home run is a hit (it gets you on base and improves your batting average), but not every hit is a home run (which requires the successful batter to get all the way around the bases).

THE INGREDIENTS OF A CONTRACT

There are multiple and fancy definitions of a contract, but the essential ingredients are the following:

- **Capacity to Make a Contract**
  Capacity relates to having the requisite legal status to make a contract: some aspects include being of age (eighteen in many states); not having a cognitive incapacity that impairs one's ability to understand that one is making a contract; and not being too drunk or something similar. The law presumes one is capable of making a contract. Thus, any party who wants to escape a contract on capacity grounds must establish that he or she lacked capacity to make the contract.[19]
- **Offer and Acceptance**
  There is no tennis-like service ace when making a contract; there must be a return of serve. The offer is the serve and the acceptance is the return. When there's been acceptance, two parties are in a contract. An offer is more than just a promise, just like a contract is more than just an agreement. An offer involves someone (the offeror) making an invitation to the other party that is specific enough that if the other party says yes to the invitation, they realize they will have made a contract.[20] For an offer to be valid, it has to be sufficiently specific to show that it is seriously intended. That means an offer needs terms. The statement, "I'll sell you my car if you say you'll buy it," isn't an offer because there are no details to the offer, such as what car and what price. Likewise, the statement, "I'll buy your car if you ever sell it," isn't an offer because it is an illusory promise by being so indefinite.

  The acceptance needs to be an unconditional, positive response to the offer. Beyond responding with something in the range of "I accept your offer," the party accepting the offer (the offeree) needs to provide what is asked for in the offer. This is often known as the mirror-image rule.[21] For example, if an offer is made on social media to sell a lamp for $100, contingent on an email acceptance of the offer and cash payment, an in-person acceptance with a check would be insufficient because it is not made in the manner required by the offer. Although most acceptances need to be affirmatively given, it is possible for silence to constitute acceptance in a few instances, such as where prior dealings between the parties show that only a rejection needs to be given.[22]

- **Legality**

  A contract made with an illegal purpose, where at least one of the parties needs to do an illegal act, is void (having no effect). Examples include agreements to buy contraband, agreements to engage in price fixing, and agreements to lend money at an illegal interest rate.

- **Consideration**

  This is the key to what makes an agreement a contract. A contract involves an exchange between both parties that creates a mutual, legal obligation. The formal term for that is "consideration." Whenever you are wondering if something is a contract (hint), start with finding the exchange in the agreement. If there's no exchange, historically called quid pro quo, then there's no contract. By way of example, a promise to make a gift is generally unenforceable because it is one-sided: no one does anything to receive a gift, other than accepting it. And, for gifts, acceptance is when the giving of a gift is legally binding. Promising to give someone your used car is much different from saying you promise to sell someone your used car because they promised to pay you $10,000. When you are obligated to keep your promise to me because I am obligated to keep my promise to you, we are in "mutuality of obligation," which is synonymous with consideration, and we are in a contract. (There are exceptions to the requirement of contract consideration and mutuality of obligation, but they are beyond the need of this chapter.) An illustrative case involved a law student who sued her school for breach of contract. After being expelled for a number of reasons, she sued the dean and the law school over a lack of disability services she said the dean had promised her by letter, which services were not provided. In dismissing the suit, the federal court noted that there was no contract in existence because there was no existing mutuality of obligation between the dean and the student. She didn't promise anything in exchange for the dean's alleged promise to provide extra disability services, which made his promise gratuitous and, therefore, unenforceable.[23] Another way of thinking about this case is to realize the dean (or, by extension, the institution) wasn't obligated to keep the promise because the student hadn't promised anything in return. One is only legally obligated to keep a promise to do something when the party receiving that promise is legally obligated to keep his or her own return promise.

THE CONSEQUENCE OF BREACHING A CONTRACT

Because a contract is a legally binding agreement, when a contract is breached, there are court-determined consequences unless the parties reach an out-of-court settlement. Alternatively, a contract can require the parties to arbitrate, rather than litigate, their dispute. Avoiding traditional litigation through using some alternative dispute resolution (ADR) mechanism, including arbitration, saves time and money. It also provides a private forum for resolving the dispute, rather than the open-access court system. Arbitration is not a settlement device because the arbitrator or arbitration panel is given the power by the parties' arbitration agreement to decide the outcome. And, once the arbitration decision (called an award) is made, a key purpose of arbitration—its finality—is evident in that the ability to appeal an arbitrator's award to an appellate court is severely limited.[24]

In a breach of contract suit, the plaintiff's monetary recovery, called "damages," would be compensation for the loss suffered; an award of damages is intended to put the plaintiff in as good a position as if the contract had been fully performed. For example, if one fails to pay for a product costing $1,000, that party (the defendant) would owe $1,000 to the one who provided the product, plus any other incidental costs of the breach, which might include interest for the time the payment was missing and perhaps the plaintiff's legal fees (if awarded by the court). A plaintiff can also be awarded consequential damages, which are the foreseeable and negative results of the breach and which the parties contemplated at the time they made their contract.[25] Going back to the prior illustration, suppose the seller (in this case, the defendant) failed to deliver the $1,000 product on time to a buyer (in this case, the plaintiff) who was going to resell it to a third party for $2,000. And suppose the defendant was aware that the product was to be resold for $2,000, and suppose the third-party buyer of the product purchased a replacement product, causing the plaintiff to have to resell that product to someone else for $1,600. Under that circumstance, the plaintiff could recover as consequential damages $400, which would allow the plaintiff to get, in effect, $2,000 as compensation for the originally intended resale.

Monetary damages can include what are called "liquidated damages," which is a predetermined sum of money stated in the contract that would have to be paid in the event the other party breaches the contract.[26] Liquidated damages are valid where they are a reasonable predictor of the loss that could occur in the event of breach and are not a penalty for breach. For example, a landlord-tenant contract could require the tenant to pay a fee for missing the rent deadline, but a fee as high as a year's rent would be unreasonable and unenforceable.

THE TAKEAWAY

A contract is more than simply an agreement. It is a legally enforceable agreement, which means that parties who have capacity to make a contract must have exchanged promises (the consideration) about doing something legal. Contracts are made upon the acceptance of the offer, which leads to the performance of the contract terms, or the possible breach of contract. Breach-of-contract disputes can be resolved in court or by settlement or by arbitration.

Is a Syllabus a Contract?

You Make the Call

- **The Case of the Unkept Promise of Practicum Time**

Three graduates of a sign-language–interpreter training program in Illinois sued their college, alleging that it failed to fulfill its contractual obligations to them and engaged in consumer fraud by failing to adequately prepare them to be certified sign-language interpreters. The students alleged that the college's course catalog and a professor's course syllabus promised a total of fifteen credits and three hundred hours in total practicum time. In fact, the grading criteria for the course syllabus in question told students of the points required to achieve a certain grade. Of the 1,000 maximum available points that could be earned, the syllabus said 600 of those points related to "Observation and Interpreting Hours (300)." The students did not receive the required practicum hours, including the training hours at an appropriate training facility. One student in the lawsuit said that, as a result of this unkept promise, she failed the sign-language–interpreter certification exam. She then spent money to hire a tutor and also to attend the needed instructional seminars so she could pass the test, claiming those costs and her lost wages during that time totaled over $50,000.

Did the college breach a contract to those students by failing to provide the necessary hours of practicum time, as stated in the course catalog and that course's syllabus?

(The answer will be given at the end of the chapter. Consider how the principles in this chapter affect your decision and reasoning.)

A syllabus is not a contract. As well intended as the archetype of "syllabus as contract" may be, it does not comport with contract law or higher-education law. At first blush, it seems that a syllabus is a written contract, to the extent that a syllabus lists the professor's various "promises" to perform (semester schedule, learning objectives, exam dates, etc.) and details the consequences for students' failure to perform according to the syllabus's preset terms. Consequences, however, are not exclusive to the world of contracts, and putting prospective penalties in writing does not create a contract.

As discussed in the first chapter, students are in contractual relationships with their colleges and universities. Students have brought a variety of breach-of-contract suits against their colleges, including, for example, one involving a private university in Massachusetts where a federal appellate court permitted a graduate to bring a breach-of-contract claim against that university because his degree was being withheld, pending the resolution of a sexual-harassment investigation.[27] And, sometimes, a court will find that a student and a university are in an implied contract, which is a type of contract based more on the contractual-like behavior of the parties, rather than on expressed and exchanged contract terms. But that does not mean, by extension, that students and professors are in contractual relationships by virtue of course syllabi. From my research, no court, in response to a student's claim, has ever declared a syllabus a contract. Furthermore, if the millions of syllabi generated each year were contracts, then their terms could be disputed or enforced in court, and the ramifications of that for an already jam-packed American legal system are staggering. And having arbitration clauses in syllabi as a way to avoid the court system would create its own legal and logistical complications.

There might not appear to be much legal risk for college instructors who say their syllabi are contracts. But we all would do well to heed the aphorism, "Be careful what you wish for," because there is a real difference between thinking that one's syllabus is a contract and saying that it is. The risk posed by calling a syllabus a contract will be explained later, but, at this point, it is important to examine why a syllabus is not a contract.

SYLLABI LACK CONTRACT CONSIDERATION

Students and professors aren't exchanging anything of legal value with each other by virtue of being in a course together. Assuming, for the sake of argument, that instructors make promises in syllabi, even if students are required to sign a syllabus page and submit it to the instructor, that doesn't mean those signatures are made *in exchange* for what the instructors promise in the syllabi. A contract is a two-way street, so thinking of a contract as something that obligates only the instructor is to neglect the other side in such a purported agreement. (One Florida university's website on syllabi tries to thread this needle by telling instructors that both parties to a syllabus should be expected to abide by it and that it's unfair to change syllabus requirements mid semester.)[28] If a syllabus really was a contract, a professor would be able to sue his or her students for breach or—even better—insert a fee schedule (liquidated damages) to be paid in the event of absenteeism or late-submitted assignments, or whatever else the professor thought constituted nonperformance. That would make for a brilliant retirement funding plan, but not a contract.

A plagiarism mini-scandal in a class, which of course led to a lawsuit against a professor, gives breath to the declaration that syllabi aren't contracts. In the case, a professor in an immunology class assigned a 450-word report to the class and used the antiplagiarism software Turnitin, which showed that many students plagiarized parts of their papers. Consequently, she told the students of her dissatisfaction and then gave them what became known as the "free pass policy," in which she said, "I am giving everybody, well most people anyway a *free pass* on one sentence copied for this paper. *I am not going to write up everybody* for copying one sentence." The student who ended up suing was one whose paper contained many more than one plagiarized sentence. The professor reported the student for plagiarism, and the student was eventually given a failing grade. The student's federal lawsuit included discrimination claims as well, and sought over $1,000,000. Among other allegations (including that the student was wrongfully denied an exam bathroom break), the student claimed that the professor's syllabus constituted a contract between the professor and students and that, since the syllabus made no mention of a "free pass policy," the professor breached the contract by not giving him the free pass, while other students in the class fell under its benefits. Speaking to the breach-of-contract claim while dismissing the case, the federal court said all valid contracts require certain elements, including mutual agreement and valuable consideration. Unlike a contract, though, the court concluded that, "[a] course syllabus—which commonly outlines reading requirements, test dates and the like—does not have any such attributes."[29] And, in a 2014 case from Florida, a federal court allowed a student to continue her discrimination and breach-of-contract suit against her university but noted in a footnote that the student could not continue the part of her breach-of-contract claim that was based on the syllabus from the course that was the catalyst for the various federal claims.[30]

INSTRUCTORS HAVE A PRE-EXISTING DUTY TO DO WHAT THE SYLLABUS SAYS THEY WILL

Another problem with the syllabus-as-contract assertion is that one's promise to do what one is already obligated to do can't be the consideration in a contract. (Inversely, one can't make a contract by promising not to do something that person is not allowed to do in the first place.) Pre-existing duties can't be recycled for new contracts. For example, if I am chronically late to class and I ask my students to pay me $100 every time I arrive on time, their collective promise to pay me is meaningless because I'm already supposed to come to class on time. They don't have to pay me even if they promise they will. And, as it concerns syllabi, professors create those at the behest of their employers—before those syllabi are given to students. Even if one were to accept the proposition that faculty make promises in syllabi, those promises are really acknowledgments of their pre-existing obligations to their employers to do what they are being paid to do.

SYLLABI AREN'T NEGOTIATED BETWEEN INSTRUCTORS AND STUDENTS, AND THERE IS NO OFFER AND ACCEPTANCE

Syllabi are created before a semester begins and distributed en masse on paper or online to groups who have had no chance to dispute the contents or ask for alternate terms. That alone doesn't make them invalid because many contracts we make, including various "terms of service," are given to us in a take-it-or-leave-it way. But those types of contracts are known as "adhesion contracts," in that one party with so much power or leverage over the other sticks the contract onto the other party without any chance for negotiation beforehand. Adhesion contracts are subject to a more careful review and are occasionally declared to be so oppressively one-sided they are considered "unconscionable" and void.[31] Giving students your written rules of the course to which they must agree or else drop the course isn't an advisable way to make an agreement, much less a contract. It is possible and maybe worthwhile in certain upper-level or graduate courses to allow students to have a say in certain aspects of a syllabus. For instance, you might allow students to choose a range of how papers and tests will be weighted toward their final grade, to give agency to those who test more poorly than they perform on projects that they have more time to revise. However, granting students some ability to affect a syllabus's terms wouldn't make a syllabus a contract for the reasons stated above and below.

INSTRUCTORS ARE ALREADY JUDGED (AND BENEFITED) BY THE ARBITRARY AND CAPRICIOUS STANDARD

As discussed in the first chapter, the professional judgment of college instructors is evaluated against the arbitrary and capricious standard. Because courts do not recognize educational malpractice, when faced with litigation over a faculty member's professional decision-making, courts only inquire if there is any evidence that the decision was arbitrary and capricious, or was made in bad faith. That safety zone would encompass the way a syllabus is created or deviated from. In effect, a student's breach-of-contract claim that relates to an instructor's syllabus should be swallowed by a legal doctrine that already protects instructor actions relating to course management and decisions. And one of the very first lawsuits over a course syllabus shows this is how courts respond.

In *Collins v. Grier*[32] (1983 and 1986), which was a "You Make the Call" case from Chapter 1, a professor's syllabus listed how a student's final grade would be calculated but didn't discuss whether grade-rounding would be done or was even a possibility. The student's final grade for the course was very close to an A, but he was given a B, while a few others in the course who had slightly higher grades than he were rounded up to an A. The student sued his professor, and his lawsuit included the claim that the syllabus was a contract the professor breached by failing to round up the student's grade while doing so for others. Noting that courts will not review matters of purely academic decisions, absent some showing of bad faith or arbitrary or capricious conduct, the appellate court (1983) affirmed the dismissal of the lawsuit. The court reaffirmed without citing any legal authority the longstanding view that neither a syllabus nor university guidelines create a contract between a professor or instructor and a student. It also reaffirmed the universal doctrine that unless a professor's conduct toward a student is alleged to be arbitrary or capricious or to be made in bad faith, it is not justiciable (capable of being decided by a court). However, the student was granted a trial against his professor on the last count of his suit, which was that the professor changed the grades of other students during the university grievance procedures initiated by the student-plaintiff, in order to justify his grading of the student-plaintiff. But the student lost that claim at trial and the appealed that decision to, the Ohio Court of Appeals (1986), which agreed with the trial court that there was no evidence that the professor acted arbitrarily, capriciously, or in bad faith with respect to that student.

Later courts have applied the arbitrary and capricious standard to syllabi controversies. In a 2015 case from Louisiana, a student sued because she was dismissed from a nurse anesthesia program due to a low grade in a pass/fail course. The student said her grade was calculated in violation of the method listed in the syllabus. The court decided against her. Blending principles of education law with those of contract law, the court said that, even if one assumed the syllabus constituted a contract, the professor's decision on how to calculate her students' grades was covered by the arbitrary and capricious standard.[33]

THE TAKEAWAY

A syllabus is not a contract. A syllabus has aspects of a contract and an appearance that some may believe is similar to that of a contract, but it lacks the essential elements of a contract, including an exchange of value between students and instructors.

The Risk Posed by Calling Your Syllabus a Contract

You Make the Call

- **The Case of the Orally Amended Syllabus**

A law student taking a contract-law class (too on the nose?) during a spring semester at a law school in Massachusetts got a D for the course, and his theory of breach of contract was tied to how the professor changed the syllabus in class. The syllabus stated that, "[b]eginning in February, we will have optional review/quiz sessions on late Friday afternoon." The student missed some of those class sessions and their quizzes. Upon seeing his D, the student went to the professor to find out what happened, and the professor said the missing quizzes hurt his grade. Astonished, the student reminded the professor that the syllabus said those quizzes were optional and didn't count toward the final grade. It was at this point that the student claimed to have learned that the professor said he told everyone at the first class of the semester that he was amending his syllabus and would be by adding sporadic pop quizzes that would count toward the final course grade. This alleged syllabus change was oral only. In the grade appeal that ensued, the professor said he also repeated this oral amendment to his syllabus several times in later classes. The school's legal counsel was appointed to investigate the matter and issued a report that led to the D being upheld. Consequently, the student was suspended for poor academic performance and a letter stating that the student was not in good standing was added to his academic file. After being unable to transfer to another law school, the student sued the school, representing himself pro se, alleging the syllabus was a contract that the professor breached by orally changing it without notice.

Can a professor orally amend a written syllabus in a way that alters the course grading scale? (Is this different from asking if this syllabus was a contract?)

(The answer will be given at the end of the chapter. Consider how the principles in this chapter affect your decision and reasoning.)

If you have been convinced that a syllabus is not a contract, you might be asking yourself, *so what?* That's a fair question. Not all mistaken beliefs result in a worrisome consequence. I've been told repeatedly that I'm wrong to believe Wilt Chamberlain is the greatest basketball player ever, but so far no one has attacked me for it or refused my credit card—even in Chicago. But I would argue that college faculty who believe or who have been told to believe that a syllabus is a contract face a risk if they tell their students that syllabi are contracts. They risk being treated like they are in a contract because of what is known in the law as the doctrine of promissory estoppel.[34]

This legal principle (which originated in courts of equity in England) prohibits someone from denying the existence of an unenforceable promise, in light of another person's detrimental reliance on that promise. Estoppel subjects the promisor to an otherwise unnecessary liability. A 2007 case involving law-school tuition is directly on point and reads like a fable. In it, a man wealthy enough to lease a Bentley at $50,000 a year suggested to a friend and neighbor that she should go to law school and that he would pay for her to go if she was accepted. The woman was recently out of college and had some school loans, but she quit her full-time employment and went to law school. The rich friend made two monthly tuition payments but issued a stop payment for the second payment's check. In an email on this controversy, the friend then said he would pay the student's tuition once she finished school and passed the bar exam but later threatened her with a restraining order if she continued to contact him. He never paid, and she sued. Even though gift promises are unenforceable and aren't contract offers, the woman was awarded over $87,000 in law-school tuition because the court concluded 1) his promise was reasonable for her to rely upon; 2) she relied on his promise, suffering harm because of her reliance; and 3) it would have been unjust to allow him to avoid keeping his promise.[35]

Because of the risk of estoppel, even a minimal one, faculty need to avoid calling a syllabus a contract. Where a professor has stated that his syllabus is a contract, and where the professor fails to follow his syllabus's terms or applies an exception to one student but not another, a student suit based on breach of contract could result in a court applying the doctrine of estoppel in favor of the student. It is worth pointing out that, in the previously discussed cases where courts specifically held that a syllabus was not a contract, there was no evidence presented that any of the professors who were sued had ever generally claimed to their students that a syllabus was a contract or specifically stated that their syllabi were contracts. Supposing instead that those professors had made such assertions, then their legal arguments to the contrary might have fallen on deaf ears.

Students have claimed promissory estoppel in relation to syllabi claims. In one case from Massachusetts, a master's student was dismissed from his program due to a low grade in a course where the professor calculated the final grades without giving the final exam, which the syllabus said was worth 15 percent of the total points. Demonstrating what one might not call best practices, the professor emailed the students during the last week of the semester to tell them that he had already completed the course grades and that they were posted. The student sued for breach of contract and promissory estoppel, making what I think is a reasonable argument: that, had he been able to take that final exam, his grade would have been satisfactory. But he lost, and the court called his argument "no more than conjecture."[36] To be clear, no evidence was presented that the professor referred to his syllabus as a contract.

Moreover, where institutions maintain the fiction that a syllabus is a contract, they risk having the doctrine of estoppel apply to them as well. A student-plaintiff might argue that her college made statements affirming that it viewed syllabi to be contracts and that the student detrimentally changed her position in reliance on the affirmations made in the syllabus. That could make reliance a more reasonable claim and might cause the institution to be liable for something the instructor did that would not have made the instructor liable on his or her own. To my knowledge, such an argument has never been made, but it might be some day and may prove persuasive.

THE TAKEAWAY

Tell your students that your syllabus is *not* a contract. Control the narrative at the beginning, and counteract any mistaken beliefs that could lead to claims that you breached the contract you made with them or that they detrimentally relied on your syllabus promises, if you deviate from your syllabus.

The Value in Thinking of Your Syllabus as a Contract

The syllabus is such an integral part of college teaching that its purposes include serving as a permanent record for the benefit of accrediting bodies and faculty reviews as well as a learning tool that expresses the instructor's philosophies on teaching and learning.[37] (A later chapter will discuss whether a syllabus is protected by copyright and, if so, who owns it.) The characteristics of syllabi that could be part of demonstrating best practices include that they are detailed but user-friendly; they are well organized with clear goals; they include the instructor's rationale for assignments; and they can be inspirational.[38]

Even though no student has yet to successfully convince a court that a syllabus is a contract, and even though it is risky to call one's syllabus a contract, there is no harm in faculty having a contract outlook. In fact, with respect to syllabi, thinking like a lawyer (which often includes worrying about and planning for the what-ifs) may be beneficial. Having such a mindset could enhance teaching effectiveness in that it is both client-centered and self-protective. Faculty who prepare syllabi as if they were drafting a contract can create a document that is purposeful and consistent, while still being learning-centered and motivational. That does not mean a law license is required. A few, contract-like guidelines are worth considering when drafting syllabi:

- **Imagine the Possibilities of Your Policies**
  Write your specific policies with an eye to how readers could reasonably interpret them to their advantage. For instance, if you have an absentee policy that includes exceptions for "emergencies," think about what you mean by an emergency and what you don't mean and then redraft the policy to minimize opportunity for forcing into the exception that which doesn't belong. If you allow students to work in groups for graded work, do you limit the size of the group or require evidence of individual effort toward the group outcome, so that you won't have to give the nonparticipant the same grade after the other group members complain about that student's languidness? If you don't allow cell phones to be used in class, does that include a prohibition on texting? Do you claim ownership in the work you make available for students, such as your PowerPoints or study aids or even your tests (assuming you've created them all)? If not, what would you think of an entrepreneurial student who sought to sell their written experiences from your course, like the questions from the tests you distributed, for example? If you are a grade-rounder, should you provide a range of when you will consider the bump or what would cause you to increase a grade? And, as it concerns the first chapter's discussion of AI, make sure to include a well-considered section on what is prohibited and, perhaps, allowed use of AI or ChatGPT, as well as your process for reaching a conclusion about cheating.
- **Avoid the Risk of Overpromising and Underdelivering**
  To paraphrase musical icon Bo Didley, be careful about letting your syllabus write checks your schedule can't cash. For example, do you promise that you will return all emails or grade all work within a certain timeframe? Can you guarantee you'll meet that time frame without failure? In online classes in particular, students can easily chafe at what they believe is instructor apathy, an opinion that may have germinated while reading the syllabus that promised them an almost-immediate response time. Formally giving yourself more time will not only minimize the chance of inadequate performance but also could engender goodwill and more positive course evaluations when you beat your own stated deadline. Write the parts of your syllabus where you assert what you'll be doing (and when) in a way that provides you some wiggle room.
- **Consider Using a Definitions Section**
  Although adding a definitions section to a syllabus may seem like gilding the lily, it is worth contemplating, especially if the number of students in your class leaves you little time to spend debating your syllabus or how it could be interpreted. There is a legal doctrine in contract law with an expensive title, the "contra proferentem rule," and it is worth mentioning here. This sound

doctrine says that, when a contract has ambiguous terms, they should be interpreted against the party who drafted the contract. Bearing that in mind when preparing your syllabi should be helpful. When you define terms like, "lateness," "absence," "pop quiz," or even "class participation," they mean what you intend, which can go a long way toward preventing unnecessary indignation and time spent rationalizing how you interpreted those undefined terms.

- **Minimize the Minutiae through Incorporation by Reference**
  There is no need to distribute an obese syllabus, stuffed full of all the standard, institutional boilerplate. Students do not care. Instead of copying and pasting all those paragraphs of school-wide policies, make reference to them and then include hyperlinks to where they can be found in full.
- **Include Your Version of a "Force Majeure" Clause**
  In contract law, a force majeure (French for "superior force") clause relieves a party from its obligations in the contract due to certain circumstances that are outside its control and that make performance inadvisable, illegal, or impossible. For example, as inarticulate as the term "Act of God" is, it often is included in force majeure discussions. Without such a clause, the parties in a contract are subject to strict contract doctrines about what excuses performance. You might want to include in your syllabus your own version of such an escape clause, one that gently acknowledges your prerogative to alter the schedule of topics covered or the test dates, for instance, if unforeseen circumstances necessitate such changes. Without one, you might be forced to formally defend your decision to go against your stated game plan.

THE TAKEAWAY

When preparing a syllabus, think of it like a contract, to the extent that such an outlook helps you be mindful of how students might interpret or find loopholes in it. Be careful of overpromising and underdelivering. Err on the side of your students when your syllabus is ambiguous.

Final Takeaways

- A contract is the kind of agreement that involves parties exchanging promises with each other about a future and legal performance. This exchange, called the consideration, is what makes the agreement legally enforceable.
- Breach of contract occurs when one party fails to perform its side of the exchange, and breach-of-contract disputes can be resolved in court or by settlement or by arbitration.

- Courts have uniformly concluded that a syllabus is not a contract, because syllabi lack the essential elements of a contract, including an exchange of value between students and instructors.
- The risk in saying a syllabus is a contract is that students might be able to win the legal argument, promissory estoppel, that they reasonably relied on that assertion and then suffered a loss because the syllabus was not followed.
- Rather than stating a syllabus is a contract, tell your students that your syllabus is not a contract, to avoid causing any misimpression that it is a contract in the event you deviate from it.
- Thinking of your syllabus as a contract can help you prepare a document that is consistent and subject to clear interpretation but still learning-centered. Be careful of overpromising and underdelivering. Err on the side of your students when your syllabus is ambiguous.

How Did You Make the Calls?

1 – The Case of the Individually Graded Group Project

In this case, an undergraduate nursing student at the University of Medicine and Dentistry of New Jersey was part of a six-member group, working on a two-part project in a health and multiculturalism course that included a written paper and an in-class presentation. The student did not like the project and, during his portion of the class presentation, he spent his time criticizing the assignment rather than discussing the group's efforts. After class, the other members of that group told the professor how difficult their experience with that student was and asked that their project work be graded separately from the work of that student. The professor agreed, gave the student a zero for his oral presentation, and told him to submit a separate, written project. The combination of those two grades earned the student a non-passing D. The student then got a do-over, thanks to his own lawyer going outside the grade appeal process, but that project, which was graded by someone else, was also insufficient. The student had to retake the course with the same professor and got an F. He sued the professor and university for breach of contract, arguing that the course syllabus was a contract that the professor breached by deviating from the portion that clearly explained how the group project would be graded.

Did the student win his breach-of-contract claim? May the professor deviate from the grading method described in her syllabus?

Decision: The Superior Court of New Jersey, Appellate Division, upheld the trial court's dismissal of the student's lawsuit.[39] Not much was written in the court's opinion about whether the professor's syllabus constituted a contract because this court said it was approving without explanation the trial judge's reasons for dismissing the lawsuit. But that judge issued a ruling that the syllabus was not a contract from the bench, orally and not in writing. Evidently, both courts thought the argument that a syllabus was a contract didn't warrant a written analysis.

2 – The Case of the Unrequited Accommodations Assurance

In this case, a student who earned multiple degrees from the College of Notre Dame of Maryland and who received multiple attention deficit disorder–related accommodations during her thirteen years there, was dismissed from her PhD program for failing, and failing again, the maximum permitted number of final exams. Her lawsuit was based on breach of contract, in that the disability services coordinator agreed by email to the student's request for a solitary environment in which to take her exams. That was important to her case because the solitary environment accommodation was more than was required by law and because she didn't get it for the three exams she failed the first time. Someone else with a disability accommodation was in the same room taking their own exams. The student was then given permission to retake those exams, with open books and open notes. She failed them a second time and asked to take them a third time because she didn't have the promised solitary environment the first time, and she claimed the noise of the other student affected her test performance. That request was rejected, and among the allegations in her lawsuit was that the disability services coordinator made a contractually binding promise to her when agreeing to provide her with the requested solitary environment.

Did the college's affirmative email response to the student's request for a solitary exam environment create a contract with the student?

The Decision: A federal district court ruled that the disability services coordinator's email did not constitute the making of a contract with the student and was, therefore, not binding or enforceable.[40] In discussing that an agreement needs consideration to make it binding, the court first pointed out that the disability services coordinator's email was really an affirmation of a pre-existing legal duty to provide the required accommodations, and so it couldn't be consideration to make a contract. Then, as it concerned the extra, solitary-environment promise, the court concluded that the student didn't exchange anything of value to get a solitary environment. She tried to argue that her tuition payment was her exchange for the solitary-environment promise, but the court said that was paid before she asked for the solitary environment. Therefore, the solitary-environment promise wasn't binding.

3 – The Case of the Unkept Promise of Practicum Time

Here, sign-language–interpreter students sued MacMurray College over the failure to receive promised hours of practicum time, which would help them prepare for the required interpreter certification exam. The students alleged that the college's course catalog and a professor's course syllabus promised a total of fifteen credits and three hundred hours in total practicum time. It was undisputed that the grading criteria for the course syllabus in question told students of the points required to achieve a certain grade. Of the 1,000 maximum available points that could be earned, the syllabus said 600 of those points related to "Observation and Interpreting Hours (300)." The students did not receive the required practicum hours, including the training hours at an appropriate training facility, and one student in the lawsuit said that, as a result of this unkept promise, she failed the sign-language–interpreter certification exam. She alleged she then spent thousands of dollars on a tutor and instructional seminars so she could pass the certification. The lawsuit alleged the college made and breached a contract with the students about the promised practicum and training hours.

Did the college breach a contract to those students by failing to provide the necessary hours of practicum time, as stated in the course catalog and that course's syllabus?

Decision: The Illinois Court of Appeals decided in favor of the college, concluding the syllabus did not constitute a contract, making the promised practicum hours nonbinding.[41] The trial court had already dismissed the suit on the grounds that it was really a veiled attempt at an educational-malpractice claim, which (discussed in the first chapter) courts don't accept. As it concerned the promised practicum or training hours, the appellate court didn't read the course catalog as promising any set of interpreter training time or hours. The syllabus, however, explicitly listed 300 practicum hours that students would receive in the course but were not even close to being provided. Yet, the court said the syllabus wasn't contractually binding on the college but was rather a "variable metric devised by the individual course instructor . . . that imposes a requirement on the student and is subject to change," based on factors that are unrelated to a contractual obligation to students in the class.

There was a dissenting opinion in that case, however, and I agree with it. The dissenting judge thought the case should not have been dismissed but should have been returned to the trial court so the students' litigation could have continued. In this judge's view, there was enough evidence to allow the students to allege breach of contract against the university. Without saying the syllabus by itself was a contract, the dissenting judge thought that it, combined with the course catalog and other university documents, created a contract with the students, who could receive money damages if they could prove breach of those promises about practicum time.

4 – The Case of the Orally Amended Syllabus
In the legal system, this kind of case would be called "on point" because its facts and legal analysis couldn't be more relevant to the issue at hand. A law professor at the Massachusetts School of Law at Andover, teaching a contracts-law course (you're welcome) distributed a syllabus that said in part, "[b]eginning in February, we will have optional review/quiz sessions on late Friday afternoon." A student in the class missed some of those classes and got a D in the course, to his shock. When he asked the professor about the course grade, the professor said that the quizzes the student missed contributed to his low course grade. The student countered with the syllabus statement on optional quizzes, but the professor said that, on the first day of class, he amended the syllabus by telling everyone that he was adding sporadic pop quizzes that would count toward the final course grade. Evidently, the student missed whatever quizzes were given in class and which now mattered, so he appealed his grade. The law school's attorney investigated the matter and found in favor of the professor, and the student was suspended. He couldn't get into another law school, and he sued his professor for breach of contract. Representing himself, he alleged the syllabus was a contract that the professor breached by unilaterally and orally changing it.

Can a professor orally amend a written syllabus in a way that alters the course grading scale? (Is this different from asking if this syllabus was a contract?)

Decision: The United States District Court ruled in favor of the professor, concluding his syllabus was not a contract and, therefore, not subject to a breach-of-contract lawsuit.[42] In deciding against the student, the court acknowledged similar case precedent from other jurisdictions, all of which ruled that a syllabus was not a contract. A footnote in that case is worthy of ending this chapter: "even if the syllabus unambiguously stated that no quizzes would ever be graded, the Court is not prepared to hold that professors are precluded from amending a syllabus without first obtaining their students' agreement."

Notes

1. https://www.redcross.org/take-a-class/resources/articles/eating-before-swimming-myth#:~:text=No%20major%20medical%20or%20safety,increase%20the%20risk%20of%20drowning.
2. K. Matejka and L. B. Kurke, "Designing a Great Syllabus," *College Teaching* 42, no. 3 (1994): 115–17.
3. J. Parkes and M. Harris, "The Purposes of a Syllabus," *College Teaching* 50, no. 2 (2002): 55–56.

4. J. Slattery and J. Carlson, "Preparing an Effective Syllabus," *College Teaching* 53, no. 4 (2005): 159–63.

5. B. Thompson, "The Syllabus as a Communication Document: Constructing and Presenting the Syllabus," *Communication Education* 56, no. 1 (2007): 54–71.

6. K. Zucker, L. Baker-Schena, and M. Pak, "The Course Syllabus: Contract, Culture, and Compass," *Teaching Professor* 24, no. 1 (2010): 3.

7. M. Luwig, A. Bentz, and H. Fynewever, "Your Syllabus Should Set the Stage for Assessment of Learning," *Journal of College Science Teaching* 40, no. 4 (2011): 20–23.

8. Id.; R. Theilheimer and B. Cahill, "This Is Your Class": Theorizing What Syllabi Say about Relationships between Instructors and Students in Early Childhood Teacher Education Classrooms," *Contemporary Issues in Early Childhood* 5, no. 1 (2004): 4–18.

9. https://www.chronicle.com/article/the-syllabus-as-a-contract/.

10. K. Kauffman, "A Legal Analysis and Contrarian Approach to the Syllabus-as-Contract Perspective," *Journal on Excellence in College Teaching* 26, no. 2 (2015): 177–97; M. M. Rumore, "The Course Syllabus: Legal Contract or Operator's Manual?" *American Journal of Pharmaceutical Education* 80, no. 10 (2016); S. Neaderhiser, "Having Students 'Sign on the Dotted Line': The Implications of Treating the Syllabus as a Contract," *Syllabus* 5, no. 1 (2016); D. P. Fernandez, A. Figares, and H. W. Cecil, "Preparing Syllabi: The Art of Self Defense," *University of Baltimore Law Review* 51, no. 3 (2022): 2.

11. https://www.buffalo.edu/catt/develop/teach/syllabus.html#title_257545052.

12. https://www.cmu.edu/teaching/designteach/design/syllabus/index.bak.html.

13. https://grad.rutgers.edu/professional-development/teaching-skills-ta-project/teaching-resources/what-put-syllabus.

14. https://stearnscenter.gmu.edu/knowledge-center/designing-your-syllabus/.

15. https://www.lsu.edu/cas/earnbettergrades/tipsandtools/thesyllabushandout.pdf.

16. https://teaching.utk.edu/teaching-resources/fundamentals/purposes-of-a-syllabus/; https://citl.illinois.edu/citl-101/teaching-learning/resources/teaching-strategies/creating-a-syllabus; https://pressbooks.nebraska.edu/onlineteaching/chapter/syllabus-design-purpose/.

17. https://hbsp.harvard.edu/inspiring-minds/syllabus-as-a-contract-setting-mutual-expectations.

18. Restatement (Second) of Contracts, § 1 (1981).

19. *Sooner Federal Savings and Loan Association v. Smoot*, 735 P.2d 555 (Okla. 1987).

20. Restatement (Second) of Contracts, § 24 (1981).

21. *Trout v. Apicella*, 78 So. 3d 681 (Fl. App. 2012).

22. Restatement (Second) of Contracts, § 69 (1981).

23. *Di Lella v. University of D. C. David A. Clarke School of Law*, 570 F.Supp.2d 1 (D.D.C. 2008).

24. 9 U.S.C § 10 (West, 2010).

25. Restatement (Second) of Contracts, § 347 (1981).

26. Restatement (Second) of Contracts, § 356 (1981).

27. *Sonoiki v. Harvard University*, 37 F.4th 691(5th Cir. 2022).

28. https://cat.fiu.edu/resources/developing-and-teaching-a-course/writing-a-syllabus/.

29. *Gabriel v. Albany College of Pharmacy and Health Sciences—Vermont Campus*, 2012 WL 4718678 (D. Vt. 2012).

30. *Orzechowez v. Nova Southeastern University*, 2014 WL 1329890 (S.D. Fla. 2014).

31. *Cabatit v. Sunnova Energy Corporation*, 274 Cal.Rtr.3d 720 (Cal. Ct. App. 2020).

32. 1983 WL 5148 (Ohio Ct. App. 1983); 1986 WL 6812 (Ohio Ct. App. 1986).

33. *Guidry v. Our Lady of the Lake Nurse Anesthesia Program Through our Lady of the Lake College*, 170 So.3d 209 (La. Ct. App. 2015).

34. Restatement (Second) of Contracts, § 90(1) (1981).

35. *Conrad v. Fields*, 2007 WL 2106302 (Minn. Ct. App. 2007).

36. *Vilbon v. Boston University*, 2016 WL 1085454.

37. J. Parkes and M. B. Harris, "The Purposes of a Syllabus," *College Teaching* 52, no. 2 (2002).

38. J. F. Slattery and J. Carlson, "Preparing an Effective Syllabus," *College Teaching* 53, no. 4 (2005).

39. *Yarcheski v. University of Medicine and Dentistry of New Jersey*, 2008 WL 5133687 (N.J. Super. Ct. App. Div. 2008).

40. *Hoppe v. College of Notre Dame of Maryland*, 835 F.Supp.2d 26 (D. Md. 2011).

41. *Miller v. MacMurray College*, 2011 WL 10482615 (Ill. App. Ct. 2011).

42. *Odema v. Devlin*, 2015 WL 13376541(D. Mass. 2015).

CHAPTER 3

Academic Freedom and the First Amendment's Protection of Faculty (and Student) Speech

You Make the Call

- **The Case of the Bawdy Analogist**

A tenured communications instructor at a public university in New Hampshire taught technical writing, which focused on helping students write technical reports. Not exactly the most exciting topic, for sure. So, to spice things up, the instructor—as he would later write to a university administrator investigating the matter—described his approach to teaching the subject this way:

> I compared focusing the thesis statement of a technical report with the sexual relationships between persons and how familiarity and experience are part of the communication, if focus is to occur. This comparison was on an intellectual plane and the purpose was to relate an abstract concept to everyday experiences most students are familiar with . . . Focusing is the second stage of the writing process after collecting information. Focusing on the central idea of a long technical report is a complex task for freshm[e]n in their second semester. The relationship of the writer to her subject must have intimacy and proximity similar to the sexual relationship between people.

And, early in the semester in question, the instructor told his students this: "I will put focus in terms of sex, so you can better understand it. Focus is like sex. You seek a target. You zero in on your subject. You move from side to side. You close in on the subject. You bracket the subject and center on it. Focus connects experience and language. You and the subject become one."

He also analogized technical writing to belly dancing and told his students, in an attempt to increase their interest and understanding of his approach to technical writing, "Belly dancing is like jello on a plate with a vibrator under the plate." He claimed he used this jello-vibrator analogy for over a decade, but, on the day in question, when he said it in class, six female students went to a professor from their own department, Applied Animal Sciences, to complain about what happened. The students said they didn't want to go to the tenured instructor because they didn't want to be alone with him. When confronted, the instructor implied that, if the students write reports about animal breeding and he's not offended at that, they shouldn't be offended at his analogies. Well, they were offended and they filed harassment complaints against him. One student wrote in her complaint, "I find [the instructor's] constant referrals to sex offensive. He has yet to hold a class in which he did not make a sexually suggestive, or bluntly sexual statement. I felt demeaned and embarassed [sic]. I am not a prude, but this is not an appropriate way for a writing teacher to communicate with his students." The conclusion of a lengthy investigation, which included other allegations of harassment or invasive actions, resulted in the instructor being found in violation of the university's sexual-harassment policy. He was suspended for a year without pay, ordered to get counseling by a university-chosen therapist, and told not to contact any of the students who filed complaints against him. The instructor then brought a civil-rights lawsuit against various administrators and the university, seeking reinstatement to his job and back pay.

Did the instructor get his job back, which would mean he won the argument that his sex-linked analogies in class were within his academic freedom to make?

(The answer will be given at the end of the chapter. Consider how the principles in this chapter affect your decision and reasoning.)

Although this chapter is centrally focused on the academic freedom faculty have in their teaching and out-of-class statements, it is important to recognize that academic freedom has three interconnected and, at times, conflicting aspects.[1] First, there is the academic freedom an educational institution has to be free from intrusive, governmental control over its own actions. Then there is the freedom that college or university faculty consequently have to use their professional judgment in choosing how or what to teach and research without being unreasonably regulated or restricted by their employer or the government. Thirdly, there is the academic freedom that students have to learn and think and express themselves without being abused or mistreated by their professors.

None of these freedoms exists in a vacuum; nor do they exist independently. A faculty member's academic freedom may, occasionally, interfere with a student's freedom. Likewise, a college or university's authority to institutionally exercise its academic freedom will, at times, encroach on the academic freedom of faculty. Such was the case when a tenured, public-university professor in Pennsylvania was suspended with pay for repeatedly inserting his religious views (over the objection of the administration) and using a nonapproved course syllabus in his Introduction to Education Media course. Despite the professor's claim of First Amendment protection, the federal court concluded that an instructor's academic freedom does not include his autonomy over the school's curriculum, in violation of what the school has chosen in its exercise of academic freedom.[2]

The above case was cited by another federal court in the first round of litigation filed by Florida professors and students against the state's Orwellian-titled "Individual Freedom Act," more popularly known as the "Stop Woke Act." In the case, which is on appeal as of this writing, a federal court blocked the law on the grounds that Florida had, through what the judge called "its own Ministry of Truth," shut down the "marketplace of ideas" and restricted public-university professors' discussion of eight specific concepts.[3] Ending its extensive ruling, the judge wrote, "[T]he First Amendment does not permit the State of Florida to muzzle its university professors, impose its own orthodoxy of viewpoints, and cast us all into the dark."[4] (In 2024, a part of the Stop Woke Act that restricted how Florida businesses chose to handle race and diversity issues was declared unconstitutional.)[5]

Case law such as this forms the shape of our understanding about academic freedom, so it is distressing to realize that a research study published in 2016 showed that faculty lose many more academic freedom–based lawsuits than they win. With a sample size of 210 written court opinions, issued between 1964 and 2014, the research showed that colleges or universities won 73 percent of these cases.[6] One conclusion the study's author made, in light of the data, was that faculty mistakenly have too broad a view of what speech is constitutionally protected.

While that may be the case, you don't need me to remind you that not all speech is protected by the First Amendment; unprotected speech includes harassment, threats, defamation, child-sexual-abuse material, and incitements to insurrection. Notice that hate speech is not included in the list. Hate or similarly offensive speech, particularly that which is made in political contexts, has repeatedly been ruled to be protected speech.[7] So, while we accept that government can't restrict odious expressions only on the grounds of their odiousness, we see all around governmental attempts to prohibit or punish the teaching of various concepts or theories. I think of critical race theory (CRT), of course. CRT has become both the monster and the cash cow for the outrage industry, an industry that ironically, for decades, expressed its opposition to group think, which it blames for fostering the un-American "political correctness" that led to speech codes and blanket bans of certain ideas. How a body of scholarship first formulated by law-school professors in the 1980s became ground zero in the fight over who determines what faculty can discuss should impel all instructors to familiarize themselves with the legal notions of academic freedom.

In 2024, Indiana passed a law that continues a recent inclination of state legislatures to tread on academic freedom under the guise that faculty use such freedom to the detriment of students. Among other things, the law (known as

SB202) puts alumni state-university board-of-trustee seats in the hands of the legislature, mandates that boards reject the tenure applications of those who are unlikely to meet yet-unestablished "intellectual diversity" standards, and imposes post-tenure review that penalizes professors who aren't providing intellectual diversity within their disciplines. The bill's principal author served for years as the deputy chief of staff of a former Purdue University president. So, one might expect his bill to be supported with mountains of evidence that faculty in the state (or at least at Purdue West Lafayette's campus) rashly penalized students for expressing their own views, or that students are denied information relevant to class, information that faculty don't like others knowing, or even that contrarian faculty are denied curricular or research freedoms. Yet, confirming that the law is a wrong institutional solution in search of a specific problem, he told *Inside Higher Ed* that the law is an attempt to fight the "perception" that higher education discourages conservative views.[8] Not only do public-university faculty and faculty groups across the state believe this law is a breathtaking encroachment on academic freedom but also Indiana University's president said about the bill that she was "deeply concerned about language regarding faculty tenure that would put academic freedom at risk, weaken the intellectual rigor essential to preparing students with critical thinking skills."[9]

Sources of Academic Freedom

Academic freedom is a lofty concept and worthy of admiration and protection. But figuring out what it means in the trenches, in the day-to-day world of teaching and researching, can be like trying to catch the wind without a sail. One might say about academic freedom what Supreme Court Justice Potter Stewart curiously and famously said about the practical difficulty in defining obscenity: "I know it when I see it."[10] Another way to define academic freedom might be to say, "I know it when it's not there." Even if the contours of academic freedom are hard to find, the sources are clear. They would include academic tradition, constitutional law, and contract law.

THE TRADITION AND CUSTOM OF ACADEMIC FREEDOM

Before the US Supreme Court issued decisions that were supportive of academic freedom in the mid-twentieth century, academic freedom existed as a customary expectation accorded to the academic world. American notions of academic freedom are borrowed from the European model, which helped move the continent from the Middle Ages to the Enlightenment.[11] When the Catholic church began to grant limited autonomy to thirteenth-century universities over their internal functions, freedom of inquiry began to germinate and grow, thanks in part to the printing press.[12] Enlightenment-era German and French universities, in particular, provided a freedom of scholarship and teaching that was untethered from the requirement of meeting the approval of the ruling Catholic or Presbyterian churches, which was a freedom of expression not existing for those outside the university.[13] In Germany, *Lehrfreiheit* (freedom to teach) and *Lernfreiheit* (freedom to learn) were part of the more general concept of *Akademische Freiheit* (academic freedom). But the rise of the Third Reich spelled the end of German academic freedom, as intellectual self-determination and Jewish professors were replaced due to nationalistic dogma.[14]

In America, academic freedom was adjacent to the individual liberties that already existed and that were foundational to the American experience: freedom of thought and expression. The primary defender of academic freedom, the American Association of University Professors (AAUP) was founded in 1915, by Arthur Lovejoy and John Dewey. When thinking about the AAUP's founding purpose and its role in defending academic freedom, we should appreciate that Arthur Lovejoy resigned from Stanford in 1901 because a university trustee had a colleague fired over that faculty member's politics, and that Lovejoy was denied appointment to the philosophy department by Harvard's president on the grounds that Lovejoy was a "troublemaker."[15] In its history, the AAUP has issued important and often-cited statements on academic freedom, and it has its own scholarly publication, the *Journal of Academic Freedom*. Key AAUP statements on academic freedom are summarized below:

- "1915 Declaration of Principles on Academic Freedom and Academic Tenure"
  This statement establishes three elements that comprise academic freedom: 1) freedom of inquiry and research; 2) freedom of teaching within the university or college; and 3) freedom of extramural utterance and action. (Extramural speech is that which occurs outside the metaphorical walls of a college or university. It will be discussed later in the chapter.) The Declaration also emphasizes the need for an "independent professoriate," for reasons including that "education is the cornerstone of the structure of society and . . . progress in scientific knowledge is essential to civilization."[16] The 1915 Declaration has fallen into some recent criticism, including that it lacks specificity and links academic freedom to tenure.[17] The connection between academic freedom and tenure is covered in detail in Chapter 7.
- 1940 Statement of Principles of Academic Freedom and Tenure (and 1970 Interpretive Comments)
  The 1940 Statement is a central pronouncement on academic freedom that has been endorsed by over 250 scholarly and professional organizations. The Statement says that teachers are entitled to "full freedom in research and in

the publication of the results, subject to the adequate performance of their other academic duties," and to "freedom in the classroom in discussing their subject." The Statement also connects academic freedom and tenure, and it also discusses faculty rights and responsibilities concerning extramural speech.

The 1970 Interpretive Comments are inserted as footnotes to the 1940 Statement, and these comments acknowledge that the principles of academic freedom have been refined since 1940. Consequently, the 1940 Statement is less of a "code" and more of a foundational document upon which layers of new understanding are to be added. For example, whereas the 1940 Statement says teachers "should be careful not to introduce into their teaching controversial matter which has no relation to their subject," the 1970 connective, Comment 4 says, "[t]he intent of this statement is not to discourage what is 'controversial.' Controversy is at the heart of the free academic inquiry which the entire statement is designed to foster. The passage serves to underscore the need for teachers to avoid persistently intruding material which has no relation to their subject."

- 2007 Report by Committee A on Academic Freedom

  A subcommittee of the AAUP's Committee on Academic Freedom drafted a report, "Freedom in the Classroom"[18] in 2007, responding to the sundry criticisms made by private groups about academic freedom in teaching. Chief among those criticisms were that 1) instructors indoctrinate instead of teach; 2) instructors deprive students of balance or diversity of thought by unfairly presenting conflicting views on contentious subjects; 3) instructors are intolerant of students' religious, political, or socioeconomic views, which creates a "hostile learning environment"; and 4) instructors inject their own personal and irrelevant views into the course content. This cogent and well-researched report was prophetic in its logical and rational rejoinders to then-current threats to academic freedom, which I would submit are now greater than they were in 2007. It speaks forthrightly to the view held by far too many politicians then and now that instructors should not do or say things that are offensive to their students' world views because that creates a "hostile learning environment." Here, the Report states that not only should educators not be expected or required to avoid the risk of challenging students' views, but also that teaching cannot take place in an environment where faculty fear retribution for potentially offending a student.

ACADEMIC FREEDOM AS A CONSTITUTIONAL RIGHT

This may seem too obvious for acknowledgment, but the Bill of Rights protects expressions that are unpopular because that which is already popular doesn't need constitutional cover. Popular expressions have the support of the majority, culturally and politically. Yet, regardless of the perceived dominance of an idea, when the government attempts to ban any expression outright, sometimes referred to as "prior restraint," one must ask what perceived harm the expression poses. In America's current state of tribalism and the growth industry that is education paranoia, ideas themselves are the great enemy. According to PEN America, from July to December 2022, there were 1,477 instances of individual books being banned, affecting 874 unique titles, a notable increase from the prior six months.[19] Unsurprisingly, Texas and Florida led the country in book bans. Tragically, George Orwell's *1984*, which introduced even the casual reader to terms like "Big Brother," "Doublethink," and "Ministry of Truth" and which has been on some lists as the greatest political novel of the twentieth century[20] (and which is my son's favorite book from high school), is repeatedly banned—in the Soviet Union until 1988[21] and in parts of America.[22] What could be more anti-American than various governmental bodies banning the expression of ideas because those ideas are labeled . . . anti-American?

During the McCarthy era of the Cold War, various state laws were passed requiring public employees to affirm in writing that they didn't belong to subversive groups, chief of which were communist groups. Eventually, courts were needed to decide whether such loyalty-oath statutes violated the US Constitution's freedom of association and freedom of speech, leading to a development of constitutional law in the area of academic freedom. The first mention of academic freedom as a construct of free-speech rights came in a dissenting opinion of a 1952 Supreme Court case, *Adler v. Board of Education*, which upheld the legality of loyalty-oath statutes.[23] That same year in the contrasting case of *Wieman v. Updegraff*, the Supreme Court ruled against an Oklahoma taxpayer who sought to deny the payment of salaries to state-college faculty who refused to sign that state's antisubversive-group-association law.[24] In a concurring opinion in this case, one justice said, "Teachers must . . . be exemplars of open-mindedness and free inquiry. . . . They must have the freedom of responsible inquiry, by thought and action, into the meaning of social and economic ideas, into the checkered history of social and economic dogma."

Two other Supreme Court Cases on academic freedom are directly on point and should be summarized:

SWEEZY V. NEW HAMPSHIRE (1952)

In this case,[25] a professor at the University of New Hampshire was questioned by the state attorney general about the professor's supposed communist affiliations. While acknowledging his preference for Marxism over capitalism, the professor refused to discuss his lectures or writings on the grounds of academic freedom. Building on the wisdom of the concurring opinion in *Wieman v. Updegraf* mentioned above, the court concluded that the professor's constitutionally protected liberty and political-expression rights with respect to his academic freedom were violated. In so doing, the court outlined what it called the "four essential freedoms" of a university: to determine for itself on academic grounds 1) who may teach, 2) what may be taught, 3) how it shall be taught, and 4) who may be admitted to study. With respect to the value of academic freedom, the Chief Justice wrote as follows:

> The essentiality of freedom in the community of American universities is almost self-evident. No one should underestimate the vital role in a democracy that is played by those who guide and train our youth. To impose any strait jacket upon the intellectual leaders in our colleges and universities would imperil the future of our Nation.

KEYISHIAN V. BOARD OF REGENTS (1967)

Here,[26] faculty at the State University of New York at Buffalo were fired for refusing to sign documents swearing they were not members of the American or New York Communist Parties. In ruling for the faculty, the court overturned the 1952 *Adler* case, expressly placing academic freedom under the First Amendment's protections. While accepting the proposition that New York had a right to protect its education system from subversion, it nevertheless forthrightly stated as follows:

> Our Nation is deeply committed to safeguarding academic freedom, which is of transcendent value to all of us and not merely to the teachers concerned. That freedom is therefore a special concern of the First Amendment, which does not tolerate laws that cast a pall of orthodoxy over the classroom.

There is an alternate view to the accepted proposition that the US Constitution protects academic freedom as an adjunct of the First Amendment. This disquieting assessment holds that academic freedom is only a professional norm and that if there is a constitutional right of academic freedom, it belongs to universities, not individual professors. One can see this viewpoint in a decades-old federal case from Virginia,[27] where a law was passed prohibiting state employees from accessing sexually explicit materials on their state-owned or state-leased computers. When six professors sued, arguing the law infringed on their academic freedom and First Amendment rights by prohibiting academic research on subjects that could fall under the statute, the first court to get the case agreed with them.[28] But, ultimately, a majority of the Fourth Circuit Court of Appeals ruled that the statute was constitutional.[29] After conducting its own historical review of academic freedom and finding that the concept lacked case-law consistency, the court declared that professors possess no greater First Amendment rights than any other state employee. It also said that, since the law didn't violate the free-speech rights of nonacademic state employees by denying them access at work to online sexually explicit material, there was no reason to treat academic state employees any differently.[30] A lengthy dissent disagreed with the majority's conclusions about the relevant case law on academic freedom and raised the specter that even the works of Toni Morrisson or academic commentary on her works would run afoul of the law.[31] The US Supreme Court declined to hear the case.

ACADEMIC FREEDOM ACQUIRED BY CONTRACT

As discussed in the prior chapter, contracts are the result of legally valid exchanges between parties that make the future performances obligatory. Colleges and universities make contracts with their students but also and obviously with their employees. And where colleges and universities declare or affirm that their faculty have academic freedom, those statements can be contractually binding. (Whether or not a handbook or policy statement is contractually binding, which is critical for faculty to understand, is discussed in Chapter 7.) While that may not be needed for faculty teaching at public institutions, where instructors teach within a First Amendment zone of academic freedom, it is essential for teachers at private colleges and universities.

Thanks to the yeoman's work the AAUP has done to support academic freedom, many colleges have incorporated various parts of the AAUP's positions on academic freedom in both in-class and extramural settings. So, even without having constitutional backing, faculty at private colleges should rely on the application of contract law as incorporating into their employment contracts or collective bargaining agreements any employer-endorsed statements supporting academic freedom. For those teaching at for-profit and, in particular, online-only for-profit colleges, instructors need to be careful to search for any statements that either grant or hinder academic freedom. The AAUP has spoken to this issue and raised valuable points worthy of inquiry.[32]

THE TAKEAWAY

Academic freedom is an essential aspect of that which is entrusted to a college instructor when teaching or engaging in scholarly activities or even when speaking in an off-campus setting. Academic freedom is first accorded to a college or university, and it is also granted to students (at least those attending public colleges or universities). For college faculty, its existence is found in academic tradition, in constitutional law, and in employment contracts.

Faculty and the Germaneness Standard for Course-Related Speech

You Make the Call

- **The Case of the Offensive Word Association**

A white adjunct instructor at a community college in Kentucky had been teaching in the communications department for several years and always received outstanding student evaluations and department reviews. During the semester in question, the instructor was teaching an Introduction to Interpersonal Communication class, where the subject for one class was language and social deconstructivism. In order to show how language has been used to marginalize minorities and other oppressed groups, he repeated an exercise he had used in prior semesters, where he asked students to provide examples of words that are used by the dominant culture in which they arise. Almost every student participated, and some of the responses included "girl," "lady," "f*gg*t," "n*gg*r," and "b*tch." One of the nine African American students in the class objected to the B-word and N-word being used in class and discussed it with the instructor and an administrator. The student believed the use of those words violated the instructor's policy on offensive language, which was included in the course syllabus and which said, "In order to make all class members feel comfortable enough to participate, there will be no abusive (i.e. sexist, racist, or otherwise derogatory) language in discussion." The instructor apologized to the student for any unintended offense. The student then contacted a local minister and civil-rights activist, who told the college administration that he would not "allow our kids to come to an institution and be berated with the 'N' word and the 'B' word." The instructor met with the acting dean and in that meeting was told that a "prominent citizen" had threatened the school's already-declining enrollment if something wasn't done. At the end of that semester, another administrator left a voicemail for the instructor, telling him there were no available classes for him to teach the following semester. The instructor was never asked again to teach at that college, and he filed a federal lawsuit, summarily alleging that he was fired in retaliation for his exercise of his rights of free speech and academic freedom.

Did the instructor win? Another way of thinking about this is to ask if the instructor's academic freedom covered the exercise that led to the offensive words?

(The answer will be given at the end of the chapter. Consider how the principles in this chapter affect your decision and reasoning.)

Faculty face an ever-escalating urgency to keep their students' attention. Whether, as some believe, the social media world in which we are immersed has caused many people to get bored quickly, there is an accepted belief that our attention spans just aren't what they used to be. TED Talks have an eighteen-minute time limit for that reason.[33] Yet, despite the commonly held refrain that students can only handle ten to fifteen minutes of lecture time, some research shows that belief to be unsupported by evidence.[34] Nevertheless, in that struggle to be relevant and memorable, or perhaps even edgy, we sometimes say or do things that others might find inappropriate or offensive. Furthermore, as we know all too well, some course topics or discussions are controversial or risk offending some students—or anyone else that feels like being offended. That can't be avoided, unless there is a complete abandonment of the ideal that higher education involves an open inquiry and exchange of ideas. And where those instances result in lawsuits, the arbitrary and capricious standard, discussed in the first chapter, is not controlling; the "germaneness standard" is.

WHEN ARE YOU SPEAKING ON MATTERS OF A PUBLIC CONCERN?

Whereas the arbitrary and capricious standard is akin to asking how far from rational was a professor's judgment about a grade, the germaneness standard asks how close the professor's statements or class activity was to the subject matter at hand. It's a legal form of the game horseshoes. And when the instructor works at a public institution, the starting point for this analysis is to ask whether the instructor's statement was about a "matter of public concern." The public concern standard comes from a 1968 US Supreme Court case, *Pickering v. Board of Education*, where a school teacher sued the school board for firing him after he wrote a letter to the editor of the newspaper, criticizing the board and the superintendent over their handling of attempts to raise revenue.[35] In ruling for the teacher, the court viewed the letter as speech that touched on a matter of legitimate public concern, in that he was speaking as a citizen on something that affected the community.

Some years later, the Supreme Court ruled the other way in a case, *Connick v. Myers*, where an assistant district attorney sued her boss (the father of singer and actor Harry Connick Jr.) after being fired for distributing a survey seeking other employees' opinions on their morale, in light of the district attorney's office's recent staffing changes and what the assistant district attorney thought were compelled political activities.[36] In ruling against the employee who alleged her firing violated her protected right of free speech, the court concluded that her actions did not implicate the First Amendment because they did not touch on a matter of public concern, which the court declared was speech "relating to any matter of political, social, or other concern to the community."[37] Essentially, the court's contextual and content review of the assistant district attorney's communication led the majority to conclude that she was speaking as an employee on mostly internal or private matters.

Garcetti v. Ceballos is another free-speech case involving a district attorney's office where an assistant district attorney was demoted for writing a memo criticizing what he thought were unlawful practices by the sheriff's department. In this case, the court once again ruled that such speech was not about a matter of public concern.[38] To the court majority, a public official speaking in his or her official capacity is not speaking as a private citizen for First Amendment purposes. To the dissent, this case's ruling would constrict the historically accepted right of academic freedom in scholarship and teaching. However, the majority thought it unnecessary to consider how its analysis would apply to academic settings.[39] Following this case, some, but not all, courts have carved an academic exception in certain contexts, mostly where teaching or scholarship is at issue.

Teaching and "Matters of Public Concern"

There is some good news for public-university faculty in that, as one court wrote, "Because the essence of a teacher's role is to prepare students for their place in society as responsible citizens, classroom instruction will often fall within the Supreme Court's broad conception of 'public concern.'"[40] To continue the horseshoes analogy, the further an instructor's controversial class speech gets from course-related content, the less likely it is to meet the public-concern test in order to be considered germane. But context matters when deciding whether the use of offensive words relates to matters of public concern. For example, a literature professor discussing *Huckleberry Finn* and its use of the N-word (and saying the word) or a film professor talking about director Quentin Tarantino's use of the N-word in his films (total count at 214)[41] would be speaking on a matter of public concern. But a college basketball coach who used the N-word in a half-time speech for motivational purposes (after asking and receiving permission from his Black players to say it) was ruled not to be speaking on a matter of public concern and was not protected by academic freedom after being fired.[42] (Black players from the coach's team joined him as plaintiffs in his wrongful-termination suit. He later became LeBron James's high-school basketball coach.)

In a unique case from Ohio, an assistant professor of obstetrics at a public medical school claimed he was fired in retaliation for disagreeing with the department chair over whether C-sections should be recommended. In clinical and other medical-school settings, the professor advocated that forceps-assisted vaginal deliveries were more advisable than what he thought were unnecessary C-sections, and a key issue in the case was if his speech was about a matter of public concern. The medical school argued it wasn't, in part because the professor had no publications on the topic and because he wasn't speaking in a class when discussing his C-section views. But the court said lack of publications wasn't fatal to whether he was "speaking" on a matter of public concern; nor was that his professional views were expressed outside of a traditional classroom. In siding with the professor, the court said, "Universities should be the active trading floors in the marketplace of ideas."[43]

In a case that in some settings would come with a trigger warning, a community-college English professor was suspended for regularly swearing in his class, saying some of the following: "f*ck," "c*nt," "p*ss*," and "*ss." He discussed necrophilia in reference to what he called "butt-f*cking" and made disrespectful Monica Lewinsky references. Lest you think he was teaching a class on Quentin Tarantino's films, none of these statements was in any way related to the course and, therefore, these statements were nowhere close to being judged to be on matters of public concern and, consequently, were found not to be germane.[44] But the court also concluded that, with respect to a sexual-harassment investigation, the professor's actions in distributing a student's sexual-harassment complaint against him, along with his satirical response (for which he was disciplined), did constitute speaking on a matter of public concern. Those actions were protected speech in that they involved him speaking on issues like harassment and the sanctity of the First Amendment.

THE TAKEAWAY

Faculty at public colleges and universities have First Amendment protection for their speech that qualifies as being about a public concern. That includes course-related speech. What is a matter of public concern is that which relates to any matter of political, social, or other concern to the community. Faculty speech made in a teaching setting generally is considered to be on a matter of public concern.

THE GERMANENESS STANDARD IN OPERATION: WHEN IS SOMETHING RELATED TO THE PEDAGOGY?

The cliché about avoiding religion and politics in conversation is unworkable in certain classes, although adhering to that chestnut could help some professors avoid entanglement with political and religious firestorms. One of the more noteworthy examples comes from Florida in 2013, where an instructor teaching an intercultural communications class on the power of symbols asked students to write "JESUS" on a piece of paper and then stand on it. It didn't matter that the instructor was known to be a born-again Christian, a follower of Jesus, and a Sunday School teacher.[45] And it didn't matter that the exercise came directly from the textbook's instructor's manual[46] and that no student was forced to engage in or penalized for refusing to engage in the exercise.[47] It also didn't matter that the in-class activity was absolutely germane to the subject matter. All that mattered (after a student complaint led to press involvement) was that pundits and conservative politicians wanted the instructor fired. He was placed on administrative leave but thankfully got his nontenured position back.[48]

The AAUP has issued various statements in support of academic freedom in the teaching sphere, including its "1940 Statement on Academic Freedom and Tenure" and its "Freedom and Classroom" report, issued in 2007 by the Committee A on Academic Freedom.[49] The 1940 Statement's section on academic freedom has this relevant quote: "Teachers are entitled to freedom in the classroom in discussing their subject, but they should be careful not to introduce into their teaching controversial matter which has no relation to their subject."[50] In the 2007 report, the committee stated "It is neither harassment or discriminatory to hold up to close criticism an idea or viewpoint the student has posited or advanced. Ideas that are germane to a subject matter in a classroom cannot be censored because a student . . . might be offended." Later, the report said, "So long as an instructor's allusions provoke genuine debate and learning that is germane to the subject matter, they are protected by 'freedom in the classroom.'"

Of course, the AAUP has no enforcement power, so courts ultimately decide what is or is not germane, and the decisions are not necessarily consistent. Take, for example, an English instructor who was fired because of an in-class exercise that led to students swearing in class. The appellate court said there was no academic freedom in the instructor's exercise, even though the majority acknowledged the exercise was "initiated for legitimate pedagogical purposes."[51] In his writing class for pre-freshmen, the instructor used a "clustering" exercise—designed to help students avoid using repetitive words in their writing—where he asked students to choose any topic and then brainstorm out loud, saying related words. Of course, the students chose "sex" as the topic. Their shouted contributions ranged from "marriage," "wedding ring," and "children," to "penis," "fellatio," "f*ck" and much more. (Those students could have written quite a blue Mad-Libs story.) Despite no student complaining about the ten-minute exercise, and despite the court majority thinking the exercise was germane, the court nevertheless agreed with the university that the exercise went too far and its use risked the school being made liable for sexual harassment. But the case law precedent cited by the court came from high-school cases, and a strongly worded dissent stressed several points, including that the students—not the instructors—said the controversial words, that the college's sexual-harassment policy was too vague, and that the college's own academic-freedom statement basically mirrored the AAUP's 1940 statement. While the dissenting judge noted that he had no fondness for the clustering exercise the instructor used, he recognized his personal view had no bearing on whether the exercise was part of the instructor's academic freedom, which that judge believed it was.

The Curse of Cursing and Discussing Sex in Class

The case law in this area shows that coarse language often is, in a worst-case scenario, what will land a faculty member in court, having to defend the usage as part of a legitimate pedagogical purpose or as being germane to the subject matter. In a case from Texas, an economics instructor not only failed to contain his ire at his students' poor performance but also berated them as if he was a drill instructor and they were boot-camp draftees. He told them their attitude "sucks" and was "a bunch of bullshit," and he repeatedly used "hell" and "God damn" when talking to them. Students rightfully took offense to his excoriations and, after being warned repeatedly to tone it down, he was fired. In ruling for the university after the professor filed suit, the court stated that nothing about the instructor's expletives implicated his academic freedom because the expletives were not germane to his subject matter and had no educational function.[52]

That case has been approvingly cited in many cases, including one involving a former tenured, early-childhood education professor at Louisiana State University, who was fired over her in-class language and language used at elementary schools where she observed student teachers. The case became a cause célèbre in academic circles and involved various federal appeals, all of which the professor lost. And the US Supreme Court refused to take her case.[53] The facts of the case are a long and winding road involving the professor (who was soon to be promoted from associate to full professor) discussing her sex life and the purported sex lives of her students, using profanity and making sexually explicit jokes. Some of the students in her class, and a school superintendent who came to know some of the professor's comments at student-teaching visits, complained about what they believed was offensive and intrusive commentary, with one student calling it humiliating. A university committee investigating the matter concluded that the professor created a "hostile learning environment," recommending censure while criticizing the university for due-process violations that harmed her defense. The university, however, sought to terminate her employment, and the crux of the legal dispute was whether her language had a pedagogical purpose. The AAUP and the Foundation for Individual Rights in Education (FIRE) supported the professor,[54] endorsing her argument that the controversial language she used was germane and had an educational connection, in that it was meant to prepare students for what they might face in their working world. Her humor, she said, was meant to help students understand their own feelings about sexuality and to help prepare them for future interactions with families with different backgrounds than their own. But every federal court refused to accept that position, concluding that her speech was not on a matter of public concern (and not protected by the First Amendment) because it was "clearly not related [to] the training of pre-K–Third Grade teachers."[55]

It can be hard to see where the line is drawn between gratuitous sexual speech and speech that is closely connected enough to pedagogy to be germane. In a federal case that makes some cases that were described earlier in the chapter seem less controversial, a tenured English instructor at a community college won his free-speech claim after being disciplined for creating a hostile learning environment. The accusation was made against the instructor for focusing much of the in-class statements in his remedial English class on pornography. He told the students that he had written for "Playboy" and "Hustler" magazines and proved it by reading some of his articles in class. He had students write about pornography, he used profanities and vulgarities that some female students believed were directed at them in a harassing manner, and he had students discuss topics like cannibalism and pedophilia in what he called a "devil's advocate" style. The instructor's saving grace was that he was for years known to teach in this intentionally shocking way (all without consequence), and the court thought the college's sexual-harassment policy, which was the catalyst for his discipline, was too vague.[56]

Title IX, Sexual-Harassment Codes, and Free Speech

It may come as a surprise that the AAUP has expressed concern that Title IX, the monumental 1973 law that prohibits sex discrimination in education, has been used in conjunction with vaguely worded sexual-harassment codes to hamper free speech on campus. Its 2017 report, "The History, Uses, and Abuses of Title IX,"[57] examines the tension between interpretations of Title IX and the increasing use of faculty suspensions related to faculty speech. In focusing much of its emphasis on the US Department of Education's own rules on Title IX (which obviously influence how college administrations act), the report categorized perceived threats to academic freedom, including the following:

- The failure to make meaningful distinctions between conduct and speech or otherwise to distinguish between "hostile-environment" sexual harassment and sexual assault.
- The use of overly broad definitions of hostile environment to take punitive employment measures against faculty members for protected speech in teaching, research, and extramural contexts.
- The tendency to treat academic discussion of sex and sexuality as contributing to a hostile environment.

THE TAKEAWAY

Academic freedom *should* protect an instructor whose controversial or even offensive teaching-related statements or activities are made in connection to a legitimate pedagogical purpose. Provocative comments or activities that are germane to the subject matter are within the faculty's discretion to make or engage in. But being provocative or profane just for the sake of it is unwise.

Faculty and Extramural Speech

You Make the Call

- **The Case of the Controversial Blog Post**

A tenured political-science professor at a Catholic university in Wisconsin ran his own blog. A post he wrote about another faculty member led to a rancorous conflict, resulting in his unpaid suspension and then a lawsuit against the university. The matter became a national news story. The background to this case involves the professor coming to know that, in a philosophy-of-ethics class on campus, a graduate-student instructor allegedly told a student, who had disagreed with the instructor's pro-gay rights views, that the student was wrong to think that gay rights was a topic open to discussion in class because everyone agrees with her. Part of this conversation included the instructor telling the student that his "homophobic comments" would not be welcome in class and that the student should consider dropping the class. The student secretly but legally recorded their conversation and gave the recording to the blog-writing professor who quoted parts of the instructor's statements on his blog and put a link to that instructor's contact information and her website. Among the statements included in the blog post was that the instructor's refusal to allow the student to present a view on gay rights counter to the instructor's views was "typical among liberals now." Soon after, the instructor began receiving emails or other communications, including threats to her safety, from those who thought she was stifling her own students' views. She filed a university complaint against the blogging professor. The dean suspended the professor without pay and sought to have the professor terminated on the grounds that his "conduct clearly and substantially fails to meet the standards of personal and professional excellence that generally characterizes University faculties."

A faculty hearing committee was formed, including having on it one member who had already expressed her view on the matter in an open letter to the local newspaper, excoriating the professor for his blog post about the instructor. The professor's demand to have that committee member removed was denied. The committee concluded the professor's blog post violated university policies on professionalism and recommended a one-to-two–semester, unpaid suspension. The university president essentially accepted that recommendation, issuing a suspension conditioned on the professor admitting wrongdoing before returning to campus. The professor sued the university on breach-of-contract grounds. The essence of his argument was that the university's academic-freedom statement in its employee handbook, which was a cut-and-paste job from the AAUP's 1940 Statement on the Principles of Academic Freedom and Tenure, contractually permitted him to exercise that freedom in the extramural manner he did. The relevant part of the 1940 Statement on extramural speech is as follows:

> The college or university teacher is a citizen, a member of a learned profession, and an officer of an educational institution. When he/she speaks or writes as a citizen, he/she should be free from institutional censorship or discipline, but his/her special position in the civil community imposes special obligations. As a man/woman of learning and an educational officer, he/she should remember that the public may judge his/her profession and institution by his/her utterances. Hence, he/she should at all times be accurate, should exercise appropriate restraint, should show respect for the opinions of others, and should make every effort to indicate that he/she is not an institutional spokesperson.

Did the professor win his argument that his blog post was protected by the university's official policy statement on academic freedom?

(The answer will be given at the end of the chapter. Consider how the principles in this chapter affect your decision and reasoning.)

As shown in the "You Make the Call" case above, the AAUP's position on extramural speech is textured. It recognizes the right faculty have to be free from retribution for speaking outside of class on matters affecting the public. But it also implores certain restraints, including mindfulness about how the public might interpret a faculty member's communication, in light of the dual communities faculty populate: the academic one and the public one. Civility should be an essential part of extramural speech but, obviously, the question then becomes who gets to determine when the civility line has been crossed. The AAUP's position (coming from 1964's Committee A Statement on Extramural Utterances) on whether extramural statements exceed the civility standard comes down to this: "[t]he controlling principle is that a faculty member's expression of opinion as a citizen cannot constitute grounds for dismissal unless it clearly demonstrates the faculty member's unfitness to serve."[58]

Revisiting Matters of Public Concern

As stated earlier in the chapter, faculty working for public institutions have a First Amendment right to speak on matters of public concern, which is that "relating to any matter of political, social, or other concern to the community."[59] To help determine whether something is of a public concern, a probative question to ask is if a public faculty member is speaking "as a citizen,"[60] or if, instead, he or she is really speaking as a public employee about a nonpublic matter.

Just because a public employee's speech is on a matter of public concern does not guarantee its status as protected, where the employee's motive for speaking is personal or private. In a 2023 case from a public university in Florida, after the university president denied faculty the right to teach remotely in the fall 2021 semester, a full professor of English, who was planning on teaching remotely, shared with his students two email exchanges he had with his department chair over the controversial, nonremote directive. His chair and other administrators thought this was so unprofessional as to warrant a permanent probation and unpaid suspension. The professor sued, but the case was dismissed on the grounds the emails were employee-only communications, which were nonpublic matters.[61] Sharing them with his students did not change their content into that which was First Amendment–worthy. (This case is revisited in Chapter 7, which is about disciplining tenured professors.) And, in a case from a public college in New York City, internal departmental politics concerning a chairperson election got so acrimonious that one professor's employment was eventually terminated. That professor sued, but the court ruled that his job-risking communications were examples of public-employee speech on a nonpublic issue, not citizen speech on matters of public concern and, therefore, were unprotected.[62] In another 2023 case that shows the tension about what qualifies as a matter of public concern, a tenured education professor at a public university in North Carolina sued his university for retaliating against him over the anti–diversity, equity, and inclusion (DEI) views he expressed to colleagues (for which he was called a bully) and for anti–woke-in-education sentiments he placed on his personal blog. In ruling that there was no retaliation shown for his blog post, the Fourth Circuit Court of Appeals also concluded that his at-work statements weren't about matters of public concern because they were unprofessional attacks that did not relate to teaching or scholarship.[63] The dissenting judge concluded the opposite: the professor's statements were protected by free speech—even if they lacked collegiality—because his dissatisfaction with DEI's influence on education was a matter of a public concern.[64]

Sometimes, faculty members might also be students, and, when such persons express themselves outside of class, they are likely to be evaluated by employee standards when their speech is controversial. A University of Nebraska graduate student who had been recently appointed to teach English part-time was removed from class and her employment was eventually terminated because of a verbal altercation she had on campus with an undergraduate student who was setting up a Turning Point USA table in a "free speech" zone. (Turning Point USA, created by right-wing provocateur Charlie Kirk, operates a "Professor Watchlist" blog that seeks to "expose" professors that discriminate against conservative students. Liberty University in Virginia was for some years the locus for the Falkirk Center, a think tank named in recognition of Jerry Falwell Jr., Liberty University's disgraced former chancellor, and Charlie Kirk, who has no college degree.) The graduate student gave the undergraduate student the finger and, among other things, said "F*ck Charlie Kirk." The undergraduate student filmed the event and posted it online, leading to threats and more controversy than the university wanted. The graduate student sued after her part-time–lecturer contract was not renewed, but her case was dismissed in 2022. (The AAUP temporarily censured the University of Nebraska over how the matter was handled.) In dismissing the lawsuit, the federal district court judge listed multiple consequential factors, including that there was insufficient evidence presented that the part-time lecturer's communications were on matters of a public concern.[65]

THE TAKEAWAY

Public-university faculty have extramural speech rights that are protected by the First Amendment when they are speaking as citizens—not as public employees—on matters of public concern. Extramural speech rights are not without limitation, as indicated by AAUP policy statements and case law.

Do Private University Faculty Have Extramural Speech Rights?

Because so much of the case law on faculty speech rights concerns an interpretation and application of the First Amendment, one might naturally conclude that faculty at private colleges and universities have no extramural speech rights. And, for those who work at religious colleges, the Free Exercise Clause and the Establishment Clause of the First Amendment allow those colleges and universities not only to restrict in-class and off-campus speech but also to require faculty to adhere to religious doctrines that impact off-campus behavior. But religious institutions risk losing their tax-exempt status through policies that promote racial discrimination, like the prohibition of interracial dating for example. The US Supreme Court said this in 1983, in *Bob Jones University v. U.S.*, declaring there is no tax-friendly approval for that which is "contrary to fundamental public policy" and which "violates deeply and widely accepted views of elementary justice."[66]

But, as stated earlier in the chapter, private-college or -university faculty can secure extramural speech rights through contract law. When a college includes clear affirmations for the speech rights of faculty in its employee handbooks, mission statements, collective bargaining agreements, or other policy documents, courts have concluded that those statements are incorporated into faculty employment contracts.[67] (Chapter 7 more specifically discusses whether faculty handbooks are contractually binding in protecting faculty rights.)

THE TAKEAWAY

Faculty at private educational institutions are not protected by the First Amendment when it comes to extramural speech. But, where private or public universities incorporate vibrant statements affirming the speech rights of faculty into their employee policies or other equivalent documents, then faculty acquire extramural speech entitlements through contract law.

Students and Their Free Speech Rights

You Make the Call

- **The Case of the Salty Salutation**

A master's degree candidate in the Material Sciences Department at a state university in California was denied his degree due to his thesis, but not in the way one might suspect. Titled "The Morphology of Calcium Carbonate: Factors Affecting Crystal Shape," the thesis was submitted and found worthy, but what happened in between his thesis guidance committee's thumbs-up and the conferring of the degree led to a federal lawsuit against the members of the guidance committee, the school's dean, and the library director. As submitted and formally approved by all three committee members, the thesis had no acknowledgments page. Per the university's policy, master's theses were placed in the library as a prerequisite to earning a degree. But, after his thesis was approved, the student inserted in the document a two-page "Disacknowledgements" section, which began, "I would like to offer special *F*ck You's* to the following degenerates for of [sic] being an ever-present hindrance during my graduate career." Among those receiving the student's written kiss-off were the dean, the graduate-school staff, the library administration, the former California governor, and even "Science." Someone in the library with an editorial eye noticed the "Disacknowledgements" page, and it hit the fan. The student then submitted a new version without the vulgar invectives in his "Disacknowledgements," but the thesis committee decided the thesis did not meet professional publication requirements because the student had altered the thesis after the committee originally approved it. Of note to the committee was that the Graduate Student Handbook's section on theses said, "You *and your committee* [emphasis added] are responsible for everything between the margins. The organization, presentation, and documentation of your research should meet the standards for publishing journal articles or monographs in your field." And the guidelines mentioned the purpose of an acknowledgments section. The dean said the student would receive his degree upon removal of the now profane-free "Disacknowledgements" section, but the student refused to remove it. After multiple layers of failed internal appeals, the student missed the allotted time required to earn a master's degree, but it was ultimately awarded to him. He then sued, claiming that his First Amendment rights had been trampled by his thesis committee seeking to remove his "Disacknowledgements" section and that his due-process rights were violated by not ever receiving a formal hearing on the matter.

Did the thesis committee violate the student's First Amendment rights by refusing to allow him to have his degree because of his thesis's "Disacknowledgements" section? And did the university violate his due-process rights?

(The answer will be given at the end of the chapter. Consider how the principles in this chapter and in the first chapter affect your decision and reasoning.)

What the First Amendment grants to public-institution faculty in the performance of their work is largely extended to their students. As a result, faculty and colleges may not restrict student speech on the grounds that it is or could be considered offensive. In fall 2015, a gender-studies professor at a public university in the state of Washington issued a syllabus with in-class language prohibitions that included using "oppressive and hateful language" and specifically outlawed words such as "illegal alien," "female," and "male." Part of the syllabus said, "Use of racist, sexist, homophobic, transphobic, xenophobic, classist or generally offensive language in class or submission of such material will not be tolerated."[68] Repeated use of language in violation of the syllabus subjected students to punishments ranging from the removal of participation points to Fs on assignments to "failure for the semester." After news of the syllabus broke, the university issued a statement that it would not allow blanket bans of words that students use, including words others might find offensive.[69] Also that same semester, a professor teaching at a public university in Texas caught a bit of hell, so to speak, when it came to light that his syllabus included a prohibition on saying, "God bless you" in class. It may have been—as was asserted by the university—a discouragement against potentially disruptive in-class behaviors, but, after students protested that their First Amendment rights were being infringed, the university issued an announcement that the line was removed from the syllabus.

Student-speech protections cover words and also that which qualifies as symbolic speech. As shown by *Texas v. Johnson*,[70] the 1989 case where the US Supreme Court ruled flag burning was protected by the First Amendment as political protest, "speech" includes expressive conduct. But, even before *Texas v. Johnson*, the US Supreme Court ruled in 1969 that public high-school students had a First Amendment right to wear black armbands to class to protest the Vietnam War.[71] And, in 2010, a federal court ruled that two college students' First Amendment rights were violated when they were told they were not allowed to wear empty holsters to class to protest a campus policy prohibiting concealed firearms.[72]

THE TAKEAWAY

Students at public colleges and universities have First Amendment rights to express themselves in class and on campus. Blanket bans, including in syllabi, of speech that faculty or universities consider unwelcome or offensive impede the academic ideal and are likely to be unconstitutional.

LIMITATIONS ON STUDENTS AND THEIR IN-CLASS SPEECH: SUBSTANTIAL DISRUPTION OF THE LEARNING ENVIRONMENT

You might recall from the first chapter the case where a speech professor at a public college was found liable for berating a student in class when the student gave a speech that was in opposition to same-sex marriage, including reciting Bible verses. The First Amendment safeguards that student's views. Yet, in a case around the same time, a community-college speech professor won a case where he was sued by a student because the professor wouldn't allow the student to give a speech on abortion.[73] Although the professor in the second case did not engage in openly malicious behavior like the professor in the first case, why would the professor in the second case win what would seem like a classic example of violating a student's First Amendment's right to speak about a matter of public concern? The answer is that, in the second case, the professor told the class what persuasive speech topics, including abortion, were off-limits because he thought giving speeches on those topics would be too disruptive. In ruling for the professor, the court respected the professor's professional judgment that the focus for that speech, which was communication skills, would be improperly shifted if students gave speeches on topics he thought were too combustible. The student also lost the claim that the B he earned for his speech was retaliation.

The restriction threshold for student speech in learning environments is that faculty may limit or restrict speech they believe will cause a substantial disruption of the learning environment or interfere with rights of others to learn. That doctrine was established in the 1969 Supreme Court case, *Tinker v. Des Moines Independent School District*, where the court said that students had a right to wear black arm bands to protest the Vietnam war. That doctrine was then applied in a 1988 Supreme Court case, *Hazelwood School District v. Kuhlmeier*.[74] In *Hazelwood*, a high-school principal refused to allow the student newspaper to print a student-written article on teen pregnancy in the high school. Despite the suppression of the students' journalism, which one could say violated two parts of the First Amendment, the Supreme Court said a school need not tolerate student speech that is inconsistent with its basic educational mission, even though the government could not censor similar speech outside the school.[75] And because the student newspaper was distributed internally to the school community, it didn't qualify as a "public forum," which would have granted the students more speech freedoms.

APPLYING THE *HAZELWOOD* STANDARD IN COLLEGES AND GRADUATE SCHOOLS

A relevant issue for college faculty when thinking about the *Hazelwood* case is that it involved high-school students. In fact, the maturity level of those who would read the teen-pregnancy article was part of the court's analysis. (The *Hazelwood* case is cited in various cases involving whether junior-high students at public schools have the right to wear the "I Heart Boobies" breast-cancer–awareness bracelets and in the famous "Bong Hits for Jesus" case (*Morse v. Frederick*), where the Supreme Court said public schools have a right to restrict pro-drug messages at school-related functions.[76] (Those cases would no doubt have different outcomes in a college or graduate-school context.) Yet the *Hazelwood* court didn't discuss how its decision would impact the speech rights of college or graduate students, other than to acknowledge that very point in a footnote. But the doctrine has been applied almost without limitation to all post-secondary, student-speech conflicts. There are exceptions where federal and state courts reject the *Hazelwood* standard for college or graduate-school cases,[77] but that does not guarantee that those students will win their First Amendment arguments.

The *Hazelwood* standard allows college faculty to limit or foreclose course-related expressions that faculty, in their professional judgment, believe interfere with legitimate pedagogical concerns. Furthermore, class or course-related activities do not occur in public settings, with rare exceptions. So, there is no higher, public-forum protection for class speech; there is only the standard of whether the speech constitutes a substantial disruption of the learning environment or the legitimate pedagogical purpose of the instructor or interferes with another student's speech rights. That is why, as discussed earlier in this chapter, a student was denied the right to give a speech on abortion. There, the speech professor thought certain speech topics would be too volatile and would interfere with the communication development purpose of the speech assignment. In a case from Michigan, a student in an advanced critical-writing course was removed from the class and banned from campus for journaling about his instructor, with one entry's Van Halen–influenced title being "Hot for Teacher," and another post that compared her to one of the women from the TV show "Gilligan's Island." Various journal posts, which the student knew the professor would periodically review, were sexually explicit in discussing the student's past and present female instructors. The student's federal lawsuit argued he had a First Amendment right to journal the way he did, particularly since the student claimed the professor expressly placed no restrictions on what students could write. But the court relied on the *Hazelwood* standard in ruling against the student, concluding that his speech was not protected, because it was curricular speech that the instructor had the authority to penalize, and that the journal posts violated the university's sexual-harassment policy.[78]

The line between curricular and noncurricular speech occurring in a learning environment can be hard to find, and courts occasionally have that difficulty. In a federal case from Florida, former students in a sonography program sued their college and faculty, alleging the faculty pressured them to perform transvaginal ultrasounds on each other as part of their training and then retaliated against the students for objecting to the procedures, including threatening to blacklist them at area hospitals. The trial court dismissed their claim on the grounds that the *Hazelwood* standard allowed the school to restrict that kind of speech because it was curricular, but the appellate court thought just the opposite.[79] That court believed that the speech in question (complaints about being "forced" to submit to a highly personal and invasive medical procedure) really implicated the *Tinker* standard (the armband case) in that the students' expressions were outside of class and there was no evidence that their objections were a substantial disruption of school activities. The court also concluded that the ultrasounds some of the litigating students eventually submitted to were "searches" for the purposes of the Fourth Amendment.

THE TAKEAWAY

Courts give faculty and universities broad discretion to limit or even restrict course-related student expressions when such speech will create a substantial disruption of the learning environment or will interfere with an instructor's legitimate pedagogical purpose.

STUDENTS AND VIEWPOINT DISCRIMINATION RISKS

Occasionally, viewpoint disagreements between students and faculty can lead to legal conflicts that are consequential in a class setting. Students are entitled to hold or express views, including course-related views, that other students and faculty might disagree with or find offensive. Students might object to the content in a course or the views of the professor on aspects of the content on grounds that implicate political or religious freedoms. In these situations, faculty must be mindful not to paint with a broad brush when engaging in grading or similar, consequential actions involving students who have expressed such views. Likewise, faculty should avoid appearing punitive against a student in a way that implicates viewpoint discrimination. In a federal case from Utah, an appellate court ruled that a student in a theater course had the right to sue for alleged violations of her First Amendment rights in that she opposed saying the F-word and taking the Lord's name in vain in class exercises and auditions. In applying the *Hazelwood* standard, and while acknowledging that faculty may require students to express views that are not their own, the court still concluded that there were grounds for a jury to determine if refusing to give the student the option to not say words that were offensive to her was tied to a "legitimate pedagogical purpose" or was a "pretext" for religious discrimination against a Mormon student.[80]

In a contrasting federal case involving a graduate-level class focused on women in film, a student sued her professor for what the student claimed was grade retaliation because the student presented antilesbian views. The student lost, and the case was dismissed. Here, the court said the student was wrong to insist that, as matter of course, a public university may not restrict a student's viewpoint expression. Rather, the court (while applying the *Hazelwood* standard) said the professor exercised her pedagogical authority in asking the student to rewrite papers that expressed antilesbian views and in grading the student for failing to adequately do so. The court found that the student was grade-penalized not for being antilesbian but for failing to provide the needed, course-required analysis that was supposed to accompany her views.[81] And, in a similar case, a graduate counseling student with a theological opposition to homosexuality sued her professor for viewpoint discrimination and retaliation after being put on a curricular remediation plan that was established by the department faculty after they came to believe the student was unable to reconcile her religious views on homosexuality with the neutrality requirements of her course-related counseling duties. In dismissing the student's suit, the court noted that the faculty were clear in showing that they weren't proscribing the student's views on homosexuality as a sinful lifestyle choice but were expecting all students to engage in judgment-free counseling, as required by the applicable ethics code incorporated into the curriculum.[82]

THE TAKEAWAY

To prevent the risk of appearing to penalize a student because his or her views disagree with yours, including views that intersect with course content, make sure to demonstrate how you've connected your grading to the course learning objectives or to the student's specific, pedagogical inadequacies.

STUDENT SPEECH OUTSIDE THE LEARNING ENVIRONMENT

Students have more extensive speech rights outside of class and on their own time than they do in learning environments. That was made clear in a 2021 US Supreme Court case involving a high-school freshman who was suspended from the junior-varsity cheerleading team for expressing her significant unhappiness at being passed over for the varsity cheerleading team. Via a post to her own Snapchat account from home on a weekend, the student delivered multiple F-word kiss-offs, including "F*ck school f*ck softball f*ck cheer f*ck everything."[83] In once again applying the *Hazelwood* standard, the court acknowledged that schools may regulate speech that "materially disrupts classwork or involves substantial disorder or invasion of the rights of others." But that wasn't the case here, the court concluded about this kind of off-campus speech, which it believed was a parental issue and not a school issue. Interestingly, though, in a footnote from a concurring opinion from the case (an opinion where a judge in the majority wants to express his or her own rationale for his vote), a justice wrote that he believed this case had no bearing on public college or university students.[84]

This is not to say that college or graduate students at public institutions can speak online consequence-free. For example, because many academic programs of professional study have ethics codes, student speech that violates those standards of conduct, much less speech that threatens other academic-community members, is not protected by the First Amendment. In a way, this is a tug of war between a student's freedom of expression and a university or faculty's academic freedom. A noted case showing how courts reconcile this conflict involves a nursing student at a public college who was expelled because of his Facebook posts, all of which were made off campus. Of the three grammatically challenged posts printed below, two were made to another student and a third was generalized but more threatening:

- "Glad group projects are group projects. I give her a big fat F for changing the group powerpoint at eleven last night and resubmitting. Not enough whiskey to control that anger."
- "[Y]ou keep reporting my post and get me banded. I don't really care. If thats the smartest thing program you stupid b*tch . . . And quite creeping on my page. Your not a friend of mine for a reason. If you don't like what I have to say than don't come and ask me, thats basically what creeping is isn't it. Stay off my page."
- "Doesnt anyone know or have heard of mechanical pencils. Im going to take this electric pencil sharpener in this class and give someone a hemopneumothorax with it before to long. I might need some anger management." [A hemopneumothorax is a traumatic puncture to the lung cavity.]

The student filed a federal suit alleging his First Amendment rights were violated, in that his Facebook posts were made out of class, were unrelated to any class assignments, and violated no specific rules. The court, however, agreed with the school that his posts demonstrated a lack of professionalism and fitness for a nursing career; they violated various parts of the American Nurses Association Code of Ethics, which the student handbook required students to uphold.[85] Nothing about this case, according to the court, showed the ethics code was being used as a pretext for the faculty to engage in viewpoint discrimination.

Other cases show court willingness to allow faculty to sanction a student for off-campus speech that is considered, in the strict sense, unprofessional. A mortuary-science student at a state university in Minnesota received an F in a class because her sarcastic social media posts on cadavers (including a reference to the 1989 dead-body comedy "Weekend at Bernie's") was viewed to be unprofessional, in light of a state statute on how morticians are to treat dead bodies.[86] Here, the court spurned the *Hazelwood* standard in declaring that faculty may restrict a student's social media if the regulation is tied to established professional conduct standards. But, of course, the student wasn't yet a mortician, the group to which that statute was directed. And, in an odd case from Hawaii, a public-university education student's teaching application was denied on multiple grounds, including his expressed endorsement for varying forms of teacher-student sexual relationships, which the faculty viewed as reason enough for them not wanting him to represent their department as a public-school teacher-in-training.[87] One wrinkle in this case is that the student's views on teacher-student sex were known because they appeared in an assignment for which he was not penalized, which may explain why the court rejected the notion that this case was about "legitimate pedagogical concerns." Rather, the court linked its decision to the faculty's conclusion that the student's opinions showed him to lack the professional judgment required of a teacher, which, of course, was embodied in established professional standards for teachers.

THE TAKEAWAY

Before sanctioning a student for off-campus speech, particularly online expressions, that is not directly pedagogical, be sure to evaluate whether the speech is threatening to others on campus (as opposed to simply being angry or coarse or controversial) or violates an applicable code of conduct or ethical standards in a way that implicates the student's professional fitness.

SPEECH RIGHTS FOR STUDENTS AT PRIVATE INSTITUTIONS

If a vital purpose of higher education is freedom of inquiry—an exchange and challenging of ideas—then one could contend that students at private colleges and universities should have the same rights of expression that their public-institution counterparts have. But that is not the case because private colleges and universities are not state actors and, therefore, are not obligated to operate within the bounds of the Bill of Rights, as it applies to the states. The First Amendment's Free Speech Clause is not in play at a private college. And, for students at religious institutions, their speech rights are subject to more regulation because those colleges have constitutionally protected First Amendment rights to exercise their religious freedom in the domain of ensuring that students and employees speak in doctrinally conforming ways.

States, however, are free to provide more Bill of Rights protections than required by federal law, and a few states have granted certain speech rights that already exist in public-speech settings to those in nonpublic arenas. For example, New Jersey and Connecticut's supreme courts have carved out certain free speech protections in the private sphere, including among nongovernmental employees, based on interpretations of their respective state constitutions.[88] And, where a private college invites the public to attend an event that has a public-forum feel (hosting a controversial speaker, for example), courts have found that attendees have free-expression rights on par with those at a public institution.[89]

STATUTES CAN GRANT SPEECH RIGHTS TO PRIVATE COLLEGE AND UNIVERSITY STUDENTS

Legislation can grant rights to the governed, so nothing prevents a law from granting speech rights to students at private colleges and universities. Such an attempt was made at the federal level in 1991, with a bill called "The Collegiate Speech Protection Act" which would have applied the First Amendment's speech clause to "any postsecondary educational institution."[90] But the legislation stalled, some say because of an exception that would have made the law inapplicable to those institutions controlled by religious organizations.

California succeeded in passing that kind of law in 1992, doing so with almost universal support.[91] Popularly known as the Leonard Law, this statute provides private college or university students the First Amendment rights they would otherwise have if their speech or communication took place outside of campus. (This law is silent on the speech rights of faculty at private colleges or universities.) But the Leonard Law includes an exception for private colleges or universities controlled by religions organizations.[92] The law also gives students the right to sue to enforce their rights. Ten Stanford University students brought the first suit under the Leonard Law, wherein a California Court declared Stanford's speech code too restrictive and in violation of those students' Free Speech rights.[93] As of this writing, I found no curricular speech cases involving private college students suing under the Leonard Law and winning.

- **Contract Law Can Grant Speech Rights to Private-College and -University Students**

Students at private colleges and universities might have the benefit of speech rights conferred through policy statements or other equivalent assurances in the various documents that coalesce to form what is known as an express or implied contract. For example, in 2014, the University of Chicago adopted a set of principles on free speech and freedom of expression, designed to articulate the University's commitment to "a free, robust, and uninhibited debate . . . among all members of the University's community."[94] Other private and public universities, including Princeton University, Washington University in St. Louis, Johns Hopkins University, Purdue University, Columbia University, Georgetown University, Franklin & Marshall College, Arizona State University, and Colgate University, have adopted the "Chicago Statement."

THE ARBITRARY AND CAPRICIOUS STANDARD AND STUDENT SPEECH RESTRICTIONS

Then there is the arbitrary and capricious standard, discussed at length in the first chapter. Remember that, in a legal world that refuses to allow educational-malpractice claims, faculty decisions relative to their students are evaluated by the arbitrary and capricious standard, which (thankfully) provides much-needed protection. Unfortunately, though, faculty occasionally do things that courts conclude could be arbitrary and capricious, necessitating a jury to decide.

Although those cases most often involve grading or academic discipline, it is possible that a faculty's restriction on student speech could be found to lack a basis in rational, professional judgment. Take, for example, the cases discussed earlier in the chapter on syllabi that placed prohibitions on phrases or words students could use in class, and suppose those cases came from private institutions. It is one thing to be gracious in asking students which pronouns they wish to be identified by, but it is quite another to mandate that all your students not use words like "male" or "female" or not use "sexist" or "generally offensive language," particularly at the risk of a student's grade or right to remain in the class. It would not be a long walk for an appellate court's legal analysis to travel in holding that such blanket speech bans at private (and also public) colleges have no rational basis in pedagogical concerns and are an abuse of the wide latitude granted to faculty over their course control.

THE TAKEAWAY

Students at private educational institutions have no constitutional right to freedom of speech for student-related communications, on or off campus. And students at religious colleges might be subject to compelled speech that fits the school's theology or doctrine. But state constitutions, legislation, and contract law can provide students at nonsectarian, private schools the speech rights they otherwise would not have. Faculty-created student speech restrictions at all colleges, public and private, should still be made with the arbitrary and capricious standard in mind.

Final Takeaways

- Academic freedom is an essential aspect of that which is entrusted to a college instructor when teaching or engaging in scholarly activities or even when speaking in an off-campus setting. Academic freedom is first accorded to a college or university, and it is also granted to students attending public colleges or universities. It is found in academic tradition, in constitutional law, and in employment contracts.
- Faculty at public colleges and universities have First Amendment protection for their speech that qualifies as being about a public concern. That includes course-related speech. What is a matter of public concern is that which relates to any matter of political, social, or other concern to the community. Faculty speech made in a teaching setting generally is considered to be about a matter of public concern.
- Academic freedom *should* protect an instructor whose controversial or even offensive teaching-related statements or activities are made in connection to a legitimate pedagogical purpose. Provocative comments or activities that are germane to the subject matter are within the faculty's discretion to make. But being provocative or profane just for the sake of it is unwise.

- Public-university faculty have extramural speech rights that are protected by the First Amendment when they are speaking as citizens—not as public employees—on matters of public concern.
- Faculty at private educational institutions are not protected by the First Amendment when it comes to extramural speech. But, where private or public universities incorporate vibrant statements affirming the speech rights of faculty into their employee policies or other equivalent documents, then faculty can acquire extramural speech rights through contract law.
- Students at public colleges and universities have First Amendment rights to express themselves in class and on campus. Blanket bans, including in syllabi, against speech that faculty or universities consider unwelcome or offensive impede the academic ideal and are likely to be unconstitutional.
- Courts give faculty and universities broad discretion to limit or even restrict course-related student expressions when such speech will be a substantial disruption of the learning environment or will interfere with an instructor's legitimate pedagogical purpose.
- To prevent the risk of appearing to penalize a student because the student's views disagree with yours, including views that intersect with course content, make sure to demonstrate how you've connected your grading to the course learning objectives or to the student's specific, pedagogical inadequacies.
- Before sanctioning a student for off-campus speech, particularly online expressions, or any speech that is not directly pedagogical, be sure to evaluate whether the speech is threatening to others on campus (as opposed to simply being angry or coarse or controversial) or violates an applicable code of conduct or ethics standards in a way that implicates the student's professional fitness.
- Students at private educational institutions have no constitutional right to freedom of speech for student-related communications, on or off campus. Furthermore, students at religious colleges might be subject to compelled speech that fits the school's theology or doctrine. But state constitutions, legislation, and contract law can provide students at nonsectarian, private schools the speech rights they otherwise would not have. Faculty-created student speech restrictions at all colleges should still be made with the arbitrary and capricious standard in mind.

How Did You Make the Calls?

1 – The Case of the Bawdy Analogist

In this case, a tenured communications instructor at the University of New Hampshire was suspended for a year without pay and ordered to receive licensed counseling as a result of the sexual-harassment investigation into his statements made to students in his technical-writing class. His method for helping students grasp technical writing from a perspective he thought they would understand was to analogize it to sex. He made multiple references in class to how focusing their writing was similar to people in sexual intimacy with each other. He also likened it to belly dancing, following it up with this gem: "Belly dancing is like jello on a plate with a vibrator under the plate." Six students found these allusions so offensive they told other faculty about it, leading to a sexual-harassment investigation. The sexual-harassment policy of the University of New Hampshire said, among other things, that "[u]nwelcome sexual advances, requests for sexual favors and other verbal or physical conduct of a sexual nature constitute sexual harassment when such conduct has the purpose or effect of unreasonably interfering with an individual's work performance or creating a hostile or offensive working or academic environment." After the university handed down its sanctions against the instructor, he brought a civil-rights lawsuit against various administrators and the university, seeking to be reinstated to his job and to receive back pay.

Did the instructor get his job back, which would mean he won the argument that his sex-linked analogies in class were within his academic freedom to make?

Decision: In what some think may have been the first faculty challenge to a campus harassment-speech code, the instructor won (to my surprise and perhaps to yours). The United States District Court awarded the instructor the injunction he sought, giving him his job back immediately at his tenured rank, back pay and benefits for the time when he was suspended, and told the university to make arrangements to allow him to begin teaching post haste.[95] The court thought the instructor's statements were not purely personal in nature but were made for a legitimate, pedagogical, public purpose of conveying course concepts. The court concluded that the university's sexual-harassment policy, as applied here, was "not reasonably related" to a legitimate pedagogical purpose in that it was too subjective and failed to take into account the country's interest in academic freedom. Simply because six students found the sex-allusion comments offensive didn't, on its own, make the instructor subject to discipline, because of the First Amendment. In fact, as part of its analysis, the judge said the instructor's classroom statements "advanced his valid educational objective of conveying certain principles related to the subject matter of his course,"[96] and that they were made in a professionally appropriate manner. The judge thought that the belly-dancing statement was not made in a sexual nature and that the students who were offended by that were under a mistaken impression that "vibrator" automatically presumes something sexual. In ruling in favor of the instructor, the court also found that the due process afforded the instructor prior to his suspension was lacking. It is believed the case settled after the district court's decision.

2 – The Case of the Offensive Word Association
A white, part-time instructor at Jefferson Community College in Kentucky, teaching an interpersonal communications class he had taught in prior semesters, conducted an in-class exercise on language and social deconstructivism. Discussing the power words have to marginalize minorities and other oppressed groups, the instructor repeated an exercise he had used before, asking for examples of words that are used by the dominant culture in which they arise. Most students participated, and responses included "girl," "lady," "f*gg*t," "n*gg*r," and "b*tch." One of the African American students in the class objected to the B-word and N-word being used in class and discussed it with the instructor and an administrator, because she believed the use of those words violated the instructor's policy on offensive language, which was listed in the syllabus and which said, in part, "there will be no abusive (i.e. sexist, racist, or otherwise derogatory) language in discussion." The instructor apologized to the student for any unintended discomfort. The student then contacted a local minister and civil-rights activist, who implied to the college administration that he could affect minority enrollment at the college if corrective action weren't taken. That was the last course the instructor would be hired to teach, and the instructor filed a federal lawsuit, summarily alleging that he was fired in retaliation for his exercise of his rights of free speech and academic freedom.

Did the instructor win? Another way of thinking about this is to ask if the instructor's academic freedom covered the exercise that led to the offensive words?

Decision: The Sixth Circuit Court of Appeals ruled in favor of the instructor.[97] First, the court concluded that the controversial in-class discussion and exercise on race, gender, and societal power conflicts clearly were about matters of public concern. In fact, the court said that classroom instruction often comes within the ambit of a public concern because "the essence of a teacher's role is to prepare students for their place in society as responsible citizens."[98] Furthermore, the court found that the exercise that led to the use of the offensive words was germane to the subject matter at hand on the power and effect of language. And (as many readers might have realized), the court noted the students used those terms, not the instructor, much less gratuitously. Finally, the court ruled that the refusal to rehire an at-will, adjunct instructor constituted a wrongful firing because the decision was made in retaliation for the instructor's exercise of his First Amendment rights, which meant the administrators who terminated his employment had no qualified immunity for their actions (as discussed in Chapter 1). The instructor passed away from cancer the following year, but his widow reportedly continued the case.[99]

3 – The Case of the Controversial Blog Post

This headline-grabbing case involved a tenured political-science professor at Marquette University who was suspended without pay over what he posted on his personal blog, "Marquette Warrior." The background to the case is that in a philosophy of ethics class on campus, a graduate-student instructor allegedly told the class that gay rights were something everyone agreed with and there's no need to debate it. After class, a student talked with the instructor about his objection to her no-disagreement position. The instructor told the student that, if he was opposed to her view on gay rights, he should find another class. We know this to be the case because he recorded the conversation, and the recording got into the hands of the political-science professor who posted about this situation, expressing his disgust that the instructor's actions were "typical among liberals now." The professor also provided a link to the instructor's contact information and her website, which led to her receiving varying invectives, including threats. She filed a complaint against the professor. The dean sought to have the professor fired, and a hearing committee was appointed to investigate and make recommendations about the matter. One of the committee members was on record taking a stand against the blogging professor before she was appointed to the committee. The committee found the professor's blog post violated university policy on professionalism and warranted an unpaid suspension, which the president put in place, requiring the professor to acknowledge his wrongfulness before he could come back to work. The professor sued Marquette, alleging that the university's Academic Freedom Statement (which was the AAUP's 1940 Academic Freedom and Tenure Statement), located in the employee handbook, protected his blog post and that the university breached his employment contract by suspending him.

Did the professor win his argument that his blog post was protected by the university's official policy statement on academic freedom?

Decision: The Wisconsin Supreme Court ruled that Marquette violated the professor's academic freedom and breached his employment contract.[100] As a preliminary note, Marquette argued that no court had jurisdiction over the matter because, according to the university, its own hearing process was akin to an arbitration (which would prevent the court from having jurisdiction over the matter), and the court quickly dispatched that claim. Moving to the substance of the case, the court first concluded that the investigation process was biased because one of the committee members clearly expressed her view on the professor and the controversy prior to being appointed. Next, the court said the conclusion that the campus committee reached was made through reverse engineering, in that it started with the consequences of the blog post for the graduate-student instructor to determine that the post itself violated university policy. "Performing the analysis in the correct direction," the court said, "leads to the unavoidable conclusion that the blog post has nothing relevant to say about Dr. McAdams' fitness as a professor."[101] (Dr. McAdams was the plaintiff.) Moving to the relationship of the professor's extramural speech to academic freedom, the court relied upon the AAUP's position on extramural statements in finding that his statements were protected by the doctrine of academic freedom. The university argued that the AAUP's 1970 Interpretive Comments on the 1940 Statement were relevant to its decision to suspend the professor, but the court noted that even the Comments included the statement that "[e] xtramural utterances rarely bear upon the faculty member's fitness for the position." There were urgently written concurring opinions, one of which said the graduate-student instructor's initial treatment of her student violated that student's freedom of expression. And there was a strenuous dissenting opinion that, inter alia, said the majority selectively chose facts about the professor's actions that supported its conclusion, choosing to disregard those that were more harsh and indefensible.

4 – The Case of the Salty Salutation

In this case, a candidate for a master's degree in material sciences at the University of California Santa Barbara was denied his degree because, in between having his thesis approved and it being placed in the library, he added a "Disacknowledgements" section that began, "I would like to offer special *F*ck You's* to the following degenerates for of [sic] being an ever-present hindrance during my graduate career." Among those receiving the student's written kiss-off were the dean, the graduate-school staff, the library administration, the former California governor, and even "Science." The student's thesis committee refused to confer his degree on the grounds that adding the "Disacknowledgements" section violated graduate-school policy on getting a thesis approved and did not meet professional and academic standards. Although the student removed the coarse language while insisting on keeping the "Disacknowledgements" section, the thesis committee refused to budge and various appeals affirmed their denial. Eventually the department decided to award the student his degree, but he filed a federal lawsuit, arguing his First Amendment and due-process rights were violated.

Did the thesis committee violate the student's First Amendment rights by refusing to allow him to have his degree because of his thesis's "Disacknowledgements" section? And did the university violate his due-process rights?

Decision: The Ninth Circuit Court of Appeals ruled that there was no violation of the student's First Amendment rights, nor of his due-process rights.[102] The student then sought US Supreme Court review of his appeal but was denied. Concerning the First Amendment claim, the court followed the *Hazelwood* standard and ruled that the faculty's academic judgment about what constituted a satisfactory thesis outweighed the student's argument that he had a right to include a few "F-you's." Even though the court acknowledged that the controlling Supreme Court precedent came from primary- or secondary-school cases not involving adult students, it concluded the underlying legal analysis still applied, which is that faculty have broad discretion to restrict speech that is "an integral part of the classroom-teaching function of an educational institution." And, since the student's vulgarities were in his master's thesis, they clearly were curricular speech and, therefore, subject to the thesis committee's academic judgment on what is a legitimate pedagogical purpose. Moreover, the court said the faculty had their own First Amendment and academic-freedom rights enabling them not to approve that thesis.

With respect to the due-process issue, the court said all that is required is a formal and deliberate decision-making process. No formal hearing is required to be given.

Notes

1. K. Alexander and K. Alexander, *Higher Education Law* (2nd ed.) (Milton Park, UK: Routledge, 2017).
2. *Edwards v. California University of Pennsylvania*, 156 F.3d 488 (3rd Cir. 1998).
3. *Pernell v. Florida Board of Governors of State University System*, 641 F.Supp.3d 1218 (N.D. Fla. 2022).
4. Id., at 1291.
5. https://www.miamitimesonline.com/news/florida/judge-blocks-stop-woke-act-restrictions-again/article_55da28c6-4f41-11ef-b720-f3bae8ad809f.html.
6. M. LeRoy, "How Courts View Academic Freedom," *Journal of College and University Law* 42, no. 1.
7. *Texas v. Johnson*, 491 U.S. 397 (1989); *R.A.V. v. St. Paul*, 505 U.S. 377 (1992); *Snyder v. Phelps*, 562 U.S. 443 (2011); *Matal v. Tam*, 582 U.S. 218 (2017).
8. Ryan Quinn, "Indiana Bill Threatens Faculty Members Who Don't Provide 'Intellectual Diversity,'" *Inside Higher Ed*, February 21, 2024, available at https://www.insidehighered.com/news/faculty-issues/academic-freedom/2024/02/21/bill-threatens-profs-who-dont-give-intellectual#.
9. Ethan Sandweiss, "IU President Whitten Comes Out against Controversial Tenure Bill," *Indiana Public Media*, February 7, 2024, available at https://indianapublicmedia.org/news/iu-president-whitten-comes-out-against-controversial-tenure-bill.php.
10. *Jacobellis v. State of Ohio*, 378 U.S. 184, at 197 (1964).
11. J. Dayton, *Education Law* (2nd ed.) (Bangor, ME: Wisdom Builders Press, 2019).

12. K. Alexander and K. Alexander, *Higher Education Law* (2nd ed.) (Milton Park, UK: Routledge, 2017).

13. Id.

14. United States Holocaust Memorial Museum, "Higher Education in Nazi Germany," available at https://perspectives.ushmm.org/collection/higher-education-in-nazi-germany.

15. Dale Keiger, "Tussling with the Idea Man," *Harvard Square Library*, available at https://www.harvardsquarelibrary.org/biographies/arthur-lovejoy-2/.

16. American Association of University Professors, "1915 Declaration of Principles on Academic Freedom and Academic Tenure," *Policy Documents and Reports*, 297, available at https://www.aaup.org/NR/rdonlyres/A6520A9D-0A9A-47B3-B550-C006B5B224E7/0/1915Declaration.pdf.

17. Emily J. Levine, "It's Time for an Overhaul of Academic Freedom," June 9, 2021, available at https://www.washingtonpost.com/outlook/2021/06/09/its-time-an-overhaul-academic-freedom/.

18. Matthew W. Finkin, Robert C. Post, and Cary Nelson, "Freedom in the Classroom," American Association of University Professors, September-October, 2007, available at https://www.aaup.org/file/ACASO07FreedomClassrmRpt.pdf.

19. "PEN America Index of School Book Bans—Fall 2022," *PEN America*, available at https://pen.org/index-of-school-book-bans-2022/.

20. Kathy Gill, "The Best Political Novels," *ThoughtCo.*, October 23, 2019, available at https://www.thoughtco.com/top-classic-political-novels-3368080.

21. Prarthana Prakash, "George Orwell's Dystopian Novel '1984' about an Autocratic Regime that Oppresses Its Citizens Is Now a Bestseller in Russia," *Fortune,* December 14, 2022, available at https://fortune.com/2022/12/14/george-orwell-1984-book-bestseller-russia/#.

22. "More Banned Books Week at UC Press," *University of California Press*, September 30, 2023, https://www.ucpress.edu/blog/52211/more-banned-books-week-at-uc-press/.

23. *Adler v. Board of Education*, 342 U.S. 485 (1952).

24. *Wieman v. Updegraff*, 344 U.S. 183 (1952).

25. 354 U.S. 254 (1957).

26. 385 U.S. 589 (1967).

27. *Urofsky v. Gilmore,* 216 F.3d 401 (4th Cir. 2000).

28. *Urofsky v. Allen*, 995 F.Supp. 634 (E.D. Va. 2000), reversed by *Urofsky v. Gilmore,* 216 F.3d 401 (4th Cir. 2000).

29. *Urofsky v. Gilmore,* 216 F.3d 401 (4th Cir. 2000).

30. Id. at 415.

31. Id. at 438, 439.

32. AAUP, "Primer on Privatization in Online Higher Ed," available at https://www.aaup.org/issues/privatization-and-opms/primer-privatization-online-higher-ed.

33. "TEDx Rules," *TEDx*, https://www.ted.com/participate/organize-a-local-tedx-event/before-you-start/tedx-rules#:~:text=Talks%20should%20not%20exceed%2018,to%20the%20TEDx%20YouTube%20channel.

34. Neil A. Bradbury, "Attention Span during Lectures: 8 Seconds, 10 Minutes, or More?," *Advanceds in Physiology Education* 40 (2016): 509–13, https://journals.physiology.org/doi/pdf/10.1152/advan.00109.2016.

35. *Pickering v. Board of Education*, 391 U.S. 563 (1968).
36. *Connick v. Myers*, 461 U.S. 138 (1983).
37. Id., at 146.
38. *Garcetti v. Ceballos*, 547 U.S. 410.
39. Id., at 425.
40. *Hardy v. Jefferson Community College*, 260 F.3d 671 (6th Cir. 2001).
41. Garrett Gravley, "We Counted Every Curse Word in Every Quentin Tarantino Movie," *Dallas Observer*, July 30, 2019, https://www.dallasobserver.com/arts/we-ranked-every-tarantino-movie-by-the-amount-of-cursing-11721727.
42. *Dambrot v. Central Michigan University*, 55 F.3d 1177 (6th Cir.).
43. *Kerr v. Hurd*, 694 F.Supp.2d 817, at 844 (S.D. Ohio 2010).
44. *Bonnell v. Lorenzo*, 241 F.3d 800 (6th Cir. 2001).
45. Scott Jaschik, "I Was Doing My Job," *Inside Higher Ed*, March 31, 2013, available at https://www.insidehighered.com/news/2013/04/01/interview-professor-center-jesus-debate-florida-atlantic.
46. Scott Jaschik, "He Didn't Say 'Stomp on Jesus,'" *Inside Higher Ed*, March 27, 2013, available at https://www.insidehighered.com/news/2013/03/28/professor-whose-exercise-caused-stomp-jesus-controversy.
47. Rick Scott, "FAU Professor in 'Jesus Stomping' Incident Defends Himself," *CBS News*, April 2, 2013, available at https://www.cbsnews.com/miami/news/fau-professor-in-jesus-stomping-incident-defends-himself/.
48. Scott Jaschik, "An Adjunct's Vindication," *Inside Higher Ed*, June 23, 2013, available at https://www.insidehighered.com/news/2013/06/24/florida-atlantic-rehires-adjunct-center-controversy-over-class-exercise.
49. Matthew Finkin, Robert Post, and Cary Nelson, "Freedom in the Classroom," 2007, available at https://www.aaup.org/file/ACASO07FreedomClassrmRpt.pdf.
50. AAUP, "1940 Statement of Principles on Academic Freedom and Tenure with 1970 Interpretive Comments," 1970, available at https://www.aaup.org/file/1940%20Statement.pdf.
51. *Vega v. Miller*, 273 F.3d 460, at 467 (2nd Cir. 2001).
52. *Martin v. Parrish*, 805 F.2d 583 (5th Cir. 1986).
53. *Buchannan v. Alexander*, 919 F.3d 847 (5th Cir. 2019); *Buchannan v. Alexander*, 140 S.Ct. 432 (Mem) (2019).
54. Colleen Flaherty, "Fired for Being Profane," *Inside Higher Ed*, September 1, 2015, available at https://www.insidehighered.com/news/2015/09/02/aaup-report-alleges-violations-academic-freedom-due-process-new-report-professors; https://www.thefire.org/news/supreme-court-denies-cert-buchanan-v-alexander.
55. *Buchannan v. Alexander*, 919 F.3d 847, at 854 (5th Cir. 2019).
56. *Cohen v. San Bernadino College*, 92 F.3d 968 (9th Cir. 1996).
57. "The History, Uses, and Abuses of Title IX," American Association of University Professors, *2016 Bulletin*, June 2016, 69–99, https://www.aaup.org/file/TitleIXreport.pdf.
58. "Committee A Statement on Extramural Utterances," American Association of University Professors, *Policy Documents and Reports*, https://www.aaup.org/report/committee-statement-extramural-utterances.

59. *Connick v. Myers*, 461 U.S. 138 (1983).
60. *Garcetti v. Ceballos*, 547 U.S. 410 (2006).
61. *Burt v. Fuchs*, 2023 WL 4103942 (N.D. Fla. 2023). Currently on appeal.
62. *Flyr v. City University of New York*, 2011 WL 1675997 (S.D.N.Y. 2011).
63. *Porter v. Board of Trustees of North Carolina State University*, 72 F.4th 573 (4th Cir. 2023).
64. Id., at 592.
65. *Lawton v. University of Nebraska*, 2022 WL 2047600 (D. Neb. 2022).
66. *Bob Jones University v. U.S.*, 461 U.S. 574, at 592 (1983).
67. *McAdams v. Marquette University*, 383 Wisc.2d 358 (Wis. 2018).
68. Scott Jaschik, "Ban on Banning Words," *Inside Higher Ed*, August 31, 2015, available at https://www.insidehighered.com/news/2015/09/01/washington-state-u-disavows-syllabus-ban-certain-words.
69. WSU News & Media Relations, "A Statement from President Bernardo Regarding Syllabi," *WSU Insider*, August 31, 2015, available at https://news.wsu.edu/press-release/2015/08/31/public-statement-from-wsu-regarding-syllabi-issue/#.VeTUs5caPrQ.
70. 491 U.S. 397 (1989).
71. *Tinker v. Des Moines Community School District*, 393 U.S. 503 (1969).
72. *Smith v. Tarrant County College District*, 694 F.Supp.2d 610 (N.D. Tex. 2010).
73. *O'Neal v. Falcon*, 668 F.Supp.2d 979 (W.D. Tex. 2009).
74. 484 U.S. 260.
75. Id., at 266.
76. *Morse v. Frederic*, 551 U.S. 393 (2007).
77. *Oyama v. University of Hawaii*, 813 F.3d 850 (9th Cir. 2015); *Tatro v. University of Minnesota*, 816 N.W.2d 509 (Minn. 2012).
78. *Corlett v. Oakland University Board of Trustees*, 958 F.Supp.2d 795 (E.D. Mich. 2013).
79. *Jane Doe I v. Valencia College Board of Trustees*, 838 F.3d 1207 (11th Cir. 2016).
80. *Axson-Flynn v. Johnson*, 356 F.3d 1277 (2004).
81. *Pompeo v. Board of Regents of the University of New Mexico*, 852 F.3d 973 (10th Cir. 2017).
82. *Keeton v. Anderson-Wiley*, 733 F.Supp.2d 1368 (S.D. Ga. 2010).
83. *Mahonoy Area School District v. B.L.*, 594 U.S. 180 (2021).
84. Id., at footnote 2.
85. *Keefe v. Adams*, 840 F.3d 523 (8th Cir. 2016).
86. *Tatro v. University of Minnesota*, 816 N.W.2d 509 (Minn. 2012).
87. *Oyama v. University of Hawaii*, 813 F.3d 850 (9th Cir. 2015).
88. *Mazdabrook Commons Homeowners' Association v. Kahn*, 46 A.3d 507 (NJ 2012); *Trusz v. UBS Realty Investors, LLC*, 123 A.3d 1212 (Conn. 2015).
89. *Commonwealth v. Tate*, 432 A.2d 1382 (Pa. 1981); *State v. Schmid*, 432 A.2d 615 (N.J. 1980).
90. Collegiate Speech Protection Act of 1991, H.R. 1380, 102d Cong. (1991).
91. Cal. Ed. Code, § 94367 (West, 2009).
92. Id., at § 94367(c).
93. *Robert J. Corry, et al. v. The Leland Stanford Junior University, et al.*, No. 740309 (Cal. Super. Ct. Feb. 27, 1995).

94. Geoffrey Stone, et al., "Report of the Committee on Freedom of Expression," University of Chicago, available at https://provost.uchicago.edu/sites/default/files/documents/reports/FOECommitteeReport.pdf.

95. *Silva v. University of New Hampshire*, 888 F.Supp. 293 (D.N.H. 1994).

96. Id., at 313.

97. *Hardy v. Jefferson Community College*, 260 F.3d 671(6th Cir. 2001).

98. Id., at 679.

99. Times Staff and Wire Reports, "Kenneth E. Hardy, 45; Professor Fired Over Class Discussion of Slurs," *Los Angeles Times*, June 14, 2002, https://www.latimes.com/archives/la-xpm-2002-jun-14-me-passings14.2-story.html.

100. *McAdams v. Marquette University*, 383 Wisc.2d 358 (Wis. 2018).

101. Id., at 411.

102. *Brown v. Li*, 308 F.3d 939 (9th Cir. 2002).

CHAPTER 4

Intellectual Property and Faculty and Students

WHO OWNS WHAT?

You Make the Call

- **The Case of the Fight over Author Listings in a Jointly Authored Paper**

The judge who wrote the opinion for the federal appellate court that had this case succinctly captured the nub of the dispute: "If war is the extension of diplomacy by other means, this suit—like other litigation a form of warfare—is the extension of academic politics by other means." A tenure-track, assistant professor of pharmacy administration at a public Illinois university hadn't published a refereed journal article in three years, which hadn't gone unnoticed by his chair or dean. He and two other colleagues were developing a paper that was the result of their efforts in a clinical program working with practicing pharmacists. The draft of the paper seemed to be going nowhere due to differences of opinion about the paper's focus. The assistant professor gave his draft to the other primary coauthor, who read it and threw it in his office trash can. Eventually, that coauthor created a new draft, listing his name first and the assistant professor's name third. Although he claimed it was simply an alphabetical listing, it led to a nasty dispute in the department. Nevertheless, that paper was submitted to a journal where it was peer reviewed and accepted for publication. But by that time, the assistant professor had been fired, finding himself on the wrong side of "publish or perish." He then sued the university, the pharmacy-school dean, his chair, and the two other authors of that paper for various civil-rights violations, contending that they mutilated his work and stole the credit, denying him due process of law. He said that, since he wasn't listed first on the paper, as he should have been, his professional reputation was harmed, which hindered his other scholarly efforts. The university claimed that the paper was a "work made for hire" (meaning the university owned the copyright to the article because it was written by a university faculty member in the course of his academic employment), so it didn't legally matter who was listed as first, second, or third author.

Is a published academic paper a work made for hire? If the paper is not a work made for hire, is it a copyright violation for the submitting author to alter the original order of the authors?

(The answers will be given at the end of the chapter. Consider how the principles in this chapter affect your decision and reasoning.)

One hundred and fifty years ago, the wealthiest people and the largest companies in America owed the source of their fortunes to tangible things like oil, automobiles, buildings, and railroads. Now, the richest of the rich often derive their wealth from intellectual property.[1] The most valuable companies in America, as measured by their total stock market capitalization, are predominantly tech companies, where intangible assets are valued more highly than bricks and mortar.[2] Apple, the most profitable company of them all, is so much more than a seller of phones and computers; it has over 95,000 patents[3] and over 1,000 trademarks.[4] Similarly, in the legal profession, data on the highest-paying areas of law practice show that intellectual-property lawyers earn the most.[5]

Intellectual property can be a significant contributor to a university's revenue, particularly in the area of patent licensing. The University of Pennsylvania topped the 2021 and 2022 lists of US academic institutions with the most revenue from patent licensing.[6] Due in large part to its COVID-19 vaccine efforts, the University's 2022 revenue was believed to be over one billion dollars.[7] (The 2023 Nobel Prize in Physiology or Medicine was awarded to two University of Pennsylvania scientists for their efforts in the creation of the mRNA vaccine. One of them, Katalin Karikó, was years earlier denied tenure on the grounds of her insufficient grant funding. She then accepted a demotion at Penn rather than leaving the university, so she could continue her vaccine research efforts.)[8]

Who owns what is a real question for more than just university-licensed patents. It is worth thinking about as you prepare your syllabi, write exams, or record yourself teaching in class for use on podcasts or vodcasts. It matters if you publish papers or books or produce artistic works. Perhaps the most manifest concern about faculty intellectual property is the ownership or licensing of what is shared through educational learning management systems, like Brightspace, Canvas, Blackboard Learn, or Moodle. Finally, there is the question of the ownership rights students have in the works they create, including their own patentable items. There is even a real question as to whether class notes belong to the student who wrote them or the faculty who provided them.

THE INTELLECTUAL PROPERTY FAMILY TREE

Intellectual property can be thought of as three siblings and a cousin. The cousin is in the family, but not as closely related as the siblings. Trademarks, patents, and copyrights are the siblings, and the trade secret is the cousin. While all of them can be valuable, only trademarks, patents, and copyrights get their economic value from being publicly known. (What is to be gained by a secret, unused invention, or a corporate logo no one has ever seen? What is a song worth if no one will ever hear it?) A trade secret, on the other hand, gets its value from the fact that it is not publicly known. In America, the most famous trade secrets one often thinks of are the Kentucky Fried Chicken ingredient list and the Coca-Cola syrup recipe.

You can also think about intellectual property as creations of the mind that can be legally protected. As such, the US Constitution gives Congress the power to grant limited-term monopolies to authors and inventors "[t]o promote the progress of science and useful arts."[9] But a trade secret, unlike trademarks, patents, and copyrights, is not covered by traditional intellectual property statutes and can last as long as the information thought to be valuable is protected against disclosure.

Trademarks

A trademark is a brand identifier. It can be a word, symbol, design, or some combination thereof that identifies goods or services. Marks can be "trademarks" (for goods) or "service marks" (for services). One can search the US Trademark Office database for existing trademarks.[10] Trademarks in use don't have to be registered, but trademark registration provides stronger, national protection and rights. Trademark law is generally governed by a federal law, the Lanham Act,[11] which was passed in 1946 and which has been amended multiple times. To qualify for trademark registration, the mark needs to be "distinctive," which is usually the result of the mark being arbitrary (Apple, as used for a computer company), fanciful (a made-up word like Dasani), or suggestive (Coppertone). A mark that is merely descriptive or generic can, over time, acquire "secondary meaning" trademark worthiness if it becomes strongly associated with the product or service (Holiday Inn). Marks that are used ubiquitously to refer to a class of goods rather than the single provider of those goods can become generic and lose their trademark status (Aspirin, Thermos, Jacuzzi). A trademark has a ten-year term but can last forever, provided it is continually in use and the required registration maintenance documentation is timely filed as required during the multiyear intervals. "Trademark infringement" is the unauthorized use of another owner's exclusive mark, and "trademark dilution" is using another's famous trademark in a way that diminishes its value (selling a brand of diapers called BMW).

Patents

A patent is granted to an inventor, providing the inventor exclusivity over all rights to his or her invention. Federal law says a patent may be obtained for whoever "invents or discovers any new and useful process, machine, manufacture, or composition of matter, or any new and useful improvement thereof."[12] Patents can also be acquired for sufficient modifications made to an already patented product, or when new uses have been made that are different from what the original patent holder proposed. For instance, a patent was awarded for a baldness treatment that involved topical application of an already-patented ointment intended to soften cow udders.[13] Abstract ideas (the meaning of life), laws of nature ($E = mc^2$), and natural phenomena (naturally occurring genes or DNA) are not patentable.[14] There are utility patents (vaccines), design patents (the traditional Coca-Cola bottle shape), and plant patents (the Cosmic Crisp apple). One may search for patents on the US Patent Office's search database.[15] Utility and plant patents last twenty years from the date on which the first provisional application is filed. Design patents last for fifteen years from the issuance of the patent grant. When it comes to a conflict over whose invention came first, federal law gives priority to the first person to file a patent application, rather than the first to invent. Patent infringement (committed in America) is a violation of a patent holder's rights to manufacture, use, or sell his or her property.

Copyrights

A copyright is the exclusive ownership, with respect to an original work, of authorship fixed in a tangible medium of expression.[16] Consequently, it is the expression of the ideas, rather than the ideas themselves, that are protected by copyright. The 1976 Copyright Act is the controlling federal law for copyrights. Copyright protection begins at the moment the creative work is put in a tangible medium of expression; however, obtaining a copyright registration after creating the work is necessary for bringing infringement lawsuits in America. There are eight categories of copyrightable works, including literary works (which includes software), musical works, audiovisual works, and pictorial works. The copyright term lengths are as follows for works created as of 1978: individual copyright lasts for the life of the author plus seventy-five years; joint ownership copyright lasts for the life of the last surviving author plus seventy years; and works made for hire (with corporate ownership, for example) last for ninety-five years from the first publication or 120 years from the year of creation, whichever expires first. For copyright purposes, joint authors own the work without regard to who put the most effort or content into the final product, and they own what is known as an undivided interest, which means each coauthor owns the whole work. Copyright protection includes ownership of derivative works (translations, motion-picture versions of literary works) and compilations (a greatest-hits album, a website consisting of text and pre-existing photos or other graphics). But ideas, facts, slogans, and lists of ingredients aren't protected by copyright.

Trade Secrets

A trade secret is any information a business believes is commercially valuable to its success and whose value derives from the information not being publicly known. A business must make a reasonable effort to protect the information against disclosure for it to qualify as a trade secret. A business might consider making a trade secret out of something that can't qualify for traditional intellectual-property protection. For example, a list of ingredients isn't copyrightable, but it can be a trade secret. Other examples of trade secrets include Google's search algorithm or the method used to assemble the *New York Times* Best Seller List. Much of trade-secret governance is promulgated by state law as opposed to federal law, but the Economic Espionage Act of 1996 criminalizes the theft of trade secrets at the federal level, and the Defend Trade Secrets Act of 2016 permits federal lawsuits for the misappropriation of trade secrets. Trade secrets may last forever, provided the information is protected against disclosure, which can be aided by a nondisclosure agreement (NDA). However, one may lawfully discover and use a trade secret through reverse engineering, which involves working backwards to figure out the trade secret, like replicating the McDonald's Big Mac Special Sauce for a secret recipe book. The book, unlike the recipes inside, however, could qualify for a copyright.

THE TAKEAWAY

Intellectual property includes trademarks, patents, and copyrights (which derive value from being disclosed and are generally governed by federal law) and trade secrets (which derive value from not being disclosed and are generally governed by state law). It is possible that a trademark and a trade secret can last forever, but patents and copyright have term limits.

FACULTY AND THEIR PATENTS

In 1967, Dr. Robert Cade, a medical researcher at the University of Florida, offered to sell to his employer the patent for a sports-purposed drink created by him and a few other researchers, which he named Gatorade, for ten thousand dollars. The university turned him down. By 1971, after Gatorade became a national phenomenon, the University of Florida sued him and two other inventors for ownership. The case was initially dismissed because the research funding for Gatorade came from the National Institutes of Health (which also sued him) and because Dr. Cade somehow never signed the university's standard inventor's agreement that assigned 75 percent of any royalties to it.[17] Eventually, a settlement was reached, allowing Cade and the other inventors to retain the lion's share of future royalties, including those related to the trademark, which has a longer life than a patent. By 2015, the university's own share of Gatorade-related royalties reached over 250 million dollars.[18]

In 1980, a federal statute commonly called the Bayh-Dole Act was passed,[19] allowing universities, nonprofit research institutions, and small businesses to own, patent, and commercialize inventions developed under federally funded research programs at their organizations. Although this law does not require the commercialization of patents, for universities with the capacity for bringing and the motivation to bring the Bahy-Dole Act to fruition, the results have been eye-opening. According to the National Academy of Inventors, which has been keeping records on this since 2013, the University of California led the nation in university patents during the intervening decade with 570.[20] Universities have collectively generated billions in revenues from their patents by either selling them or licensing their use to businesses who might pay fixed fees or share revenue or both. But, among other key provisions under the Bayh-Dole Act and its accompanying regulations, the US government retains "a nonexclusive, nontransferable, irrevocable, paid-up license" to use the invention.[21]

But do faculty or nonfaculty researchers whose work led to those patents have claims to ownership or monetization rights? Yes, and also a big no. First, the law is clear that an invention belongs to the inventor,[22] but there are exceptions that can swallow the rule, including intellectual-property policies in faculty employment contracts, and situations where the law presumes the employer has rights to the invention.

Intellectual-Property Policies and Faculty Patents

While one might legitimately argue that faculty control over their own inventions is part of academic freedom, that has essentially become moot in a world where faculty employment comes with acquiescence to intellectual-property policies incorporated into hiring and retention contracts. For example, the University of Pennsylvania, which is at the top of recent lists of universities with the highest revenues from patent licensing, requires as a condition of employment that all Penn faculty and other similarly situated researchers sign an intellectual-property participation agreement that, among other things, assigns all rights in patents to the university, with certain limited exceptions.[23] In situations where the University of Pennsylvania receives an ownership stake in a company as a result of licensing or transferring a patent, the inventors receive 30 percent of that equity stake, and they can receive royalties from their assigned inventions.[24] At Yale, faculty inventors can receive up to 30 percent of the net patent royalty income from their university-owned inventions.[25]

Hired to Invent and Shop-Right Doctrines

If you do research that could lead to patentable property and have not looked at your university's policies on patent ownership or assignment, then, to paraphrase the inventor Benjamin Franklin,[26] don't leave that until tomorrow. Assuming your college or university has no intellectual-property policies that are incorporated into your terms of employment, it is still possible for your employer to claim ownership of, or at least the right to freely use, your invention. If one is hired by an employer to do the work that inventors do, then courts can—and do—find that those inventions belong to the employer under the hired-to-invent doctrine. This doctrine can apply to a university researcher. Furthermore, the shop-right doctrine is another court-created (common law) doctrine establishing that, where an employee uses his or her employer's resources, such as funds or labs, in creating an invention, even during nonworking hours, the employer has the right to use the invention. Purdue University has explicitly made those common-law doctrines part of their intellectual-property policy by saying it owns all inventions "made in the course of employment by the University or through the University resources."[27]

THE TAKEAWAY

While it is true that an inventor is the owner of an invention, faculty who create patented property generally are not the owners due to employment contracts incorporating intellectual-property language that mandate the assignment of any work-related inventions. But such statements can include various forms of equity or revenue sharing in instances where those patents are licensed or otherwise monetized.

Faculty and Copyright: Who Owns What?

You Make the Call

- **The Case of the Copyrighted Curriculum Materials**

Proving once again that no good deed goes unpunished, this case involves an instructor and part-time administrator at a college in Illinois who, while being tasked with creating a new program at the college, completed her own employer-required master's degree, only to be told her degree was insufficient. Her employment therefore was eventually terminated. Next came the fight over the ownership of the curriculum materials she created for that new program. This former, full-time instructor of travel and tourism was also the program's director and coordinator, and that title and responsibility came with an additional stipend. When her employer sought to transition the travel and tourism program from a program awarding a certificate to a program awarding a bachelor's degree, it told the instructor she needed a master's degree to be qualified to teach courses in the new program. The instructor's direct supervisors advised her on where to apply and wrote her reference letters for her application. Yet, after completing that master's program, her college informed her that it was unaccredited and, therefore, insufficient. She was told to earn another master's degree in her discipline and given a new deadline to do so. During the time that the instructor was earning her eventually unaccepted master's degree, she was tasked with doing what was needed to create the upcoming bachelor's-degree program in tourism, sport, and hospitality management. Naturally, she detailed in her annual self-evaluation her efforts in creating this new degree program, including saying she would "continue to work on curriculum development and required paperwork." One thing she didn't mention in her self-evaluation was that she filed copyright registrations with the US Copyright Office for two of the curriculum materials she created. Her annual employment contract was not renewed after she postponed signing it. She postponed for a few reasons, including that the contract required her to earn the second master's degree by a certain date and it did not promote her or provide a pay increase for having the first master's degree. She then sued the college for age discrimination (she was in her fifties, which is over the federal, age-protected status of forty) and for copyright infringement. She claimed that she owned the curriculum materials she created and copyrighted, which were being used in the new bachelor's-degree program she brought to life.

Does the instructor own the curriculum documents she created and officially copyrighted?

(The answer will be given at the end of the chapter. Consider how the principles in this chapter affect your decision and reasoning.)

From syllabi to exams to journal articles to musical compositions, faculty engage in multitudinous activities that have copyright implications. And, where copyright is at issue, so are ownership and licensing implications. General principles often give way in specific situations, and one of those specifics to keep in mind is that institutional policies on faculty-created intellectual property can supersede traditional copyright doctrines.

WORKS MADE FOR HIRE AND FACULTY COPYRIGHTS

Assuming for the sake of argument that a syllabus is copyrightable, it would be initially correct to presume that the author owns it, since that is the law.[28]

But the law also says that when something is a "work made for hire," the copyright belongs to the author's employer or whoever the work was created for.[29] The most common way to be in a work-made-for-hire situation is to be employed where creating copyrightable works for your employer is in the scope of your employment. For example, employees of the Hallmark card company don't own those pithy sayings they write on the cards we buy; Hallmark does. The second work-made-for-hire situation involves being specifically hired to create one of nine categories of work—which includes instructional texts and test questions and answers—if both parties' signatures confirm the written work-made-for-hire arrangement.[30] This is a transfer of copyright in an independent-contractor situation. Indeed, the copyright for this book was transferred to the publisher by way of a jointly signed, work-made-for-hire agreement.

Because the 1976 Copyright Act doesn't define "employee" or "scope of employment," our courts, including the US Supreme Court, have grappled with the issue of when someone is in a work-made-for-hire situation and have said that agency law is controlling.[31] Without getting too far into the weeds of agency law, a number of factors are weighed to determine whether one is an employee or an independent contractor, including the following: 1) whether the hiring party has the right to control the manner and means by which the work product is accomplished (which is often viewed as the most probative factor); 2) whether the employed party's actions serve the hiring party's larger purposes; 3) whether the tax structure in the arrangement suggests the hired party is an employee or an independent contractor; 4) whether there are employee benefits; and 5) where the work is being done.

But, even if one is an employee, that doesn't end the analysis on whether something is a "work made for hire." For example, if I have an acoustic guitar in my campus office and play it from time to time to break up my work day, and I create a song on my guitar in my office and record it on my iPhone, does my university own the song because I created it in my office during regular working hours? Of course not, because it's not the kind of work I create in the scope of my employment as a business law professor. But suppose I play the recorded song in a class to demonstrate how copyright works, which means I'm using it in a teaching setting, and suppose that class is recorded by the university. Now who owns the song?

Full-Time versus Part-Time Faculty Status and the Work-Made-for-Hire Doctrine

Applying those variables to full-time faculty, it seems evident that they are employees for the purposes of the work-made-for-hire doctrine. But what about adjunct faculty? When I was an adjunct faculty member, I occasionally taught at more than one college in the same semester. I showed up for classes and then went home, having very little contact with any department employees during the semester. Rarely did anyone know, much less control, what I was doing in my classes, other than in my calamitous first semester at one college where I would have quit within weeks of starting had I not needed the money for groceries.

Independent of whether one receives a W-2 Wage and Tax Statement Form, one might argue, based on agency law, that part-time faculty aren't employees, but they most likely are. In fact, a US Tax Court ruled in 2011 that an adjunct economics professor who only taught online courses was an employee for tax purposes.[32] In this case, the conflict was over whether the instructor could deduct work-related expenses as business expenses, which employees may not do. In applying agency-law principles while ruling against him, the tax court acknowledged that, even though adjunct teaching is inherently independent, colleges and universities still exercise—or have the right to exercise—control over adjuncts, as they do over their employees. Consequently, the teaching materials adjunct professors create for their classes likely qualify as the property of the institutions.

THE TAKEAWAY

The copyright code's work-made-for-hire statutes create two situations where the hiring party owns the copyright in the work created by the hired party: 1) when the hired party is an employee who created the work in the scope of his or her employment; and 2) when an independent contractor transfers ownership of certain, named works to the hiring party in a document signed by both parties. What makes one an employee is often answered by analyzing the employer's right to control the employee's work and assessing whether the employee's actions serve the employer's goals. Part-time faculty are employees for the purposes of the work-made-for-hire statutes.

THE TYPES OF COPYRIGHTABLE WORKS FACULTY CREATE

In light of the work-made-for-hire doctrine, one might sadly conclude that all copyrightable works belong to the college or university where the faculty member's efforts were in the scope of his or her employment. Even service activities that include writing letters or promotional materials, and even more so the traditional teaching and research activities that result in tangible work products, are conducted as part of one's employment, including part-time employment. So, does that mean that faculty have no copyrights in any works of authorship they create in furtherance of their employment? Let's start by looking at the common types of works of authorship faculty create.

Administrative or Noninstructional Works

Regardless of your gifts at turning a student recommendation letter into a work of art, or your ability to wordsmith a faculty committee's tenure-review memo into something so elegant that others should study it line by line, those works are not yours. Likewise, administrators or faculty with administrative responsibility are acting within the scope of their employment when drafting memos, reports, letters, or similar documents, whether these are written on campus or at home. Even where academic freedom would support that faculty have the prerogative to conclude what they want and express themselves in the manner they believe is best in those documents, the expressions are still made in an employment context and concern college or university matters.

Course Syllabi and Exams

Who writes your syllabi? Perhaps the operative verb should be "assemble," rather than write, because I would argue that most syllabi are copy-and-paste jobs, a well-organized pastiche of required and suggested sections that have been passed down from the efforts of prior instructors, the mandates of your department or school, or the amazing efforts of learning specialists at your campus's teaching and learning center. Syllabi are the starter yeast of academia. And, if it's not original, it's not worthy of copyright. That applies even to Taylor Swift, who initially won a copyright-infringement case brought against her by two song writers who said they first wrote the lyrics for her 2014 mega-hit "Shake it Off." There, the judge said those lyrics ("haters gonna hate hate hate") were so "banal" that they didn't qualify for copyright.[33]

Courts have rarely spoken about syllabi ownership, but, in one case, the Missouri Court of Appeals said that syllabi were protected by copyright and were owned by faculty, even though the case curiously involved the University of Missouri asserting its right not to disclose them.[34] That case is more of a one-off rarity because, traditionally, courts tend to rule that syllabi are the kind of documents that are owned by employers, not faculty.[35] In a case from a junior college in Colorado, a professor who was fired for, among other things, making inappropriate in-class statements, sought copyright ownership on a course outline he drafted on his own time at home. While acknowledging that faculty put in hours upon hours of at-home work, the court still concluded the course outline was created in the scope of his employment and belonged to his former employer.[36]

Exams, like syllabi, are created in the scope of a faculty member's employment and, if presented in a sufficiently original manner, would be copyrightable. But—like syllabi—exams get swallowed by the work made-for-hire rule. A court said as much in a high-school case where a fired teacher argued to no avail that his tests, quizzes, and homework problems belonged to him. Part of the teacher's argument was that he created them outside of work and on his own time. But the court concluded that they were classic work-made-for-hire materials and that it was customary for teachers to create those works outside of class.[37] Furthermore, the court concluded that the "teacher exception" to work made for hire (discussed later in the chapter) did not apply.[38] Even so, faculty may still act as if their exams belong to them. For example, an assistant professor at a private university in California sued his students for copyright infringement for appropriating his exams by posting them on the study-assistance website, CourseHero.com. One problem: he doesn't know who those students are, so—as of this writing—he is seeking to compel Course Hero to turn over their names to him.[39]

Class Presentations and Notes

Copyright doesn't protect ideas. It protects that which is "fixed in any tangible medium of expression."[40] Consequently, if your class sessions aren't recorded, then what you're saying isn't copyrighted. If you record your own classes using your own technology, you might have an argument that the recording is your property—if it weren't for the work-made-for-hire doctrine. If your school records classes as a matter of course, or if you record your classes using your school's provided technology, including archiving the recordings, your employer would most likely be the owner. As well, since notes are in a fixed medium of expression (on paper, on PowerPoint slides, etc.), they are copyrightable, provided they aren't copied from a pre-existing copyrighted source, such as a publisher's instructor manual. But, if you created your class notes or PowerPoint presentations, it is fair to consider them as works made for hire.

Universities can provide specific exemptions to everything from syllabi to class recordings. Some, including the University of North Carolina at Chapel Hill and the University of Missouri, inform faculty that they own their course materials.[41] But even when a university tells its faculty that they own their instructional materials, often there are "carve-outs," which include the university retaining various rights to use the materials (more on that quagmire later in the online course materials section), or the university claiming ownership if the course materials were specifically contracted, like if an instructor was personally commissioned (paid) to create a new course.

One sticking point about institutions disclaiming certain faculty works as works made for hire is that, when something is a work made for hire, its copyright can only be transferred to the employee by way of a document that the employer and employee sign.[42] And so it seems insufficient for a faculty handbook or policy statement to assert that faculty own certain copyrightable property that are really works made for hire, like instructional materials. For example, in a case involving Brown University, a campus photographer who was a victim of downsizing sought ownership of the photos he took while employed there. He relied on a campus policy that said Brown disclaimed ownership of copyrightable works created in the performance of one's university duties. But the federal district court said the Copyright Act was clear and the only way an employer could disclaim a work made for hire was through a jointly signed agreement.[43] And the teacher exception didn't apply because the photographer wasn't faculty.

Of course, if my opinion is correct, we're all back to the work-made-for-hire doctrine's starting point and we don't own our work anyway—unless the teacher exception applies. Not all legal scholars (or universities) agree with my view and believe that copyright law allows universities, by fiat, to disclaim work-made-for-hire status for certain items.[44] I'm confused, too.

Software

Computer software is copyrightable as a literary work. But software can also qualify as patentable, if it qualifies as a new and useful process, machine, manufacture, or composition of matter, or any new and useful improvement.[45] When faculty create software in the scope of their employment, courts are likely to classify it as a work made for hire. As evidence of that, in a case from a public university in Iowa, animal-science research professors brought a copyright-infringement case related to software they created and had originally transferred to the university's research foundation. Part of the case's outcome involved the federal court's conclusion that the software qualified as a work made for hire (using agency-law variables).[46] Furthermore, the court shot down the professors' argument that the faculty handbook and its intellectual-property policy transferred the copyright back to faculty because—as required by the Copyright Act for altering a work-made-for-hire copyright—there was no express, signed document showing a transfer back to the professors.[47] (Handbook statements and their legal significance are discussed in greater detail in Chapter 7, which concerns employment rights and tenure policies.)

Scholarly Works, including Musical or Other Creative Works

A 1951 paper, titled "Protein Measurement with the Folin Phenol Reagent," published in the *Journal of Biological Chemistry*, is by far the most-cited research paper in history, with over 305,000 citations.[48] The authors were from the Washington University School of Medicine in St. Louis. On its website, the university promotes the primary author's career and that famous article but makes no claim that the work belongs to it. Despite everything one might know about the work-made-for-hire doctrine, all the paper's authors owned the copyright to that forever-cited article, at least initially. But to have your scholarly works published, it is often necessary that you transfer at least some of your copyright in those works to the publishers. And so it is with books that aren't self-published, because a copyright transfer is a common part of a publishing contract.

While some journal publishers might allow authors to transfer less-than-full ownership (such as giving the publisher a license for distribution rights or the right to make copies of the work rather than the full copyright), publication of scholarly works often means you will likely lose at least some rights to your work. Even in an open-access publishing world, where certain journals or other similar repositories allow other free online access to what is published, authors still might be required to transfer rights that are similarly given in traditional publishing arrangements.

Faculty working in the arts also create copyrightable works, from poems to scripts to paintings to musical compositions. Understanding the nuances in how those works are characterized can be challenging at times. For example, the Berklee College of Music allows faculty and staff to retain ownership interests in their own musical compositions but claims ownership in research papers, where research is part of the creator's job duties.[49] And for those creative works to be published in the traditional sense, faculty might need to assign or transfer parts, if not all, of their respective ownerships.

Little is said in work-made-for-hire case law about whether a college or university is actually the owner of faculty-authored journal articles or other scholarly works. Unless one is not expected to publish at all as part of one's faculty appointment, then wouldn't all scholarly works belong to the university, because they are clearly written in the scope of academic employment, as are syllabi or exams? Weirdly enough, here is where custom outdistances the law, because the longstanding tradition is that faculty own their scholarly works. For example, Brown University's intellectual-property policy says, "In keeping with 'academic tradition,' the University does not claim ownership to scholarly works, and traditional works of authorship . . . of Academic Appointees."[50] Cynically, one might think universities don't claim ownership in faculty-created scholarly works because there is no financial value in those kinds of works. But, where an educational institution would claim ownership of scholarly or creative works as part of its work-made-for-hire rights, an important question arises: Does the "teacher exception" to the work-made-for-hire doctrine apply? See the next section for that discussion.

THE TAKEAWAY

Of the works of authorship that full- or part-time faculty create in the scope of their employment as faculty, most of them would qualify as works made for hire under the legal analysis courts traditionally apply when those questions arise. One notable outlier is scholarly or creative works, which traditionally have been thought to belong to faculty. But, often, publication of scholarly or creative works requires the author to transfer at least some aspects of their copyright.

IS THERE A TEACHER EXCEPTION TO THE WORK-MADE-FOR-HIRE DOCTRINE?

Perhaps, like the Loch Ness Monster or a work-free weekend, you've heard of something called the teacher exception to the work-made-for-hire rule but aren't sure if it really exists. Because the work-made-for-hire doctrine is an exception to the rule that authors own their copyrights, the teacher exception is really an exception to an exception, doubling back on itself. So much has been written about the teacher exception, but most of it focuses on not if it ever existed, but if it still exists. That's because its life wasn't in doubt until after the passage of the 1976 Copyright Act, when, to many legal scholars (and some courts), the explicit nature of the work-made-for-hire statute eliminated the court-created teacher exception.

A famous court case from 1929, which is thought to be the first case on the teacher exception, involved a military-college instructor who wrote a book based on his lectures. In a copyright fight related to that book, the court ruled that the instructor owned the book's copyright, and his employer, the US government, did not.[51] And, in 1969, a California court ruled that a faculty member personally owned his class lectures and any derivatives from them, like class notes—even though they weren't recorded.[52] That case is discussed later in the chapter in the section involving the ownership of student notes, and a lengthy part of the case was the court's explanation of why the professor's employer, UCLA, could not be the owner of the professor's copyrightable works. Included in the court's analysis was that it made no logical sense for UCLA to own lectures because, among other things, that would prevent the professor from teaching those subjects again somewhere else.

Arguments against and for the Teacher Exception's Continuation

Soon after the 1976 Copyright Act's passage, a new legal position began, propounding that the explicit language in the work-made-for-hire statute made the teacher exception no longer viable. And, in a case from 2010, which is repeatedly cited approvingly in legal journals across the country, a federal court said the teacher exception no longer exists.[53] In that case, professors asserted copyright in a proposal they drafted on their own time for a new graduate program at the University of Puerto Rico, on the grounds that the teacher exception to the work-made-for-hire rule applied. In shoveling dirt on the teacher exception, the federal court looked at the history of copyright law and the changes brought by the 1976

Copyright Act, the language of the work-made-for-hire statute, and a lack of reference in the legislative history to the teacher exception.[54] Forebodingly, the court concluded that recent interest in colleges monetizing faculty work for distance learning altered one of the rationales for the teacher exception, which was that colleges wouldn't have any need to own faculty works of authorship.[55] Uh oh.

But two cases from the Seventh Circuit Court of Appeals (a federal appellate court covering federal courts in Illinois, Indiana, and Wisconsin) stand strongly in support of the continuation of the teacher exception. The first case, from 1987, was the subject of an earlier "You Make the Call" case and involved a fight over whose name was listed first in a jointly authored paper. (The author of that court opinion was, for many years while serving as a judge, a senior lecturer at the University of Chicago Law School and the author of the most-cited law-review article on corporate law.) Part of that dispute involved whether the university was the owner of the research paper or whether the fighting faculty members were. In rendering its decision (found at the end of the chapter), the Seventh Circuit Court of Appeals told the lower court, which had gotten the case first, that it was wrong to declare the paper to be a work made for hire in the first place.[56] Instead, the court found support for the teacher exception in an academic tradition that "covers scholarly articles and other intellectual property."[57] One year later, the second case affirming the teacher exception was decided. Notably, the court's opinion was written by Judge Richard Posner, the author of almost forty books and who is the most-cited legal scholar of the twentieth century.[58] Judge Posner also taught for decades at the University of Chicago Law School. While the case involved high-school teachers, the teacher exception analysis was tailor-made for universities.[59] Interestingly, Judge Posner first intimated that the work-made-for-hire doctrine might not even apply to academic writings at all (making the teacher exception unnecessary) because universities don't supervise faculty writings or have the ability to financially exploit them. Then, while assuming the work-made-for-hire doctrine would cover academic writings, Posner wrote that, even if that was the case, the teacher exception likely would still apply because there was a lack of evidence that the teacher exception was terminated by current copyright law.[60]

If the Teacher Exception Still Exists, What Would It Include?

Even though many jurisdictions have rejected, or at least have not acknowledged, the teacher exception to the work-made-for-hire doctrine, it is still a viable doctrine recognized by some courts and is endorsed by the AAUP.[61] In fact, as will be shown later, the teacher exception is inferentially incorporated into many universities' intellectual-property policies. But, assuming a teacher exception still exists, that doesn't mean everything faculty create is protected under its umbrella. Traditionally, the teacher exception has been applied to scholarly works of authorship, rather than purely instructional works of authorship, despite having "teacher" in its name. Courts that have approached the issue usually focus their discussion on books and journal articles or other similar works that traditionally are thought of as works within one's academic discipline. That doesn't mean syllabi or exams would be always outside the teacher-exception orbit, because they are often studied in scholarship-of-teaching-and-learning inquiries and research. But courts that move quickly to apply the work-made-for-hire doctrine in faculty copyright claims almost always do so in cases involving instructional or course-related materials.

THE TAKEAWAY

The teacher exception to the work-made-for-hire doctrine is a court-created exception that holds that faculty continue to retain their copyright in their intellectual property in what would seem to be work-made-for-hire situations. Since the passage of the 1976 Copyright Act, a majority of legal scholars and courts say it no longer exists. If the teacher exception still exists, its application primarily concerns faculty work that is more scholarly in nature.

How University Policies Affect Faculty Copyrights, including in Distance or Remote Learning

You Make the Call

- **The Case of Faculty Fighting for Ownership of Their Online Courses**

Two tenured professors, who were married to each other and taught at a public university in Arizona, created a PhD program in linguistics for their university. Included in their efforts were the preparation of curriculum and course materials as well as videorecorded lectures and related application exercises. The professors alleged they made those instructional materials, including the videorecorded lectures, with the understanding that they would be teaching the courses. As a result of internal wranglings over what the university would pay them for teaching these online courses, the professors had a parting of ways with the university's college of education and joined its college of liberal arts. When one of the professors heard that he and his wife's online courses were operational, he enrolled in one of them and—much like Charlton Heston's face at seeing the Statue of Liberty coming out of the sand at the end of *Planet of the Apes*—was stunned to realize that the course materials he and his wife put behind a password-protected wall were accessed without their knowledge, much less permission, and uploaded into a new online shell, with someone else teaching their course. They filed a grievance against the administrator who accessed and duplicated their online course materials, and they asserted that the university infringed their copyrighted course materials—which they had since registered with the US Copyright Office. And they sued. They alleged that the online course materials and video recordings were not works made for hire, but were scholarly works, which the university's intellectual-property policy exempted from being the university's property.

Do the professors own the copyrights to the online courses for the newly created PhD program they created? May the university offer those courses without the professors' permission and have them taught by other instructors?

(The answers will be given at the end of the chapter. Consider how the principles in this chapter affect your decision and reasoning.)

Across America, many colleges and universities are in never-ending battles to either save costs or increase revenue—or both. And one way to accomplish those goals is to increase the availability of online courses and online degree programs. Leaving aside the issues of quality of education or how this affects the job market for those seeking full-time faculty appointments, reusing in multiple online sections the course content that faculty have already created makes sense from a cost-benefit analysis. To facilitate this, universities could simply declare that they own as works made for hire every copyrightable product that faculty create that is job-related and then wait for claims of overreaching. Or, they could tailor their intellectual-property policies in ways that promote the historical view that faculty own their work (the teacher exception) while at the same time creating various and occasionally confusing exclusions or limitations that make use of the work-made-for-hire doctrine.

COMMON TERMS FOR COPYRIGHTABLE PROPERTY FOUND IN INTELLECTUAL-PROPERTY POLICIES

Whether your employer's intellectual-property policy was presented at a new-employee orientation or linked in an administrative email, you had no power to negotiate its terms. Being hired or staying employed was conditioned on you accepting those policies. Yet, even if you have a legal degree, you might find your institution's intellectual-property policy perplexing. As varied as those policies are, there are certain terms that are common and that bear explaining.

Traditional Works of Scholarship, or Scholarly Works, or Academic Works

Often this type of copyrighted work is defined to include works that faculty create in their teaching, research, or scholarly activities. Examples include syllabi, lecture notes, course materials (including those delivered online), research papers, books, musical scores, and various forms of art. Patentable property is, either by implication or by express statement, excluded from this category.

As to who owns traditional works of scholarship, policies might state that the university owns those works (while often exempting instructional materials) or they might state that the ownership remains with or is assigned to faculty. The University of South Carolina's policy states that those works would be works made for hire, but the policy then transfers those copyrights to faculty, "in keeping with the academic tradition."[62] That approach is a nod to the teacher exception. The conundrum there is that if those are works made for hire, the Copyright Code says employers would have to transfer ownership by way of a jointly signed agreement.[63] And some policies (like the University of South Carolina's) say faculty own those works but the university retains a license in the work. More on that later.

Instructional Copyrightable Works

The category of instructional copyrightable works, sometimes called instructional materials, is in many instances a subcategory of scholarly works, which explicitly describes teaching materials, including online-teaching materials. The ownership options for instructional materials are similar to what is described above.

Specifically Commissioned Works, or University Works, or Institutional Works

These works are created by way of an agreement the college or university makes with a faculty member for a particular work of authorship. For example, your department or school might offer a stipend or grant for the creation of a new online course. Also, these types of works might include those that are paid for by a third party. Or university works could be those created through "exceptional university support," which is generally defined as university resource support that exceeds the norm for a faculty member in one's department or field. All of these are types of specific works made for hire, and such works are owned by the university or even the third-party payor, assuming the joint signatures are in the agreement.

Administrative Works

Administrative works are nonscholarly works that college personnel, including faculty, create in the course of their administrative duties. Examples include reports or memoranda. Administrative works are classified as traditional works made for hire.

Licenses

If you see the word "license" in your college's intellectual-property policy, read very carefully. One way to deal with the controversy created by the work-made-for-hire statutes and the teacher exception is for a university to state that it transfers ownership in faculty-created instructional materials to faculty, but then to declare that faculty are granting a license back to the university to use those teaching materials. Alternatively, the policy could state that faculty own their instructional materials, but that faculty also grant to their employer a license in those materials. One advantage to educational institutions using self-granting licenses is that a license doesn't require signatures to be effective. Continuing the earlier example, the University of South Carolina's intellectual-property policy says the university's license in faculty-created teaching material is nonexclusive (meaning a faculty member could grant a license in his or her work to another entity), royalty-free (no compensation is paid to the faculty member for the license), but the license only applies to the specific semester for which the academic work was prepared.[64] Faculty also have the right to control the timing and access of those materials when they are archived in a learning-management system.

By way of contrast, my employer, Purdue University, states in its Intellectual-Property Policy that, "[e]ach Instructional or Scholarly Copyrightable Work is, by operation of this policy, subject to a perpetual, nonexclusive, royalty-free license from its University author(s) to the University to use, duplicate and distribute the Instructional or Scholarly Copyrightable Work for all research and educational purposes of the University."[65] By its language, Purdue grants to itself what are essentially ownership rights, since it can do what it wants with faculty works of authorship, including online teaching materials as well as papers, books, and musical compositions, for as long as it wants. Of course, for some works of authorship, faculty no longer have those copyrights, where they have been transferred as a condition of publication, or if they are independent contract works made for hire.

As stated earlier, colleges and universities that transfer ownership in scholarly works to faculty seem to be acknowledging the teacher exception to the work-made-for-hire doctrine. For example, the University of California's copyright property policy grants ownership of scholarly works to faculty in order to "fulfill its teaching, research, and public service mission, and in support of academic freedom."[66] But, if faculty are granted ownership in their works, then wouldn't faculty—as owners—have the power to grant licenses to allow the work to be used in online instruction, and not the other way around, as is the case in many universities?

THE TAKEAWAY

Faculty should carefully read their institution's intellectual-property policy, including the definitions section, because those policies establish the ownership and, equally importantly, the control of faculty-created works of authorship. Be alert to any language that says faculty own the copyright in their scholarly works or instructional materials but grant to their employers' nonexclusive licenses in those works. Such a license can grant use rights that are unlimited.

THE AAUP POSITIONS ON COPYRIGHT AND DISTANCE EDUCATION

The AAUP has for decades been concerned with copyright issues for faculty, especially in the age of remote learning.[67] It has a resource web page on intellectual property and copyright[68] and a Statement on Online and Distance Education.[69] In its 1999 Statement on Copyright, the AAUP expressed dissatisfaction with how the work-made-for-hire doctrine was being applied to faculty works of scholarship, including teaching materials, and disagreed with the unilateral practice of some educational institutions transferring copyright to themselves in policies or handbooks without the required signatures.[70] Concerning distance education, then in its infancy, the 1999 Statement noted a "faculty member should also be given rights in connection with its future uses, not only through compensation but also through the right of 'first refusal'[71] in making new versions, or at least the right to be consulted in good faith on reuse and revisions." In 2013, the AAUP released a Statement on Intellectual Property, which includes thoughtful analysis on copyright and patent issues for faculty, with a focus on faculty governance.[72]

WHAT IF FACULTY PARKED THEIR ONLINE COURSE MATERIALS IN THEIR OWN GARAGES?

I put all my course materials, including for my face-to-face classes, in the Brightspace learning-management system shells that my university makes available for each course. Of course, that means all of my files (every syllabus, test, assignment, extra course document, podcast, and any other media I create) are subject to my employer's discretionary reuse at any time—and without needing my consent. But what if I didn't use Brightspace? Suppose I house all those materials on a third-party server, like Google Drive, or create my own cloud-based storage system, and then provide my students access to my Brightspace alternative? Now, none of my instructional materials are free for the picking, like fruit trees in a public park. That's thinking like a lawyer, right?

Not so fast, my friend. My university has lawyers too, and an additional employee policy can simply require that all faculty use institutionally provided online instructional platforms—say, because of FERPA considerations. Or a new policy could demand that wherever faculty keep instructional materials, a copy of those materials must also be provided to the university—this time on the grounds of ensuring academic quality and college or departmental consistency of learning goals or outcomes. Counterarguing that I have the academic freedom to keep my instructional materials where I choose is foolhardy. Additionally, claiming that those materials belong to me, personally, might be correct (assuming a court in my jurisdiction agrees with my work-for-hire-teacher-exception argument), but that's not a hill I'm willing to die on. Although I'm uncomfortable with my university's claimed, free license in my instructional materials, nothing prevents me from attempting to monetize them too. But, if there is no official policy that prevents you from choosing your own online-learning platform, choosing one you control may be worth considering.

Miscellaneous Copyright Issues: Fair Use, and the TEACH Act

Two remaining copyright-law issues are worthy of inclusion and a bit of explanation in this chapter: the fair-use doctrine and the TEACH Act; both concern infringement risks faculty face in research or teaching.

THE FAIR-USE DOCTRINE

When does borrowing become stealing, for copyright purposes? The 1976 Copyright Act speaks to this question in a statute, 17 U.S.C. § 107, that codified a judicial doctrine in use for years. This statute provides a defense to a copyright-infringement claim by providing as follows:

> [T]he fair use of a copyrighted work, including such use by reproduction in copies or phonorecords or by any other means specified by that section, for purposes such as criticism, comment, news reporting, teaching (including multiple copies for classroom use), scholarship, or research, is not an infringement of copyright. In determining whether the use made of a work in any particular case is a fair use the factors to be considered shall include—
>
> (1) the purpose and character of the use, including whether such use is of a commercial nature or is for nonprofit educational purposes;
> (2) the nature of the copyrighted work;
> (3) the amount and substantiality of the portion used in relation to the copyrighted work as a whole; and

(4) the effect of the use upon the potential market for or value of the copyrighted work.

The fact that a work is unpublished shall not itself bar a finding of fair use if such finding is made upon consideration of all the above factors.

KEY POINTS ABOUT THE FAIR-USE DOCTRINE

1) The fair-use doctrine applies to teaching situations. Written before the Internet, the mention of teaching in the statute includes making copies of other authors' works. And the statute also includes scholarship and research as a fair-use purpose. But just because you're using someone else's work without permission in an education setting doesn't automatically make it fair.
2) What counts as fair use is not solved by a mathematical equation. There is no sum-specific formula that determines when a faculty member or anyone else has used or copied too much of a copyrighted work. Google even won a copyright-infringement case on fair-use grounds after it scanned millions of books in their entirety, some of them without permission from the copyright holders.[73] There are thousands of cases on what is or is not fair use, making this subject rife with confusion. Consequently, faculty are wise to err on the side of caution when using the works of others, and to be mindful employer-created fair-use policies.
3) The four parts of the fair-use statute are intended to be weighed together when determining if an unauthorized use is fair. Here are what the four factors are about.

   a. *Why are you using someone else's work?* It is better that you use it for noncommercial purposes, like teaching.
   b. *What kind of work are you using?* Claiming fair use of a work that has yet to be published is problematic (but not dispositive), because that deprives the author of his or her initial right of publication. Also, creative works have more protection in fair-use cases than do factual works, because courts tend to find the spreading of facts and information more in line with the purposes of the fair-use doctrine. (Thankfully, the Copyright Act excludes from its coverage "any work of the United States Government,"[74] like statutes, regulations, or case law, and that goes for law created and published by state governments.)[75]
   c. *How much of the total work have you used?* Again, this isn't decided by percentages or word counts, but fair-use doctrine disfavors an overly liberal portion size. And what might be considered fair use in a face-to-face class might not be in an asynchronous online setting when the same borrowed material is used over and over again without permission.

d. *Does your use of the copyrighted work harm its commercial market value?* This analysis includes whether your use could potentially harm the market value of the copyrighted work. If your college or university is profiting off your unlicensed use of others' copyrighted works, that is problematic for a fair-use evaluation. The US Supreme Court noted that this factor is "the most important, and indeed, central fair use factor."[76]

4) Providing students with web links to copyrighted materials, rather than copies or PDFs of those materials, avoids the fair-use question altogether, because you are providing a digital mechanism for accessing the copyrighted works.

The TEACH Act

Despite the fair-use statute and its limitations on using others' copyrighted works in teaching settings, there is a specific exemption to it in the Copyright Act, 17 U.S.C. § 110(1), for those teaching in nonprofit institutions. This exemption allows those faculty teaching in face-to-face settings to display copyrighted works in their entirety (without getting permission or a license), including showing movies in class where the copy of the audiovisual work being shown is a lawful copy.

In 2002, the statute was amended by adding a new section, 17 U.S.C. § 110(2), formally known as the Technology, Education and Copyright Harmonization (TEACH) Act. The TEACH Act is focused on instructional use of media in distance or remote learning environments.

Key Points of the TEACH Act

1) Its benefits only apply to "accredited" nonprofit educational institutions, unlike the benefits of the earlier statute, which doesn't require the nonprofit educational institution to be accredited. Such institutions need to have a copyright policy.
2) It allows for extensive use of copyrighted materials in a digital environment, provided the use is for teaching purposes. That includes showing the performances of all nondramatic literary or musical works.
3) It also allows for the display of "limited portions of any other work, or display of a work in an amount comparable to that which is typically displayed in the course of a live classroom session, by or in the course of a transmission." That has been interpreted by some to mean an entire film may not be displayed in a remote-learning environment, even live remote, which would bring the fair-use doctrine back into play.
4) Materials that are made or marketed primarily for online teaching are exempted from the TEACH Act, which means an instructor in a remote-

learning course may not, without permission or license, use another's online-teaching visuals or media.

5) Only students enrolled in the course are to have access to the copyrighted materials used in that course.

6) The copyrighted materials used under the safe harbor of the TEACH Act are to be available only during the time the course is being offered.

THE TAKEAWAY

The fair-use doctrine provides a defense to a copyright-infringement allegation by providing an allowance for faculty to reasonably use others' copyrighted works in teaching, scholarship, or research. The four fair-use factors are interpreted in concert when a court must decide whether one's unauthorized use is more than what is fair.

The TEACH Act allows faculty in accredited, nonprofit educational institutions to show or display almost everything in remote-learning environments as they are allowed to do in face-to-face environments. There are certain limitations or conditions applied in the TEACH Act, including that only enrolled students in a course are allowed to have access to the materials.

Students and Their Intellectual Property Rights

You Make the Call

- **The Case of the Student's Semipurloined Paintings**

A master's-level student of fine arts at a public university in Michigan was invited by her professor to contribute to a project for Mercedes-Benz that would be on display at the upcoming North American Auto Show in Detroit. The student, along with several others, attended planning meetings with Mercedes-Benz, where the idea was to have art students paint large cargo containers that would be placed around the automaker's exhibit. The student's proposed theme came to be titled "hand-to-hand." A brochure for the art exhibit was prepared, which included a photograph and short profile of each student artist along with a reproduction of each's individual work that was to be exhibited. Students each were paid $1,400 for the use of their one work and were also offered a trip to Spain to continue the exhibit at a Barcelona auto show. But, when the student saw the brochure, she realized it included three of her other paintings, which she said she had never agreed would be used. According to her, she painted those paintings at the request of her professor for the purpose of showing Mercedes-Benz what colors would be used on the cargo containers. Adding insult to injury, of the three unauthorized and uncredited works that were reproduced in the brochure, which was distributed to over two thousand press members and VIPs, one was upside down. In addition to suing Mercedes-Benz and her professor for copyright infringement, the student also sued her professor for "breach of a fiduciary relationship," in part because she said he refused to get involved when she went to him for help after first realizing the unauthorized reproductions.

Does the student own the copyright in the three paintings that she painted at her professor's request and that were also included in the auto show promotional brochure? Does the student have a legitimate claim of breach of a fiduciary relationship against her professor? (This would mean that, at some level, he violated a duty he had to her as his student.)

(The answers will be given at the end of the chapter. Consider how the principles in this chapter affect your decision and reasoning.)

I, too, was involved in projects as a student. And I took notes as a student, lots of notes in left-handed notebooks, which were basically regular notebooks labeled and opened on the backside. Students learn in different ways, including taking notes digitally or having others take notes for them, or not even writing much at all in class. But from class notes to projects to creative works to even patentable property, students face questions that are similar to those of faculty members about ownership.

DO STUDENTS OWN THEIR CLASS NOTES?

When a company, that by contractual agreement published the lecture notes and textbook of a University of Florida professor, sued another publishing company that had published the notes students took in that professor's class (these students had sold their notes to the second publishing company), one of the questions to be answered by the court was whether student notes even qualify for copyright protection.[77] The starting point is to ask what they're writing. If students are writing down what they're seeing on a board or screen, then they are copying what is already there and those notes aren't theirs. But, if students take notes in distinctly creative or newly original ways, the students might rightfully claim ownership of their notes as a "transformative use."[78] The legal concept of transformative use grows from the fair-use doctrine and holds that someone's use of a copyrighted work is not infringing if the new version has superseded or changed the purpose of the original work. That would require something more than mild creativity. For example, suppose a student creates graphic novel–like versions of her class notes. Beyond being inventive and cool, the graphic novel would likely be an original work in which the instructor's notes have been transformed into a new thing.

If an instructor is not recording his class session, then what he is saying isn't fixed in a tangible medium of expression, which would mean that the students would own any notes they took on what was said—if they were sufficiently original, rather than just being a listing of facts. But, in a case that predates the 1976 Copyright Act (which codified the work-made-for-hire doctrine by including it in the Copyright Act), a California court ruled that a professor owned his lectures (even though he didn't record them) and that he could sue to stop the publication of the student's notes from his classes.[79] Of course, if the college, rather than the instructor, is recording the class session (or owns the equipment doing the recording), one might safely conclude that the college, not the instructor, owns the recording. There are valid arguments on both sides concerning the efficacy of class recordings. Some law schools prohibit making any class recordings for a variety of reasons, including protecting the organic nature of the Socratic method and its effect on class discussion. A political-science and public-policy professor at UCLA prohibits students from recording her classes (at the risk of failing) because she believes allowing the publication of student discussion on controversial topics is unwise. She believes academic freedom covers her decision, which is not without controversy.[80] Yet, once again in Florida, where it is a felony to record a conversation without the consent of all the parties involved,[81] a 2021 law was passed giving college students the right to secretly record their classes.[82] Federal litigation ensued for the obvious reasons one might suspect, and, as of this writing, there has been no decision on the constitutionality of what the legislature titled without any sense of irony "The Campus Free Expression Act."

Prohibitions on Students Monetizing Their Class Notes

Regardless of the various issues that weigh both pro and con on whether students own their notes, some universities and statutes make this an unnecessary argument by prohibiting students from monetizing their class notes. For example, the University of North Carolina at Chapel Hill, which has a web page dedicated to helping students take worthwhile class notes,[83] prohibits students from profiting from their notes, as stated in its University Copyright Policy.[84] The University of California, Berkeley, has a similar policy.[85] California even has a law that prohibits students from commercializing their own class recordings or notes.[86]

DO STUDENTS OWN THEIR COURSE SUBMISSIONS?

Students do own the copyright in their papers and assignments and other written or artistic works, provided they qualify on their own as being sufficiently original. If one were to make the counterpoint that faculty might have some right to such course submissions as works made for hire, because such submissions had been specifically assigned, none of the work-made-for-hire conditions apply, starting with the fact that students aren't the employees of faculty. Some years ago, four enterprising high-school students brought a copyright-infringement lawsuit against Turnitin, the plagiarism-detection company, because their term papers, along with tens of thousands of others, were archived in Turnitin's database. That allowed Turnitin to use archived papers in its plagiarism-searching database. While ruling that the students did own their term papers, the court still ruled Turnitin's use to be allowable under the fair-use doctrine, in part because the students never lost the first right to publish their papers and because Turnitin was using the information in the archived papers in a transformative and entirely different function than the students' use.[87]

University policies often codify this realization by stating that students own or retain the intellectual property that they create in their for-credit classes without compensation.[88] Some universities, however, like the University of Minnesota, reserve in their student copyright policies the right to use their students' work, consistent with the rules of the student's college or department, or even make reproduction or display rights a condition of enrollment in a course.[89] The problem with such a university-friendly policy is that it envisions students enrolling in a class as if they were consciously making a contract that comes in exchange for their giving up some of their intellectual-property rights. There are difficulties with that conception, including that students likely have no idea they are "voluntarily" giving up any intellectual-property rights when they are taking a course and giving them up without any compensation.

THE TAKEAWAY

Students don't own a copyright in their class notes where the notes are transcriptions of the instructor's class notes or where the notes are simply listings of facts. Unless a university policy or state law has precedence, students might have a valid claim of copyright ownership in their notes if the notes are created in such a transformative way that they qualify as an original work of authorship.

Students generally own their copyright-worthy coursework, provided it was created without compensation. Some institutions include in their intellectual-property policies the right to use or display student work without compensation as a condition for course enrollment.

AI Technology and Copyright

Among the many questions resulting from the proliferation of generative and conversational AI is whether the user owns what AI provides. Legally, AI systems, whether chatbots or image or music generators, cannot be the author of the material they "create" because what they generate is simply a culmination of prior, human-made work. For example, if I ask AI to produce something in the manner of F. Scott Fitzgerald, the AI tool I'm using has to have in its database sentences from Fitzgerald's works. And much of which has been Internet-harvested by bots (called web-scraping) to produce a response is likely copyright-protected. Litigation is currently underway to answer the question of whether a large language model AI provider is infringing on the copyright of the sources it has read in order to respond to a given prompt.

Independent of the immediate ramifications of cheating, if your students engage in intellectual dishonesty and create course-related work products using AI, do they even own the work at all? The US Copyright Office has an answer: no, but it depends. According to a 2023 Copyright Guidance Statement, if a machine produces what would otherwise be thought of as a creative work, with the traditional elements of authorship, the work lacks human authorship and the Copyright Office will not register it.[90] The Copyright Office stated, in part, it "will not register works produced by a machine or mere mechanical process that operates randomly or automatically without any creative input or intervention from a human author."[91] (Even a monkey was denied a copyright for its own selfie, because copyright protection starts with human authors.)[92] For example, prompting AI technology to produce a term paper or haiku involves the technology—not the person seeking the content—doing what would previously be considered authorship work. And technology can't be an author for copyright purposes.

But the Copyright Office also said it was open to deciding on a case-by-case basis if a copyright registration is warranted where an author sufficiently selects or arranges "AI-generated material in a sufficiently creative way that the 'resulting work as a whole constitutes an original work of authorship.'"[93] Imagine a writer having difficulty in revising her short story into a required word length and then using an AI tool for editing purposes. A copyright could go to the AI-supported effort because the author had the copyright in the original version. Likewise, an artist who sufficiently modifies AI output could obtain copyright protection for the human-authored aspects of the work. For example, suppose a student in an art class uses AI to get a large (not copyrightable) written paragraph about the science of color and then paints the document in a way that compliments or contrasts the message created by the words in the paragraph. This student could seek a copyright registration for the document as art but not as a literary work. Whether the student has cheated in creating that work is up to the instructor (assuming one could recognize it as cheating).

THE TAKEAWAY

AI-generated content is not protected by copyright because copyright protection is for works created by humans. But it is possible that a copyright could be granted for an AI-assisted work where a human has provided sufficient creative input with the AI content.

GRADUATE STUDENTS AND THEIR INTELLECTUAL PROPERTY

Graduate students are often treated more like faculty when it comes to university entitlements to patents or inventions. It is not uncommon for graduate schools to have their own intellectual-property polices that, for patent purposes, declare the institution as owner of any inventions those students create using institutional resources.[94] Universities have sought to enforce their polices through suing graduate students who are thought to have absconded with inventions.[95] In one amazing case, an undergraduate student at a public university in Florida went to prison after being convicted of stealing trade secrets and his own lab notebooks,[96] and the university sued him to prevent him from using what it believed was its proprietary property in the notebooks.[97] Even though he wasn't a graduate student, the litigation was based on the presumption that he had given up rights to his university-related research as a graduate student would have. Years later, that former student rejected a pardon on grounds he had done nothing wrong.[98] Graduate students can turn the tables, too, and have sued their schools over invention assignments and patent royalties.[99]

With respect to copyright-eligible works of graduate students, school policies might require students to assign the copyright in works that are specifically commissioned or that qualify as works made for hire; similar requirements are made of faculty. Otherwise, graduate students are the owners of their original works of authorship, including their theses and dissertations, even where school policy requires those works to be archived in a school library. But graduate students have sued when they think their universities have committed copyright infringement. A doctoral student at the University of New Mexico won the argument that he had a legitimate infringement case against the university for copying and archiving his dissertation draft before it was complete.[100] Because his faculty advisors had not properly reviewed his dissertation, he wanted to enter another university to complete and present that dissertation, and the court agreed that he couldn't if a copy was in the university's possession.

Where graduate students work on research with their professors, joint ownership questions arise. Outside of a contractual agreement, there is no partial or minority ownership of a creative work, so, either one is a coauthor, with equal rights to the work no matter who contributed more to the final product, or one is not an author. In a curious case from a public university in Wisconsin, an electrical-engineering professor and one of his graduate students had a falling out over the student's decision to not enroll in one of the professor's classes, leading to recriminations resulting in the professor eventually receiving a one-year suspension without pay for academic misconduct.[101] Then the professor sued the university for employment discrimination (which he lost) and the student for copyright infringement. The student and the professor had worked together on a paper (their fourth), and, after it was submitted for publication, the professor withdrew it, but the student later resubmitted it under his name only. Regarding the issue of whose paper it was, a federal court of appeals concluded that the evidence showed the paper was a joint work, because the student had contributed "significant copyrightable material,"[102] which is the needed threshold. Therefore, since the student qualified as a joint author, he could do whatever he wanted with the paper, and his only obligation to the professor was to account to him in the event there were profits from the article's publication. There weren't any.

THE TAKEAWAY

Graduate students are generally subject to patent or invention policies that similarly apply to faculty and that give colleges and universities ownership rights to whatever students discover or invent while using school resources. Likewise, students can receive royalty shares. A student is considered a joint author with his professor where the student has contributed significant copyrightable material to the work. Joint authors have full, individual rights over their papers, subject to a contractual agreement the authors might make.

Final Takeaways

- Intellectual property includes trademarks, patents, and copyrights (which derive value from being disclosed and are generally governed by federal law) and trade secrets (which derive value from not being disclosed and are generally governed by state law). It is possible that a trademark and a trade secret can last forever, but patents and copyrights have limited terms.
- While it is true that an inventor is the owner of an invention, faculty who create patented property generally are not the owners, due to employment contracts containing intellectual-property policies that mandate the assignment of any work-related inventions. But those policies can include various forms of equity or revenue sharing in instances where those patents are licensed or otherwise monetized.
- The copyright code's work-made-for-hire statutes create two situations where the hiring party owns the copyright in the work created by the hired party: 1) when the hired party is an employee who created the work in the scope of her employment; and 2) when an independent contractor transfers ownership of certain, named works to the hiring party in a document signed by both parties. What makes one an employee is often determined by analyzing the employer's right to control the employee's work and assessing whether the employee's actions serve the employer's goals. Part-time faculty are employees for work-made-for-hire purposes.
- Of the works of authorship that full- or part-time faculty create in the scope of their employment, most of them would qualify as works made for hire under

the legal analysis that courts traditionally apply when those questions arise. One notable outlier is scholarly or creative works, which traditionally have been thought to belong to faculty. But often publication of scholarly or creative works requires the author to transfer at least some aspects of his copyright.

- The teacher exception to the work-made-for-hire doctrine is a court-created exception that holds that faculty retain their copyright in their intellectual property in what would seem to be work-made-for-hire situations. Since the passage of the 1976 Copyright Act, a majority of legal scholars and courts say it no longer exists. If the teacher exception still exists, its application primarily concerns faculty work that is more scholarly in nature.
- Faculty should carefully read their institution's intellectual-property policy, including the definitions section, because those policies establish the ownership and, equally importantly, the control of faculty-created works of authorship. Be alert to any language that says faculty own the copyright in their scholarly works or instructional materials but grant to their employers' nonexclusive licenses in those works. Such a license can grant use rights that are unlimited.
- The fair-use statute provides a defense to copyright-infringement allegations by providing an allowance for faculty to reasonably use others' copyrighted works in teaching, scholarship, or research. The four fair-use factors are interpreted in concert when a court must decide if one's unauthorized use is more than what is fair.
- The TEACH Act allows faculty in accredited, nonprofit educational institutions to show or display almost everything in remote learning environments that they are allowed to show in face-to-face environments. There are certain limitations or conditions applied in the TEACH Act, including that only enrolled students in a course are allowed to have access to the materials.
- Students don't own a copyright in their class notes where the notes are transcriptions of the instructor's class notes or where the notes are simply listings of facts. Unless a university policy or state law has precedence, students might have a valid claim of copyright ownership in their notes if the notes are created in such a transformative way that they qualify as an original work of authorship.
- Students generally own their copyright-worthy coursework, provided it was created without institutional compensation. Some institutions include in their intellectual-property policies the right to use or display student work without compensation as a condition for course enrollment.
- Graduate students are generally subject to patent or invention policies that similarly apply to faculty and that give colleges and universities ownership rights to whatever students discover or invent while using school resources. Likewise, students can receive royalty shares. A student is considered a joint author with his professor where the student has contributed significant copyrightable material to the work.

How Did You Make the Calls?

1 – The Case of the Fight over Author Listings in a Jointly Authored Paper

This case may be proof of what Sigmund Freud called "the narcissism of small differences." A tenure-track assistant professor of pharmacy administration at the University of Illinois at Chicago hadn't published a peer-reviewed journal article in three years, which hadn't gone unnoticed by his chair or dean. Consequently, he and two other colleagues were working on a paper that was the result of their efforts in a clinical program working with practicing pharmacists. The dean wrote to them that he wanted this paper published. The writing process was contentious, and the assistant professor gave his draft to the other primary coauthor, who read it and threw it in his office trash can. Eventually, that second author created a new draft, which listed his name first and the assistant professor's name third. Although this change in order was claimed to be merely an alphabetical listing, the action led to more intradepartmental conflict. That author submitted the paper to a peer-reviewed journal and it was accepted for publication. But by that time, the assistant professor had been fired, having been on the wrong side of "publish or perish." He then sued the university, his pharmacy-school dean and chair, and the two other authors of that paper for various civil-rights violations, contending that they mutilated his work and stole the credit, denying him due process of law. He said that, because he wasn't listed first on the paper, as he should have been, his professional reputation was harmed, which hindered his other scholarly efforts. The university claimed that the paper was a work made for hire in the first place, so it didn't legally matter who was listed first, second, or third.

Is a published academic paper a work made for hire? If the paper is not a work made for hire, is it a copyright violation for one author to alter the order of the authors and then submit the paper for publication?

Decision: The trial court that first got this case dismissed the professor's suit, concluding that the paper was a work made for hire, per university policy.[103] On appeal, the Seventh Circuit Court of Appeals affirmed the lawsuit's dismissal but noted the lower court was wrong to say the paper belonged to the university.[104] In interpreting the university's intellectual-property policy on what constituted a work made for hire, the appellate court determined that academic papers couldn't reasonably be placed in that category for a variety of reasons, including that the university never sought copyright ownership or royalties in any of its faculty's academic publications.

As to the constitutional violations the professor claimed he was a victim of, the court said the professor wasn't fired for his views but "for not having any views, at least none recently in print." Ouch. As to the professor's claim that he got stiffed by the coauthor who listed his own name first, the court said that's not a copyright-law issue. It's a contract-law issue. Copyright law allows each coauthor to do whatever they want with their joint work (or coauthored paper), unless the coauthors made some binding agreement with each other. That includes the authors' listings, regardless of the academic disciplinary tradition of who gets listed first.

2 – The Case of the Copyrighted Curriculum Materials

In this case, a travel and tourism instructor and part-time administrator who was formerly employed at Lincoln College in Illinois (which closed in 2022) sued her former employer for age discrimination and for copyright infringement over the curriculum materials she created and for which she filed two copyright registrations. When the college sought to create a program conferring a bachelor's degree in travel and tourism, it tasked her with the responsibility of making it happen and told her she needed to have a master's degree in order to teach bachelor's-level courses. Her direct supervisor helped her choose the master's degree program and provided a recommendation letter, and the college paid for it. But, after completing the degree program, the instructor was informed that it was unaccredited and that she would need to start over. While putting together the new degree program, the instructor drafted various curriculum documents and filed copyright registrations for two of them. Her employment was eventually terminated over her disagreement with an annual contract presented to her, and she sued the college for age discrimination and also for copyright infringement, because the college used the documents she copyrighted.

Does the instructor own the curriculum documents she created and officially copyrighted?

The Decision: The federal district court dismissed her age-discrimination and copyright-infringement claims.[105] With respect to the age-discrimination suit, the court found there was no evidence presented (which would allow the claim to go forward) that the college engaged in any discriminatory actions against her based on her age. And, even though the instructor filed copyright registrations for the curriculum materials, the court still concluded that those documents belonged to the college. The court believed such documents were works made for hire. This vested the copyright in the college rather than the instructor because she created them in the course of her employment; they were the kind of documents that she (as a part-time program administrator) would be paid to create, and she prepared them at the college's request. In support of his conclusion, the judge noted that the instructor discussed her curriculum work in her annual self-evaluation. Although the instructor argued that the "teacher exception" to the work-made-for-hire doctrine applied to her, the court—while acknowledging the possible existence of the teacher exception—said it didn't apply because 1) curriculum materials aren't academic writings; and 2) she prepared the documents directly for her employer.

3 – The Case of Faculty Fighting for Ownership of Their Online Courses
Two tenured professors, who were married to each other and taught at Arizona State University, created a PhD program in linguistics for the university.[106] Included in their efforts were the preparation of curriculum and course materials, as well as videorecorded lectures and related application exercises. The professors alleged they made those instructional materials, including the videorecorded lectures, with the understanding that they would be teaching the courses. As a result of internal wranglings over what the university would pay them for teaching these online courses, the professors had a parting of ways with the university's college of education and joined its college of liberal arts. But, after hearing that their online courses were operational, one of the professors enrolled in a course and saw that their course materials, which were behind a password-protected wall, were accessed without their knowledge and uploaded and turned into new versions of their courses. The professors filed a grievance against the administrator who accessed and duplicated their online course materials and alleged that the university infringed their copyrighted course materials—which they had since registered with the US Copyright Office. And they sued. They alleged that the online course materials and video recordings were not works made for hire, but were scholarly works, which the university's intellectual-property policy exempted from being the university's property.

Do the professors own the copyrights to the online courses for the newly created PhD program they created? May the university offer those courses without the professors' permission and have them taught by other instructors?

The Decision: Despite the well-known and controversial practice of universities using faculty-created teaching materials in online courses not taught by the original faculty, there is almost no case law on the issue. But here, the federal district court dismissed the professors' copyright-infringement case.[107] First, the judge reviewed the Arizona State intellectual-property policy, which disclaimed ownership in "scholarly works." A later part of the policy defined scholarly works to include "on-line instructional materials." That would seem to bode well for the professors, except a later part of that sentence claimed ownership in faculty works of authorship if they were "created in the course and scope of employment." The professors claimed that they created the online course materials as independent contractors when they rejected the university's offer of what they would be paid for teaching those courses. But the judge ruled that all their efforts were made as a work made for hire, in light of the key agency-law factors, including that their efforts in creating the online courses were done, at least in part, to serve Arizona State's purposes and that their status was that of tenured professors.

Consequently, the copyrights for everything the professors created belonged to the university, and it could use all of the materials for its online courses, regardless of who taught them. Since the initial controversy, the professors joined the faculty at the University of Maryland, whose own intellectual-property policy would claim similar rights over teaching materials.[108] As an aside, faculty who develop new online programs might consider asking that a separate contract be drafted for those endeavors, establishing whether the efforts are part of a work-made-for-hire arrangement and what, if any, separate compensation is to be paid. That would not change the copyright ownership, but it could minimize the chance of future conflict.

4 – The Case of the Student's Semipurloined Paintings

In this case, a master's-level student in the fine arts program at Wayne State University was invited by her professor to be part of a student contribution to the Mercedes-Benz exhibit at the upcoming North American Auto Show. She and other students were asked to paint cargo containers that Mercedes-Benz would display around its exhibit. To promote the art installment, Mercedes-Benz had a brochure created, which included a photograph and short profile of each student artist along with a reproduction of each's individual work that was to be displayed. Students each were paid $1,400 for the use of their one painting and also were offered a trip to Spain to continue the exhibit at a Barcelona auto show. At the request of Mercedes-Benz, the professor asked the student to create three more paintings, which were meant to show how various colors would look on the cargo containers. But, when the student saw the completed brochure, she realized that all four of her paintings were in it, including one that was shown upside down, even though she was paid for her efforts for the first painting only. Two thousand brochures were printed for distribution at the Auto Show. The student went to her professor to get him to stop Mercedes-Benz from using that brochure, but he refused. She then sued Mercedes-Benz and her professor for copyright infringement, and she also sued her professor for "breach of a fiduciary relationship."

Does the student own the copyright in the three paintings that she painted at her professor's request and that were also included in the promotional brochure? Does the student have a legitimate claim of breach of a fiduciary relationship against her professor? (This would mean that, at some level, he violated a duty he had to her as his student.)

The Decision: A federal district court dismissed part of the student's claims against Mercedes-Benz and Wayne State University but permitted the continuation of other claims, including the copyright-infringement claim against Mercedes-Benz and the professor and also the breach-of-a-fiduciary-relationship claim against the professor.[109] Concerning the copyright claims, the court had to deal with multiple issues involving the interplay of federal and state law and ruled against the student on a number of issues, including her claim that she was owed lost profits for the copyright infringement. She was unable to provide any evidence that her paintings lost value or that Mercedes-Benz's sales increased, due to the wrongful and unauthorized presentation of the paintings in the brochure. (Instead of lost profits, the student was awarded statutory damages, granted under the Copyright Act.) But that didn't alter the initial conclusion that the student owned the copyright in those three paintings and that her copyright was infringed on by Mercedes-Benz and her professor.

Secondly, the court refused to dismiss the "breach of fiduciary relationship" claim but noted that the student would have to provide evidence that she was in a relationship of trust with her former art professor and that his actions were an abuse or betrayal of her confidence.

Notes

1. Forbes, "The World's Real-Time Billionaires," available at https://www.forbes.com/real-time-billionaires/#3f3860d43d78.

2. CompaniesMarketCap, "Largest Companies by Market Cap," available at https://companiesmarketcap.com/.

3. "Apple Patents—Insights & Stats," GreyB Insights, April 30, 2024, available at https://insights.greyb.com/apple-patents/.

4. "Apple Trademarks," Gerben Trademark Library, May 19, 2024, available at https://www.gerbenlaw.com/trademarks/major-corporations/apple/#:~:text=A%20first%20version%20of%20their,brand%20names%2C%20slogans%20and%20more.

5. David Merson, "Highest-Paid Lawyers: Most Profitable Law Careers," *Juris Education*, December 20, 2023, available at https://www.juriseducation.com/blog/highest-paid-lawyers; Joshua Holt, "Highest Paid Lawyer Types: Which Field Is Best?" *Bigalow Investor*, March 12, 2023, available at https://www.biglawinvestor.com/highest-paid-lawyers/; Jack Crittendon, "Most Lucrative: Intellectual Property," *The National Jurist*, May 19, 2017, available at https://nationaljurist.com/lawyer-statesman/most-lucrative-intellectual-property/.

6. Ken Knickerbocker, "Penn Likely to Be Top Research Institution for Licensing Revenue, Thanks to Abington Resident," *Vista.Today*, March 27, 2023, available at https://vista.today/2023/03/penn-top-research-institutions/.

7. Gabriel Steinberg and Nilan Nandish, "Penn Ranks First in Annual Licensing Income among 153 Research Institutions," *The Daily Pennsylvanian*, April 6, 2023, available at https://www.thedp.com/article/2023/04/penn-licensing-revenue-first-national-universities.

8. Damian Garde and Johnathan Saltzman, "The Story of mRNA: How a Once-Dismissed Idea Became a Leading Technology in the Covid Vaccine Race," *STAT*, November 10, 2020, available at https://www.statnews.com/2020/11/10/the-story-of-mrna-how-a-once-dismissed-idea-became-a-leading-technology-in-the-covid-vaccine-race/.

9. U.S. Constitution, Art. I, Sec. 8.

10. United States Patent and Trademark Office, "Trademark Electronic Search System (TESS)," available at https://www.uspto.gov/trademarks/search.

11. 15 U.S.C. § 1051 et seq.

12. 35 U.S.C. § 101 (1952).

13. *In re Cortright*, 165 F.3d 1353 (Fed. Cir. 1999).

14. *Alice Corp. Pty. Ltd. v. CLS Bank Int'l*, 573 U.S. 208 (2014).

15. United States Patent and Trademark Office, "Patent Public Search," available at https://www.uspto.gov/patents/search.

16. 17 U.S.C. § 102 (1990).

17. Darren Rovell, "Royalties for Gatorade Trust Surpass $1 Billion: 'Can't Let It Spoil Us,'" *ESPN*, October 1, 2015, available at https://www.espn.com/college-football/story/_/id/13789009/royalties-gatorade-inventors-surpass-1-billion.

18. University of Florida, "Why the University of Florida Gets a ~$20M Cut of Gatorade Profits Every Year (The Hustle)," available at https://innovate.research.ufl.edu/2021/09/20/uf-gets-20m-gatorade/.

19. 35 U.S.C. § 200–212 (1980).

20. National Academy of Inventors, "Top 100 Worldwide Universities Granted U.S. Utility Patents in 2022," April 2023, available at https://academyofinventors.org/wp-content/uploads/2023/04/2022-Top-100.pdf.

21. 34 C.F.R. § 401.14 (1987).

22. *Stanford v. Roche Molecular Systems, Inc.*, 563 U.S. 776 (2011).

23. Penn Center for Innovation, "Penn Patent and Conflict of Interest Policies," available at https://pci.upenn.edu/inventors/how-it-works-commercializing-innovation/policies/.

24. Id.

25. Scott Stroble and Michael Crair, "Important Changes to Patent Royalty Sharing Practices," Yale University, September 27, 2022, available at https://provost.yale.edu/news/important-changes-patent-royalty-sharing-practices.

26. Benjamin Franklin, *Poor Richard's Almanack* (New York: Caldwell, 1900), available at https://archive.org/details/poorrichardsalma00franrich.

27. Purdue Research Foundation, "Inventors Recognition Reception," April 18, 2024, available at https://otc.prf.org/inventors/ and https://purdueinnovates.org/otc/intellectual-property/.

28. 17 U.S.C. § 201(a) (1978).

29. 17 U.S.C. § 201(b) (1978).

30. 17 U.S.C. § 101 (2010).

31. *Community for Creative Non-Violence v. Reid*, 490 U.S. 730 (1989).

32. *Schramm v. C.I.R.*, 2011 102 T.C.M. (CCH) 233 (2011).

33. *Hall v. Swift*, 2018 WL 2317548 (C.D. Cal. 2018) (overturned on appeal, and the case eventually settled).

34. *National Council for Teachers Quality, Inc. v. University of Missouri*, 446 S.W.3d 723 (Mo. Ct. App. 2014).

35. *Roop v. Lincoln College*, 803 F.Supp.2d 926 (C.D. Ill 2011).

36. *Vanderhurst v. Colorado Mountain College Dist.*, 16 F.Supp.2d 1297 (D. Colo. 1998).

37. *Shaul v. Cherry Valley-Springfield Cent. School Dist.*, 363 F.3d 177 (2nd Cir. 2004).

38. Id.

39. Colleen Flaherty, "Suing John Doe Students over Copyright," *Inside Higher Ed*, March 17, 2022, available at https://www.insidehighered.com/news/2022/03/18/suing-students-who-shared-exams-online-identify-them.

40. 17 U.S.C. § 102(a) (1990).

41. University of North Carolina at Chapel Hill Libraries, "Copyright and Usage," available at https://library.unc.edu/scholarly-communications/copyright/; University of Missouri, "FAQ: Intellectual Property and Course Materials," April 24, 2020, available at https://www.umsystem.edu/sites/default/files/media/elearning/faq-ip-course-materials-04-24-2020.pdf.

42. 17 U.S.C. § 201(b) (1978).

43. *Foraste v. Brown University*, 290 F.Supp.2d 234 (D.R.I.).

44. J. Wadley and J. Brown, "Working between the Lines: Teachers, Copyright, Work-for-Hire and a New Washburn University Policy, *Washburn Law Journal* 38, no. 385 (1999); *Pittsburgh State University/Kansas Nat. Educ. Ass'n v. Kansas Bd. of Regents/Pittsburgh State University*, 122 P.3d 336 (Kan. 2005).

45. *Alice Corp. Pty. Ltd. v. CLS Bank International*, 573 U.S. 208 (2014).

46. *Rouse v. Walter & Associates, L.L.C.*, 534 F. Supp. 2d (S.D. Iowa 2007).

47. Id.

48. GenScript, "Top 100 Most Cited Publications," available at https://www.genscript.com/top-100-most-cited-publications.html.

49. Berklee, "Copyright and Intellectual Property," August 2, 2023, available at https://guides.library.berklee.edu/copyright.

50. Brown University, "Copyright Ownership and Use Policy," October 16, 2020, available at https://policy.brown.edu/policy/copyright-ownership-and-use-policy.

51. *Sherrill v. Grieves*, 57 Wash. L.R. 286 (D.C. 1929).

52. *Williams v. Weisser*, 273 Cal.App.2d 726 (Cal. Ct. App. 1969).

53. *Molinelli-Freytes v. University of Puerto Rico*, 792 F.Supp.2d 164.

54. Id.

55. Id., at 172.

56. *Weinstein v. University of Illinois*, 811 F.2d 1091 (7th Cir. 1987).

57. Id., at 1094.

58. Fred Shapiro, "The Most-Cited Legal Scholars Revisited," *University of Chicago Law Review* 88, no. 1 (2021): 1598, available at https://lawreview.uchicago.edu/print-archive/most-cited-legal-scholars-revisited.

59. *Hays v. Sony Corp. of America*, 847 F.2d 412 (7th Cir. 1988).

60. Id., at 416.

61. AAUP, "Intellectual Property Issues for Faculty and Faculty Unions," April 15, 2020, available at https://www.aaup.org/sites/default/files/intellectual_property_issues_faculty.pdf.

62. University of South Carolina, "Copyright Policy," Policy ACAF 1.35, June 3, 2021, available at https://www.sc.edu/policies/ppm/acaf135.pdf.

63. 17 U.S.C. § 201(b) (1978).

64. University of South Carolina, "Copyright Policy," Policy ACAF 1.35, June 3, 2021, available at https://www.sc.edu/policies/ppm/acaf135.pdf.

65. Purdue University, "Intellectual Property (I.A.1)," January 26, 2017, available at https://www.purdue.edu/policies/academic-research-affairs/ia1.html.

66. University of California, "Copyright Ownership," February1, 2021, available at https://copyright.universityofcalifornia.edu/resources/copyright-ownership.html.

67. AAUP, "Resources on Copyright, Online Education, and Intellectual Property," available at https://www.aaup.org/issues/intellectual-property/resources-copyright-distance-education-and-intellectual-property.

68. AAUP, "Intellectual Property and Copyright," available at https://www.aaup.org/get-involved/issue-campaigns/intellectual-property-risk.

69. AAUP, "Statement on Online Education," January 2024, available at https://www.aaup.org/report/statement-online-and-distance-education.

70. AAUP, "Statement on Copyright," available at https://www.aaup.org/report/statement-copyright.

71. Id.

72. AAUP, "Statement on Intellectual Property," available at https://www.aaup.org/report/statement-intellectual-property.

73. *The Authors Guild v. Google, Inc.*, 804 F.3d 202 (2nd Cir. 2015).

74. 17 U.S.C.A. § 105 (2022).

75. *Veek v. Southern Building Code Southern International, Inc.*, 293 F.3d 791 (5th Cir. 2002).

76. *Stewart v. Abend*, 495 U.S. 207, at 238 (1990).

77. *Faulkner Press, L.L.C. v. Class Notes, L.L.C.*, 756 F.Supp.2d 1352 (N.D. Fla. 2010).

78. *Seltzer v. Green Day*, 725 F.3d 1170 (9th Cir. 2013).

79. *Williams v. Weisser*, 273 Cal.App.2d 726 (Cal. Ct. App. 1969).

80. https://www.insidehighered.com/news/faculty-issues/academic-freedom/2024/07/10/fs-recording-class-even-students-disabilities#

81. Fla. Stat. § 934.03 (2021).

82. Fla. Stat. § 1004.097 (2021).

83. University of North Carolina at Chapel Hill, "Effective Note-Taking in Class," available at https://learningcenter.unc.edu/tips-and-tools/effective-note-taking-in-class/.

84. University of North Carolina at Chapel Hill, "Copyright Policy of the University of North Carolina at Chapel Hill," April 18, 2023, available at https://policies.unc.edu/TDClient/2833/Portal/KB/ArticleDet?ID=132138.

85. University of California Berkeley, https://campuspol.chance.berkeley.edu/policies/coursenotes.pdf.

86. Cal. Education Code § 66450 (2001).

87. *A.V. ex rel. Vanderhye v. iParadigms, LLC*, 562 F.3d 630 (4th Cir. 2009).

88. Purdue University, "Intellectual Property (I.A.1)," January 26, 2017, available at https://www.purdue.edu/policies/academic-research-affairs/ia1.html.

89. University of Minnesota, "Copyright Ownership," available at https://policy.umn.edu/research/copyright.

90. U.S. Copyright Office, "Copyright Registration Guidance: Works Containing Material Generated by Artificial Intelligence," Federal Register, Vol. 88, No. 51, March 16, 2023, available at https://www.federalregister.gov/documents/2023/03/16/2023-05321/copyright-registration-guidance-works-containing-material-generated-by-artificial-intelligence#citation-25-p16192.

91. Id.

92. *Naruto v. Slater*, 888 F.3d 418 (9th Cir. 2018).

93. U.S. Copyright Office, "Copyright Registration Guidance."

94. Purdue University Graduate School, "Ownership of Intellectual Property," August 20, 2018, available at https://www.purdue.edu/gradschool/documents/rcr/Ownership_of_Intellectual_Property_08_20_18.pdf.

95. *Regents of University of California v. Chen*, 2017 WL 3215356 (N.D. Cal. 2017); *University of West Virginia Board of Trustees v. VanVoorhies*, 278 F.3d 1288 (Fed. Cir. 2002).

96. *Taborsky v. State*, 659 So.2d 1112 (Fla. Dist. Ct. App. 1995).

97. *University of South Florida v. Taborsky*, 648 So.2d 748 (Fla. Dist. Ct. App. 1994).

98. Seth Shulman, "A Researcher's Conviction," *MIT Technology Review*, February 1, 1997, available at https://www.technologyreview.com/1997/02/01/237363/a-researchers-conviction/.

99. *Chou v. University of Chicago*, 254 F.3d 1347 (Fed. Cir. 2001).

100. *Diversy v. Schmidly*, 738 F.3d 1196 (10th Cir. 2013).

101. *Seshadri v. Kasraian*, 130 F.3d 798 (7th Cir. 1997).

102. Id., at 803.

103. *Weinstein v. University of Illinois*, 628 F.Supp. 862 (N.D. Ill 1986).

104. *Weinstein v. University of Illinois*, 811 F.2d 1091 (7th Cir. 1987).

105. *Roop v. Lincoln College*, 803 F.Supp.2d 926 (C.D. Ill 2011).

106. Claire Lawton, "Former ASU Professors Threaten Legal Action against University for Violation of Intellectual Property," *Phoenix New Times*, March 14, 2012, available at https://www.phoenixnewtimes.com/arts/former-asu-professors-threaten-legal-action-against-university-for-violation-of-intellectual-property-6574375.

107. *MacSwan v. Arizona Board of Regents*, 2013 WL 12096526 (D. Ariz. 2013).

108. University of Maryland, "University of Maryland Intellectual Property Policy," January 10, 2018, available at https://policies.umd.edu/research/university-of-maryland-intellectual-property-policy.

109. *Rainey v. Wayne State University*, 26 F.Supp.2d 963 (E.D. Mich. 1998); and 26 F.Supp.2d 973.

CHAPTER 5

Key Questions about FERPA

DOES ANYBODY UNDERSTAND THIS STUFF?

You Make the Call

- **The Case of the College Trip to Costa Rica**

Some students, enrolled in a biology class at a college in Wyoming, took a trip to Costa Rica. The trip was led by the college's president. While in Costa Rica, one of the students began exhibiting emotionally unstable behaviors. On the first night of the trip, this student took more than her prescribed dosage of medications, which some students believed was an attempted overdose, and she began exhibiting hyperactivity and threatened to harm herself. Upon learning of the situation, the college president asked another student who had some emergency medical training to play pharmacist for the ill student and make sure she didn't overmedicate anymore. Later, the student who had threatened to harm herself made additional suicidal statements. Once, she threatened to run into the forest and never return. On one day of the trip the president allowed her to purchase a very large knife at a souvenir shop, even though she was known to be a cutter whose razors had already been given to another student for safekeeping. Once, and while holding the knife, the student ran into traffic, whereupon five of the students set off after her. Throughout these ordeals, the college president didn't attempt to get the student home and didn't contact the college's care team; nor did he seek medical help for the student in Costa Rica. After the trip's conclusion, the college's care team conducted an investigation and wrote an internal report on the matter. Its findings included criticisms of the president's actions in asking other students to watch over the student, rather than placing the student in the care of a medical professional, and in not sending the student home. When a local newspaper heard about the matter, it asked for the care team report, but the college said no. Then, when the newspaper came into possession of a leaked copy, the college went to court seeking a restraining order to prevent the newspaper from posting news stories on the trip and the report. The college argued that it would risk losing federal funding because the release of its report, which included students' names, would be a Family Educational Rights and Privacy Act (FERPA) violation. The newspaper stated that students' names would not be disclosed in its reporting.

Is it a FERPA violation for the newspaper to publish stories on the inauspicious trip, based on the college's report, which includes the students' names?

(The answer will be given at the end of the chapter. Consider how the principles in this chapter affect your decision and reasoning.)

Ask a group of people what the greatest political speeches in US history are and you can bet someone will offer the Gettysburg Address or Martin Luther King's "I Have a Dream Speech," given at the Lincoln Memorial in 1963. President Lincoln's elegant and constitutionally redefining speech, made to commemorate the Gettysburg battlegrounds cemetery in 1863, was just 272 words. Dr. King's equally powerful and needed speech was 1,667 words. The US Constitution, including the signatures, is 4,573 words. Which brings us to FERPA,[1] a single federal statute that weighs in at about 3,800 words. One statute. And then there are the pages of federal regulations the US Department of Education has issued on FERPA.[2] The immensity of it all makes understanding FERPA a discouraging task. So, let's avoid trying to understand all of FERPA and instead attempt to answer key questions about FERPA, including if faculty face personal liability risks for violating it.

Related to liability and FERPA proscriptions is the student recommendation or reference letter. Yes, it's almost guaranteed that a student request for a recommendation letter will come with a written waiver to discuss information that would be otherwise protected by FERPA. But that doesn't always happen, and when faculty discuss their students' bona fides and other subjective impressions with prospective employers or similar decision-makers, there still is the question of whether those letters or even those conversations violate FERPA. One word of caution about this chapter is that, if your educational institution's FERPA policies or assertions are different from the conclusions reached here, my advice is to follow your employer's requirements.

What Is FERPA and What Does It Do?

The Family Educational Rights and Privacy Act of 1974 (FERPA), also known as the Buckley Amendment, provides parents and students with access to students' education records while protecting the privacy of such records.[3] FERPA is augmented by federal regulations created by the US Department of Education.[4] It is important to note that FERPA's requirements and prohibitions are directed to educational institutions. States can have their own version of FERPA, which often are focused more or exclusively on K–12 settings. If a state's student privacy laws conflict with FERPA, federal law would be controlling due to the US Constitution's Sixth Amendment's Supremacy Clause. But a state could, as some do, provide more student privacy protections than are minimally required by FERPA.[5]

FERPA prohibits educational institutions from having a "policy or practice" of releasing student records without proper student consent. There are necessary exceptions made to this rule, many of which don't bear on faculty. Some of those exceptions include when the education records or personally identifiable information is released to other school officials; to officials of other schools where the student wants to enroll; in connection with financial aid; to accrediting agencies; and with respect to law-enforcement investigations or record-keeping.[6] As it concerns the status of graduated students who become teachers, at least one federal appellate court ruled in a case where someone made a public-records request to see a public-school teacher's college transcript that her transcript was not an education record when it was part of an employee file.[7] Think about that for a second or more.

FERPA also provides students the right to seek a hearing with their school if they believe their education records are in error,[8] and the related hearing procedures are detailed in the FERPA regulations.[9] In a case reminiscent of Chapter 1's discussion of faculty liability risks, a former medical student in Virginia sued some of his professors and his medical school for breach of contract and defamation over what he believed was a wrongly graded exam, which affected his status as a medical student. He claimed his rights to sue were under FERPA's grant of a hearing to challenge an education record. But the federal court believed the student was attempting to bootstrap an earlier failed grade appeal into a FERPA-violations case, concluding that FERPA is not in any way applicable to how professors evaluate right or wrong answers on exams.[10]

WHEN DO PARENTS LOSE RIGHTS TO THEIR CHILDREN'S EDUCATION RECORDS?

Parents or guardians have rights to access their children's education records when they are in K–12 schools, but those rights transfer to their children when they turn eighteen or whenever they go to college.[11] Nevertheless, colleges and universities do provide student-consent mechanisms to allow parental access to education records. For example, my college-attending son ticked the needed online boxes to provide parental access to his otherwise protected education records. And there are a variety of exceptions to the general rule that prohibits outside access to college students' records, including if the college student is, for IRS purposes, a dependent of the parent[12] or if the student is under twenty-one and the college or university believes the student violated a law or school policy related to alcohol or a controlled substance.[13]

HOW LONG DO FERPA RIGHTS LAST?

Former students who have left an educational institution still have FERPA rights; they are treated the same as enrolled students for FERPA purposes, including when they sue their former universities.[14] But FERPA protections end when a student dies.[15] This is consistent with the legal doctrine on privacy, in that privacy rights do not continue after death. A famous case on that involved the widow of Jesse James Jr., who sued the company that produced a documentary on her infamous, outlaw father-in-law. She alleged the documentary libeled her husband and, by extension, her. But the court ruled she had no claim because, since her husband was dead, he no longer had privacy interests.[16]

THE TAKEAWAY

FERPA and its regulations are designed to provide parents and guardians of pre-college students and college students of all ages the right to access their student's education records. It also prohibits educational institutions—at the risk of losing federal funding—from having a policy or practice of releasing education records or the personally identifiable information in them without proper written consent. FERPA also provides a mechanism for students (or parents) to challenge the accuracy of an education record. FERPA's coverage includes former students but does not continue for students who have passed away.

Can Faculty Be Liable for Violating FERPA?

This is the most important question for faculty, isn't it? So, let's get to it early. Thankfully, the answer is no. There are two reasons why faculty can't be liable to a student for a FERPA violation. First, FERPA isn't written to faculty: it is written to educational institutions and only to those that receive federal funding. (There are a handful of colleges, mostly religious, that refuse to accept federal funding.) FERPA offers a stick, rather than a carrot, approach by threatening to refuse to provide federal funding to those institutions that have a policy or a practice of denying rightful persons access to student education records or a policy or a practice of wrongfully releasing education records.

Second, the US Supreme Court ruled in 2002 that no plaintiff can bring a claim for monetary damages because of a FERPA violation. In the case *Gonzaga University v. Doe*,[17] a former education student sued two professors and the university for allegedly ruining his teaching employment chances through what he considered to be a defamatory FERPA violation, which included false allegations that he sexually assaulted another student. The allegations were the reason for the denial of his state-required affidavit of good moral character, which he needed to be a public-school teacher. A jury awarded him $450,000 on the FERPA claim alone. But the US Supreme Court ruled that, while educational institutions risk losing federal funds for having a policy or practice of permitting the release of education records, FERPA did not create any enforceable, federal-law entitlement right such as that provided by federal civil-rights statutes. For example, a victim of racial discrimination in employment can recover monetary damages under federal antidiscrimination laws. Other federal courts have expanded on that, concluding FERPA is the type of federal legislation that doesn't permit any federal or state lawsuit for monetary damages.[18] In a curious law-school case (as if there are any other kinds), a law student sued a professor who, the student claimed, intercepted the anonymous class evaluations for one of the student's classes before they reached their intended destination, used handwriting analysis to conclude the student was the one who wrote critical comments, and then retaliated by giving the student a D for the course. In rejecting the student's FERPA claim, the court said FERPA doesn't confer the right to sue for money.[19]

Has Any College or School Lost Federal Funding for Violating FERPA?

As encouraging as it is to know that faculty face no personal liability for failing to follow FERPA accurately, this is not to say there are no personal employment risks for violating FERPA. All faculty should do their best to follow their employer's FERPA policies, including the practice of sending or responding to student-related email exclusively through a student's official college or university email address.

And remember, the loss of federal funding hinges on whether an educational institution has a "policy or practice" of unauthorized disclosure, not on whether the institution made a single misstep. In fact, in my research and communication with the US Department of Education, I conclude no educational institution has ever lost federal funding for FERPA reasons. If a complaint filed with the US Department of Education Student's Privacy Policy Office results in a determination that there was a FERPA violation, the next step is a US Education Department–generated compliance action. And, when the school completes those compliance actions, that investigation is concluded.

THE TAKEAWAY

Faculty might commit FERPA violations that impact their employment, but they can't be held personally liable for FERPA violations for two reasons. First, FERPA is directed at educational institutions, not their employees. Second, the US Supreme Court and other federal courts have ruled that FERPA provides no availability for a plaintiff to recover monetary damages for FERPA violations, whether against colleges or their employees, since its focus is only to condition federal funding on educational institutions observing FERPA requirements.

You Make the Call

- **The Case of the Instructor's Attempt to Find the Author of the Complaining Email**

Near the end of the semester in many colleges and universities, students are invited to complete course evaluations, which allow students to do their own anonymous grading of their courses and instructors. In a case from Florida that has a similar ring, an adjunct instructor at a public college went to court to find out who in his class wrote an email to the department chair that, the instructor believed, led to him not being hired again. The student who sent the email complained about the instructor's classroom behaviors, including "his humiliating remarks to students and his unorthodox teaching methodologies."[20] Upon learning of the email, the instructor asked for a copy so he could defend against what he said were untrue accusations. But the email copy he received had the student's name redacted, which the chair said was required under both Florida and federal FERPA law because the email was "an education record." (Florida's definition of an education record is identical to the federal definition.) The instructor found this response unsatisfactory, because he believed he needed to know who the complaining student was so he could determine if this student was even able to fairly evaluate his classroom actions. (For example, did this student have ulterior motives based on a bad grade?) As the instructor—who represented himself in the litigation—said, "To me, it's just un-American that you don't have the right to know who your accuser is."[21]

Is a student email to a college administrator addressing dissatisfaction with her instructor an education record under FERPA that prevents the instructor from knowing who the author is? (Feel free to change your mind when reaching your own conclusion, because the court did the same thing.)

(The answer will be given at the end of the chapter. Consider how the principles in this chapter affect your decision and reasoning.)

What Is an Education Record?

The term "Education Record" is found over twenty times in the FERPA statute, which also provides a definition. Education records are "those records, files, documents and other materials," which

1) contain information directly related to a student; and
2) are maintained by an educational agency or institution or by a person acting for such institution.[22]

Education Records and Personally Identifiable Information

The FERPA regulations expand on this definition and state that a "Record" includes "any information *recorded in any way* [emphasis added], which includes handwriting, print, computer media, video or audio tape."[23] One would think there would be a definition of information that is "directly related" to a student, because there could be a category of information that is "indirectly related" to a student and, therefore, not part of FERPA's coverage. But neither FERPA nor its federal regulations define what information is "directly related to a student."[24] The inference to be drawn is that not much student information is needed in order to fall within the range of directly related.

FERPA and its related regulations often include the phrase "personally identifiable information," referring to information that is included in an education record and, therefore, generally prohibited from being released. That phrase is defined in the regulations, and the definition is long and includes some of the following information: a student's name; their family members' names; their social security or other identifying number; their date of or place of birth; and other information "that would allow a reasonable person in the school community, who does not have personal knowledge of the relevant circumstances, to identify the student with reasonable certainty."[25] One way to think of personally identifiable information is that it is information that would reasonably permit identification of a student. Notably, grades themselves aren't included in any definition of an education record or personally identifiable information, perhaps because that is too obvious for inclusion.

Is an Email an Education Record?

An education record for FERPA purposes is not limited to paper files or documents. The FERPA regulations define a record as "information recorded in any way," including handwriting, print, computer media, video, or audio.[26] An email would qualify as an education record if it contains information directly related to a student (as opposed to an email that was written by a student to college or university personnel but that doesn't concern the student) and if it is maintained by the college or university. Emails sent by or to college personnel would seem to be automatically maintained, and even a private email that includes information directly related to a student and that is sent to a college email address would likely qualify as an education record. In fact, some universities claim ownership of, or at least the right to access, all email that is sent by way of a university-issued email address, including student email.[27]

Maintained by the Educational Institution or Its Agent

Neither the statute nor the regulations define "maintain," which has led to some confusion. On this point, in 2002 the US Supreme Court issued a decision on whether it's a FERPA violation for students to grade each other's homework in class. In the case, a mother with three children in a public school argued that it was a FERPA violation and embarrassing to her children that their teachers have students grade each other's assignments and occasionally tell students to call out those grades in class, so the teacher can record them.[28] The US Supreme Court disagreed and issued a unanimous opinion, holding that those student-graded papers didn't qualify as education records because they weren't—at the time of being graded—in the possession of the teachers and recorded in a grade book. Analyzing what it means to maintain an education record, the court referred to filing cabinets in a record room, or secure databases, something kept by a single custodian. And the court said that, for FERPA purposes, student-graders aren't "persons acting for the education institution." The federal regulations were revised some years later to exclude as education records peer-graded papers before they are collected.

My problem with this case is that the very thing FERPA was intended to protect was released permissibly and with obvious embarrassment for some students. Suppose in an ice breaker at the start of the semester, I ask students to tell everyone what their GPA and their social security numbers are and then give a prize to the student with the highest total number. That's not going to fly and is clearly a violation of students' privacy rights, even though it would seem to be in line with the US Supreme Court's decision and not be a FERPA violation. Furthermore, if teachers write down in their grade books what students have just called out in class, then wouldn't reading the grades out loud off the grade book be a FERPA violation—even though the equivalent was already done a few minutes earlier? That isn't clear because the Supreme Court's opinion specifically put aside the question of whether a grade book is an education record, because the court focused on an education record being "maintained" when it's under the control of a single custodian. One Supreme Court justice wrote a concurring opinion in that case, which included criticizing the court for creating confusion about grade books and FERPA.[29]

Adding to the perplexity about whether a grade book would be an education record is that a later part of FERPA excludes from being an education record those "records of instructional . . . personnel" that are in the sole possession of the maker and not accessible to anyone other than a substitute.[30] That exclusion could include a grade book, yet a US Department of Education web page says that grades, by themselves, are education records.[31]

COVID Lockdowns, Virtual Class Sessions, and FERPA

In March 2020, the US Department of Education held a webinar on FERPA and student privacy issues related to classes being held virtually. Among the questions asked and answered were whether faculty could bring education records home (yes), whether it was OK to hold classes on Zoom (yes) and whether nonstudents could view the class sessions (yes, if no personally identifiable information was disclosed in the class sessions), whether virtual learning sessions could be recorded and shared with students (yes, if no personally identifiable information was recorded), and whether student-professor meetings could be held virtually from home if other members of the professor's family are in the home too (yes, if no personally identifiable information is disclosed or if the student provides e-consent to the possible disclosure).[32]

THE TAKEAWAY

Education records are hardcopy and electronic materials that contain information directly related to a student and that are maintained by the educational institution or an agent of it, like faculty. Personally identifiable information is information that would reasonably permit identification of a student and it includes student's contact information, grades, and other information that would allow someone to identify a student. Grades and email can qualify as education records. An education record is also that which is maintained by the educational institution or its agent, including faculty.

What Isn't an Education Record?

FERPA has four categories of information that are not education records, including "records of instructional, supervisory, and administrative personnel and educational personnel ancillary thereto which are in the sole possession of the maker thereof and which are not accessible or revealed to any other person except a substitute."[33]

Federal regulations specify six categories of information that are not education records, including records that are kept in the sole possession of the maker that are used only as a personal memory aid and are not accessible or revealed to any other person except for a temporary substitute for the maker of the record; records of an individual in that person's capacity as an institutional or agency employee; and medical records of an adult student that might be in the possession of an educator where education activities are part of a treatment plan.[34] An example drawn from these exceptions might be to suppose that a professor has a class list with personally written mnemonic devices on the list (e.g., "Taylor hates country music," "Sydney sits against the back window"). That would not be an education record. Likewise, class notes aren't education records. And, as stated earlier, peer-graded assignments or similar documents aren't education records before being submitted to teachers or faculty.

In one case involving what is or is not an education record, record companies sought to find out who on the campuses of Yale and the University of Connecticut were illegally downloading music and, thus, engaging in copyright infringement. In order to find the scofflaws, the recording companies needed the media access control (MAC) addresses of certain students' computers, and the universities countered that divulging that information would violate FERPA. The federal court disagreed, concluding that a MAC address is not an education record but, rather, is directory information (more on that later) that can be released by a court order.[35]

THE TAKEAWAY

Various types of information that might seem to be education records are specifically exempted by FERPA or its regulations. Peer-graded papers and instructional documents that are only in the possession of faculty are the most relevant examples of what are not education records.

What Is Directory Information and Why Does It Matter?

Directory information is personally identifiable information from an educational record that educational institutions may disclose without a student's prior written consent.[36] That is in contrast to instructional materials, which are not part of FERPA's restrictions because they are not an education record. In other words, directory information includes that which is part of an education record but which, under various circumstances, is treated as an exception to the FERPA prohibition on unauthorized release. FERPA defines directory information to include the student's name, address, telephone number, email address, dates of attendance, full- or part-time status, major field of study, height and weight of members of athletic teams, degrees and awards received, participation in sports and activities, and the school the student has most recently attended.[37]

A FERPA regulation states that directory information is that "information contained in an education record of a student that would not generally be considered harmful or an invasion of privacy if disclosed."[38] That regulation defines directory information similarly to how FERPA defines it, including in the definition the educational agency or institution most recently attended by the student and the student's ID or other personal identifier that is used for accessing or communicating in electronic systems but only if that information may not be used to access education records.[39]

When an institution intends on making directory information available, it must first provide notice of the content it classifies as directory information and allow a reasonable time for students (or parents of minor students not in college) to object to that type of information being released.[40] A college or university can accomplish this by linking a directory information opt-out or revocation-of-release form on its FERPA web page, which is often part of its registrar's office website.[41]

Institutions may release directory information about former students without complying with the public-notice and opt-out conditions,[42] which makes sense because of the difficulties and costs in contacting former students to provide them FERPA-related waivers. But a college or university could preemptively provide enrolled students methods to opt out of the directory-information disclosure in a way that continues beyond their enrollment.

THE TAKEAWAY

Directory information is personally identifiable information in an education record that may be released without a student's written consent, due to the belief that such a release would not be harmful. Examples of directory information include a student's name and contact information and participation in sports and activities. Schools must provide a mechanism for students to receive notice about directory-information policies and give students the opportunity to oppose the release of their directory information, but notice does not need to be made to former students.

How Does FERPA Impact Faculty Reference Letters or Conversations?

You Make the Call

- **The Case of the Student-Teacher (Non)recommendation Letter**

A college senior in the school of education of a state college in Indiana was assigned to an elementary school for her student-teaching semester. One of the university's school of education professors was assigned to supervise her efforts, which included making regularly prescribed visits to the student's elementary class. Although the university student-teacher handbook said supervising faculty were to make biweekly visits to observe and interact with the student, there was a dispute in the eventual litigation about whether the professor fulfilled this expectation. During the semester in question, the student took over the class when the regular teacher was hospitalized. For the student's midsemester evaluation, the supervising professor praised the student's classroom-management and lesson-presentation skills as excellent and noted she was well organized. At the end of the semester, the professor issued a formal teaching evaluation and gave the student a passing grade. Later, that school's principal contacted the professor because a teaching job was available and asked the professor for a written evaluation of the student's overall teaching abilities. In the letter, which the student eventually discovered after asking the superintendent why she wasn't hired, the professor first positively described the student as enthusiastic, willing to work, and comfortable with children's parents. But the professor did not recommend that the student be hired, noting that the student was a marginal student teacher who had certain weaknesses, including faulty grammatical skills, poor organization and execution skills with respect to lesson plans, poor discipline, inflexibility, and a resistance to criticism. The student sued the university, but curiously not the professor, for libel. Included also in the lawsuit was her allegation that the university violated her FERPA rights because she said the school of education's handbook for student teachers prohibited such a letter from being issued without her permission.

1) *Although libel law will be covered in the next chapter, feel free to give this one a try: does a professor risk being liable for libel for a negative recommendation letter like this one? Is this recommendation letter an education record that requires the student's permission (or waiver against disclosure to the student) to be issued?*

(The answers will be given at the end of the chapter. Consider how the principles in this chapter affect your decision and reasoning.)

Because we were once students and asked our professors for reference or recommendation letters, we should be gracious and helpful in doing our part, even when a few of those requests are made way too close to the deadline for the letters' receipt. Many of those reference letter requests are made in situations where students provide waivers against reviewing the letters' contents or receiving copies. That is due to FERPA and its regulations, which require that a student must provide a written waiver to give up their right to inspect the letter in the possession of the education institution.[43] Of course, without such a waiver, the letter is no longer confidential and the student's right to review the letter could affect how the letter is written. The FERPA regulation on reference letters is silent on who is responsible for securing the student's waiver, so it seems incumbent on faculty to seek a waiver if the student does not, and many universities tell their faculty to provide a university-drafted waiver form as a condition of writing a reference or recommendation letter. Be careful if a student says "I don't have to see the letter," as that is not a waiver of their FERPA rights because it is not in writing.

Reference Letters Don't Have to Include FERPA-Linked Information

One thing to bear in mind about reference letters is that they would only qualify as an education record if they contain the kind of information that constitutes the "personally identifiable information" about which FERPA concerns itself. Naturally, a letter with a GPA would qualify, but what about letters that simply discuss the letter writer's subjective impressions of the student in ways that don't address the student's academic accomplishments? If a professor writes a letter that focuses on a student's soft skills or the professor's opinion of the student rather than on the student's academic history, I would submit that such a letter is outside FERPA's scope.

For example, if a prospective employer asks for a letter focused on the student-applicant's attitude or leadership skills or how the student-applicant handles criticism, or even the student-applicant's nongraded communication skills, that letter, if written carefully, would not include personally identifiable information from an education record and would not implicate FERPA. Although this relevant case doesn't involve reference letters, a federal court said, in a lawsuit involving a high-school gym teacher's egregious mistreatment of two students and his subsequent discussion of some of the events with other students, that FERPA doesn't protect against the dissemination of information that might come from an education record but that is independently known by others.[44] Another federal court said that Congress couldn't have intended FERPA to prohibit the discussion of facts about a student that were learned independently of an education record.[45] And, in a case involving a female student athlete who brought a sexual-harassment–related claim against a public university in North Carolina, the university sought to seal some of the depositions (a deposition is out-of-court testimony made under oath) on the grounds that releasing them (which is not unheard of in litigation) would violate the student's FERPA rights.

But the court refused to seal that evidence, concluding that it concerned conversations about the student that were not information coming from an education record.[46]

There is no need to secure a student waiver when sending a reference letter that only includes information that qualifies as directory information, unless the student has complied with the university's opt-out procedure for release of directory information. Another issue to consider is that FERPA says an education record is one that is "maintained" by the educational institution or its agent. So, if an instructor mails a reference letter, then there is nothing for the instructor to maintain, unless the instructor has made a copy. As more faculty work is done from home (which is not a FERPA violation) and as more reference or recommendation letters are sent as e-documents or are completed inside the electronic systems of the receiving party (such as the Law School Admission Council),[47] then faculty might not have a copy on hand. So, unless school policy requires reference letters to be kept on file or on a university hard drive, if one deletes a reference letter that was sent on a computer, then is it "maintained?" If not, then perhaps it is not an education record.

Are Conversations about a Student Outside the Scope of FERPA?

Because FERPA concerns "personally identifiable information" that comes from an education record, as well as the actual record, a conversation about a student that included discussing FERPA-covered information would carry the same implications as a reference letter. Of course, it would be difficult to establish that a faculty member committed a FERPA violation during a conversation, but it would not be impossible. For instance, a prospective employer could tell a student that the student wasn't hired because a professor told the employer that the student tested poorly in computational parts of a course or performed inadequately in practicum activities. But conversations that faculty have with prospective employers that are limited to independently known information (the student has a problem getting to class on time) or information that isn't related to an education record (the student lacks self-awareness or maturity) are safe—at least for the faculty.

THE TAKEAWAY

When faculty write reference letters or have conversations about students, they should consider FERPA and their college or university policy. Generally, a student has the right to review a letter that would include information from an education record, unless the student has provided a written waiver or an opt-out form. However, if there is no copy of the letter on file, one could argue that there is no FERPA implication because the letter has not been maintained, per FERPA language. But letters or conversations that discuss information that does not come from an education record, such as one's impressions of a student, or that which is independently known by others, are thought to be outside FERPA's scope.

Final Takeaways

- FERPA and its regulations are designed to provide parents and guardians of precollege students and college students of all ages the right to access their student's education records. It also prohibits educational institutions—at the risk of losing federal funding—from having a policy or practice of releasing education records or the personally identifiable information in them without the proper written consent. FERPA also provides a mechanism for students (or parents) to challenge the accuracy of an education record. FERPA's coverage includes former students but does not continue for students who have passed away.
- Faculty can't be personally liable for FERPA violations for two reasons. First, FERPA is directed at educational institutions, not their employees. Second, the US Supreme Court and other federal courts have ruled that FERPA provides no availability for a plaintiff to recover monetary damages for FERPA violations against colleges or their employees, since its focus is only to condition federal funding on educational institutions observing FERPA requirements.
- Education records are hardcopy and electronic materials that contain information directly related to a student and that are maintained by the educational institution or an agent of it, like faculty. Personally identifiable information includes student's contact information, grades, and even information that would allow someone to identify a student. Grades and email can qualify as education records. An education record is also that which is maintained by the educational institution or its agent, including faculty.
- Various types of information that might seem to be education records are specifically exempted by FERPA or its regulations. Peer-graded papers and instructional documents that are only in the possession of faculty are the most relevant examples of what are not education records.
- Directory information is "personally identifiable information" (as defined in FERPA and its regulations) in an education record that may be released without a student's written consent, due to the belief that such a release would not be harmful. Examples of directory information include a student's name and contact information and participation in sports and activities. Schools must provide a mechanism for students to receive notice about

directory-information policies and give students the opportunity to oppose the release of their directory information, but notice does not need to be made to former students.

- When faculty write reference letters and engage in conversations about students, they should consider FERPA and their college or university policy. Generally, a student has the right to review a letter that would include information from an education record, unless the student has provided a written waiver or an opt-out form. However, if there is no copy of the reference letter on file, one could argue that there is no FERPA implication because the letter has not been maintained, per FERPA language. But letters or conversations that discuss information that does not come from an education record or that is independently known by others are thought to be outside FERPA's scope.

How Did You Make the Calls?

1 – The Case of the College Trip to Costa Rica

This case involves a disastrous trip to Costa Rica, taken by some students at Laramie County Community College and led by its president. While in Costa Rica, one of the students on the trip began exhibiting emotionally unstable behaviors. On the first night on the trip, the student attempted an overdose of her prescribed dosage of medications. Thereupon, the college president asked another student who had some emergency medical training to take care that the ill student didn't overmedicate anymore. Later, the ill student made multiple suicidal statements. Once she threatened to run into the forest and never return. On another day, she was allowed to buy a huge knife in a gift shop and then she darted off into traffic with it. The college president did not attempt to get the student home and didn't contact the college's care team; nor did he seek medical help in Costa Rica for that student. After the trip's conclusion, the college's care team conducted an investigation and wrote an internal report on the matter. Its findings included criticizing the president's actions in asking other students to watch over the student rather than placing the student in the care of a medical professional and in not sending the student home. When a local newspaper, the *Wyoming Tribune Eagle*, heard about the matter, it asked for the care team report, but the college said no. Then, when the newspaper came into possession of a leaked copy, the college went to court seeking a restraining order to prevent the newspaper from posting news stories on the trip and the report. The college argued that it would risk losing federal funding because it would be a FERPA violation for the report, which included students' names in it, to be discussed in the news stories. The newspaper said it would not disclose any students' names in its reporting.

Is it a FERPA violation for the newspaper to publish stories on the misbegotten trip, based on the college's report, which includes the students' names?

Decision: In a decision widely derided by free-speech advocates and those who study FERPA,[48] the judge initially granted a temporary restraining order to Laramie County Community College, preventing the *Wyoming Tribune Eagle* from publishing its story. But, eventually, the judge dissolved the restraining order and the story was published.[49] In doing so and in reviewing FERPA and its application to this case, the judge ultimately concluded that the college's claim regarding FERPA liability was "purely speculative and not supported by any evidence before the court."[50] Of course, FERPA and its prospective penalty is only directed at educational institutions and has no bearing on what a news organization does. Furthermore, the *Wyoming Tribune Eagle* never asserted it would publish any students' names (which wouldn't violate FERPA if it had). And the student in question was not even a party to the litigation.

2 – The Case of the Instructor's Attempt to Find the Author of the Complaining Email

In this case from Florida, an adjunct instructor at Santa Fe College went to court to find out who in his class wrote an email to the department chair that, the instructor believed, led to him not being hired again. The student who sent the email complained about the instructor's classroom behaviors, including "his humiliating remarks to students and his unorthodox teaching methodologies."[51] After learning about this email, the instructor asked for a copy so he could defend against what he said were untrue accusations. But the email copy he received had the student's name redacted, which the chair said was required under both Florida and federal FERPA law because the email was "an education record." That was unsatisfactory to the instructor because he believed he needed to know who the complaining student was so he could determine if this student was even able to fairly evaluate the instructor's classroom actions. (For example, did this student have ulterior motives based on a bad grade?) As the instructor, who represented himself in the litigation, said, "To me, it's just un-American that you don't have the right to know who your accuser is."[52]

Is a student email to a college administrator addressing the student's dissatisfaction with an instructor an education record under FERPA that prevents the instructor from knowing who the author is?

Decision: With either conclusion you've reached, you are going to be right. First, the Florida District Court of Appeals ruled that the instructor had a right to know who wrote the dismissive missive. But, months later, after accepting the college's request and holding a second hearing on the matter, the court withdrew its earlier opinion and then reissued a new and opposite opinion. This time, the court concluded that the student-author's name was protected against disclosure by FERPA.[53] In the first round, the court agreed with the instructor that the email wasn't an education record because it was written by a student about a teacher. (Florida's definition of an education record is identical to the federal definition.) In other words, the email was something that was not "directly related" to a student but was directly related to the instructor. The court cited precedent from other states involving similar fact patterns mostly in high-school settings, and in those cases the courts ruled that statements or other documents that were written by students or that focused on the behavior or actions of school employees were not covered by FERPA.

But, with their second bite at the apple, the court took a different approach to what "directly related" means. Here, the court distinguished what is "primarily related" and what is directly related. Even though the email's content was primarily related to the instructor, the court believed, nevertheless, that it still was directly related to the student because the student wrote the email and the email concerned the student's impressions. The court acknowledged its decision was in contrast to those of other courts that concluded the opposite.[54] One issue the court didn't address was whether the email was "maintained" by the college, which is a second prerequisite for something to be an education record. There are a few problems with this decision. A faculty member was accused of engaging in wrongful behavior in class and was denied the opportunity to fully defend himself, including assessing the accuser's motivations. There was no evidence the instructor would have been able to retaliate against the student had the identity been made known, particularly since the instructor was not retained for the next semester. And anonymity isn't possible in much more serious situations, like in cases involving criminal accusations.

3 – The Case of the Student Teacher (Non)recommendation Letter

In this case, a college senior in the school of education at Indiana University was assigned to an elementary school for her student-teaching semester. One of her school of education's professors was assigned to supervise her efforts, which included making regular visits to the student's elementary class. Although the university student-teacher handbook said supervising faculty were to make biweekly visits to observe and interact with the student, there was a dispute in the eventual litigation about whether the professor fully fulfilled this expectation. For her midsemester evaluation of the student, the professor praised the student's classroom-management and lesson-presentation skills as excellent and noted she was well organized. At the end of the semester, the supervising professor issued a formal teaching evaluation and gave the student a passing grade. Later, that school's principal contacted that professor because a teaching job was available and asked the professor for a written evaluation of the student's overall teaching abilities. In the letter—which the student eventually discovered after asking the superintendent why she wasn't hired—the professor first positively described the student as enthusiastic, willing to work, and comfortable with children's parents. But the professor also wrote that the student was a marginal student teacher who had certain weaknesses, including faulty grammatical skills, poor organization and execution skills with respect to lesson plans, poor discipline, inflexibility, and a resistance to criticism. The student sued the university, but not the professor, for libel. The lawsuit also alleged that the university violated her FERPA rights because she said the school of education's handbook prohibited such a letter from being issued without her permission.

Although libel law will be covered in the next chapter, feel free to give this one a try: Does a professor risk being liable for libel (pun intended) for a negative recommendation letter like this one? Is this recommendation letter an education record that requires the student's permission (or waiver) to be issued?

Decision: The Indiana Court of Appeals ruled against the student on both counts, affirming the trial court's dismissal of her lawsuit.[55] Concerning the libel claim, the court believed a legal privilege against being sued for libel applied, namely that the letter was written and sent because both parties involved (Indiana University and the school district) had a "common interest" in communicating freely on these matters. The elementary school has a need in finding the best teachers, and the Indiana University school of education has a responsibility in preparing and evaluating future school teachers. This would protect the letter against a claim of libel if no one involved took advantage of this limited privilege by releasing it to parties who had no need to read it, and no one did. Beyond that, the court said there were no material facts presented that the professor who wrote the letter was motivated by any ill will toward the student. But a dissenting judge wrote that a jury should have been given the chance to decide that matter, in light of the professor's conflicting evaluations of the student and the contradictory evidence about the number of in-class observations the professor made.

As for the FERPA claim, the court ruled that, whatever the school of education's student-teacher handbook said about recommendation letters, it wasn't controlling; FERPA was. To the court, the letter wasn't even an "education record," because the school of education didn't maintain a copy of the letter in its files, since that is part of the FERPA definition of an education record. One point the court did not address, which would have been helpful, is if the contents of the professor's letter were even covered by FERPA. But the court focused on the letter not being maintained.

Notes

1. 20 USCA §1232g (1974).
2. 34 C.F.R. 99.1 et seq (1988).
3. 20 U.S.C.A. § 1232g.
4. 34 C.F.R. 99.1 et seq (1988).
5. "State Laws and Legislation," Student Privacy Compass, May 15, 2017, available at https://studentprivacycompass.org/state-laws-and-legislation/#:~:text=States%20can%20give%20students%20additional,use%20of%20data%2C%20including%20how.
6. 20 U.S.C.A. § 1232g(a)(1)(C)(iii); 20 U.S.C.A. § 1232g(b)(1)(A–L).
7. *Klein Independent School Dist. v. Mattox*, 83o F.2d 576 (5th Cir. 1987).
8. 20 U.S.C.A. § 1232g(a)(2).
9. 34 C.F.R. 99.22.
10. *Lewin v. Medical College of Hampton Roads*, 931 F.Supp. 443 (E.D. Va. 1996).
11. 20 U.S.C.A. § 1232g(d).
12. 34 C.F.R. 99.31(a)(8).
13. "Can Parents Be Informed about Students' Violation of Alcohol and Controlled Substance Rules?," Protecting Student Privacy, U.S. Department of Education, accessed MONTH, DAY, YEAR, https://studentprivacy.ed.gov/faq/can-parents-be-informed-about-students-violation-alcohol-and-controlled-substance-rules.
14. *Doe v. Massachusetts Institute of Technology*, 46 F.4th 61 (1st Cir. 2022).
15. U.S. Department of Education, "Does FERPA Protect the Education Records of Students That Are Deceased?," available at https://studentprivacy.ed.gov/faq/does-ferpa-protect-education-records-students-are-deceased.
16. *James v. Screen Gems, Inc.*, 344 P.2d 799 (Cal. Ct. App. 1959).
17. *Gonzaga University v. Doe*, 536 U.S. 273 (2002).
18. *Frazier v. Fairhaven School Comm.*, 276 F.3d 52 (1st Cir. 2002); *Langadinos v. Bd. of Trustees of University of Massachusetts*, 2013 WL 5507042 (D. Mass. 2013).
19. *Mucklow v. John Marshall Law School*, 531 N.E.2d 941 (Ill. App. Ct. 1988).
20. https://1dca.flcourts.gov/content/download/311095/opinion/11-3049.pdf.
21. Julie Hilden, "A Florida Court Allows a College Professor to Learn the Name of a Student Who Lodged a Complaint against Him: Was This the Right Result?" *Verdict*, July 24, 2012, available at https://verdict.justia.com/2012/07/24/a-florida-court-allows-a-college-professor-to-learn-the-name-of-a-student-who-lodged-a-complaint-against-him.
22. 20 U.S.C.A. § 1232g(a)(4)(A).
23. 39 C.F.R. 99.3.
24. Id.
25. Id.
26. 34 C.F.R 99.3.
27. Yale University, "1607 Information Technology Appropriate Use Policy," last modified August 11, 2020, available at https://your.yale.edu/policies-procedures/policies/1607-information-technology-appropriate-use-policy; Purdue University, "Electronic

Mail (S-7)," October 16, 2017, available at https://www.purdue.edu/policies/information-technology/s7.html.

28. *Owassa Independent School Dist. No.I-011 v. Falvo*, 534 U.S. 426 (2002).

29. 534 U.S. 426, at 436–37 (2002).

30. 20 U.S.C.A. § 1232g(a)(4)(B).

31. U.S. Department of Education, "What Is an Education Record?," available at https://studentprivacy.ed.gov/faq/what-education-record.

32. Kala Shah Surprenant, "FERPA & Virtual Learning during COVID-19," U.S. Department of Education, March 30, 2020, available at https://studentprivacy.ed.gov/sites/default/files/resource_document/file/FERPAandVirtualLearning.pdf.

33. 20 U.S.C.A. § 1232g(a)(4)(B)(i–iv).

34. 34 C.F.R 99.3.

35. *Arista Records LLC v. DOES 1-4*, 589 F.Supp.2d 151 (D. Conn. 2008).

36. 34 C.F.R. 99.3.

37. 20 U.S.C.A. § 1232g(a)(5)(A).

38. 34 C.F.R. 99.3.

39. Id.

40. 20 U.S.C.A. § 1232g(a)(5)(B); 34 C.F.R. 99.37.

41. William & Mary, "Student Records Privacy Policy and Notification of Rights under FERPA," available at https://www.wm.edu/offices/registrar/studentsandalumni/studentrecords/confidprivacy/ferpa-b/; Missouri State, "Family Educational Rights and Privacy Act (FERPA)," available at https://www.missouristate.edu/Registrar/FERPA.htm.

42. 34 C.F.R. 99.37(b).

43. 34 C.F.R. 99.12.

44. *Daniel S. v. Board of Educ. of York Community High School*, 152 F.Supp.2d 949 (N.D. Ill. 2001).

45. *Frasca v. Andrews*, 152 F.Supp.2d 949 (E.D.N.Y. 1979).

46. *Jennings v. the University of North Carolina at Chapel Hill*, 340 F.Supp.2d 679 (M.D.N.C. 2004).

47. Law School Admissions Council, "Applicant References," 2024, available at https://applicantreferences.lsac.org/Release/Logon/Access.aspx.

48. Sommer Ingram, "Judge: FERPA Not Justification for Prior Restraint in Wyo. Newspapers," *Student Press Law Center*, May 25, 2010, available at https://splc.org/2010/05/judge-ferpa-not-justification-for-prior-restraint-on-wyo-newspapers/.

49. Michael Van Cassel and Becky Orr, "Hammon Focus of LCCC Report," *Wyoming Tribune Eagle*, May 26, 2010, available at https://www.wyomingnews.com/news/hammon-focus-of-lccc-report/article_42ae632d-f60f-5fcf-b12e-596e82b7bcf0.html.

50. https://splc.org/wp-content/uploads/2018/12/WyomingTRODissolved.pdf.

51. https://1dca.flcourts.gov/content/download/311095/opinion/11-3049.pdf.

52. Julie Hilden, "Court Allows a College Professor to Learn the Name of a Student Who Lodged a Complaint against Him: Was This the Right Result?," July 24, 2012, available at https://verdict.justia.com/2012/07/24/a-florida-court-allows-a-college-professor-to-learn-the-name-of-a-student-who-lodged-a-complaint-against-him.

53. *Rhea v. Dist. Bd. of Trustees of Santa Fe College*, 109 So.3d 851 (Fla. Dist. Ct. App. 2013).

54. Id., at 857–58.

55. *Olsson v. Indiana University Board of Trustees*, 571 N.E.2d 585 (Ind. Ct. App. 1991).

CHAPTER 6

Faculty and Administrators in Defamation Cases

You Make the Call

- **The Case of the Anthropological Study in Enmity**

Proving that no conflict is as ugly as a proverbial family feud, two anthropology professors' decades-long feud with each other resulted in a defamation lawsuit. According to the court cases, each professor's research focus was on the Huichol Indian community in Mexico. The defendant in this case was the first to observe and study the religious practices of the Huichols, beginning in the 1960s. The plaintiff began his research on the Huichols in the late 1970s, whereupon he began to dispute some of the findings of the first professor, including referring to them as inaccurate. Thus began this rancorous beef. As a result, and over the years, the defendant called the plaintiff "a lousy anthropologist" in a letter to another anthropologist and explained to a museum curator why the plaintiff was unqualified to do an upcoming project on the Huichols. The defendant was also alleged to have said that he thought the plaintiff was anti-Semitic and to have referred to the plaintiff as "paranoid," "delusional," "beset by devils," "crazy," and "[having] little grasp on reality." He also referred to the plaintiff's work as "pursuing a half-assed fantasy." When the plaintiff wrote a book about his own research on the Huichols, he wrote this about the defendant's research: "I discovered what may be the most complicated and fascinating anthropological hoax of the 20th Century." That prompted the defendant to threaten the publisher with libel if the book was published, which got the book contract cancelled. The plaintiff then found a new publisher and revised what he said, producing what he claimed was now a "libel-proof" manuscript. After the book was published, the plaintiff then sued the defendant for defamation and also tortious interference with a contract, related to the cancellation of the initial book contract. (That part of the lawsuit will not be analyzed because it's unrelated to this chapter.) The defendant argued in response to the defamation claim that nothing he was alleged to have said qualified as defamatory.

Are the statements defamatory or, instead, are they something else, such as statements of opinion?

(The answer will be given at the end of the chapter. Consider how the principles in this chapter affect your decision and reasoning.)

Every now and then the headline is "Man Bites Dog: News at 11:00." Even though much of this book concerns thinking about and, hopefully, minimizing the legal risks faculty face in their teaching and research, there are times where the script is flipped. We become Howard Beale and decide we're not going to take it anymore and seek to find in the law a sword rather than a shield. Because damaged reputations are hard to reclaim, faculty file defamation lawsuits more often than you might think, due in part to the instant courage the Internet provides to those with basic typing skills and axes to grind. Whether it is on online professor-rating websites or personal blogs, some students' posts have resulted in students finding themselves on the receiving end of a libel lawsuit and a summons. A professor of communication at a public university in Wisconsin sued a former student for what the professor said was an intentional, malicious campaign of anonymous online postings defaming her as a person and professor, including an animated YouTube video that said, "I have a learning disability and Sally took every opportunity she could to degrade, demean, patronize and verbally attack me when she got me in her private [sic]."[1] (This nationally covered case settled.)[2] A professor at a state university in Texas sued a law student for falsely accusing the professor to the university's equal opportunity office of having an affair with the law student's girlfriend—who was the professor's graduate student.[3] (That case settled.)[4] A tenured sociology professor at a Catholic university in Indiana sued a student newspaper for libel, after it posted various articles the professor said wrongly represented her abortion-rights views following the 2022 overturning of *Roe v. Wade*.[5] That suit led to a discovery of letters and emails that the professor's legal filings allege were an orchestrated attempt by various members of the university community, including other faculty, to remove her.[6] And a former assistant professor at a private research university in New York City sued actor James Franco for defamation, which came after the professor had given Franco a D when Franco was a student in his graduate-level "Directing the Actor" class.[7] Evidently, Franco attended only two of the fourteen classes and, according to the suit, the actor took his D to the administration, which fired the professor.[8] (The professor's suit was dismissed because he failed to serve the lawsuit on Franco within the required time period.)[9]

Faculty and administrators sue each other for defamation, as well. A tenured professor at a state university in Illinois sued a student-affairs vice-president for defamation because, at a faculty meeting where the professor expressed consternation about recent campus police activities, the vice president, who oversees the campus police, mentioned to all in attendance that the professor had been accused of stalking a male student—an accusation the student retracted.[10] (The professor reached a settlement.)[11] Professors have sued one another for libel over claims made in academic journals,[12] while others have sued academic journals for libel, sometimes after the journals retracted those professors' publications.[13] An adjunct professor even sued a US senator for libel, after being awarded the senator's "Golden Fleece of the Month Award," which ridiculed the professor's publicly funded research.[14] (That case went to the US Supreme Court and will be discussed later in the chapter.)

Whether one should sue for defamation is not this chapter's purpose. Only you, with the advice of counsel, can make that decision. Here, the goal is to acquaint you with the key markers of defamation law and how they and their relevant impediments and defenses have been applied to faculty or administrator suits. For example, the outcome of a defamation suit can depend on the classification of the plaintiff and whether the plaintiff qualifies as a "public figure." In those instances, the plaintiff bears a higher burden of proof in a defamation case. Another issue to consider is whether a professor who believes that he or she has been falsely accused of something can even bring a defamation suit if the accusation was made in the course of a college- or university-created grievance or complaint mechanism. Included in this analysis is determining if a defendant has some level of a legal privilege or immunity against the defamation claim.

A Brief Tutorial on Defamation

Please don't stop reading, but defamation law is convoluted—so much so that legal scholars have in the nineteenth and twentieth centuries labelled it "incomprehensible."[15] One legal writer in this century said about defamation that it is "so complex that it is almost impossible to state even the most basic proposition with certainty."[16] Even a US Supreme Court justice likened libel law to a "quagmire."[17] Adding to this perplexity is that a few states include certain types of defamation as crimes. Nevertheless, defamation law can be summarized as follows.

- **False Statement or Assertion of Fact**
  The starting point for defamation is that the defendant made a statement of fact about the plaintiff that was wrong, erroneous, or false. That statement has to be capable of being proven false. For example, which one of the following statements would be defamatory?: a) Kent Kauffman is a 100 percent

certified jerk!; b) Kent Kauffman cheated his way through law school!; c) Kent Kauffman is such a bad professor, he should be "de-tenured!" The answer is b. The other two options are statements of opinion, and opinions are not defamatory. But making or implying an assertion of fact and then couching it in opinion-like language ("Kent Kauffman cheated his way through law school, allegedly") does not automatically absolve the speaker. Of course, courts are often called on to determine what legally qualifies as an opinion, contributing to the sense that defamation law is inscrutable. For example, calling someone "racist" is an opinion, but accusing someone of engaging in "racism" can be defamatory because it implies verifiable actions that (if false) are reputation damaging. Genuine evaluations of colleagues or students, based on professional judgments that involve conclusions of incompetence, even unnecessarily harsh conclusions, are accepted in the academic community and thought not to be defamatory. Hyperbole or satire is also not defamatory, as shown in a noteworthy case where a student newspaper at a state university in Virginia won a dismissal of a libel suit brought by a university administrator whom the paper had called the "Director of Butt Licking."[18]

- **Made to a Third Party (Publication)**
  A defamatory statement is made to someone other than the plaintiff. (Making a statement to the plaintiff in the presence of a third party can suffice.) That is known as publication. Those who pass on defamatory statements can also be liable to the plaintiff as republishers.
- **Fault**
  If the plaintiff is not a public figure or public official, then the plaintiff needs to show negligence (a failure to use reasonable care) on the part of the defendant in making the false statement. But where the plaintiff is a public figure (more on that later) or public official, then the plaintiff must show that the defendant was more than negligent and, instead, acted with "actual malice." That means that the defendant made the defamatory statement with knowledge that it was false or with "reckless disregard" of whether it was false.[19] That is a higher bar to hurdle, and, where faculty are considered public figures, they risk having their defamation suits dismissed unless they can show evidence of this higher standard of fault.
  Because the law is rife with exceptions, always consult an attorney from your state if you are considering bringing a defamation claim. For example, Indiana case law states that a defamation plaintiff needs to show that the defendant's statements were made with malice.[20]
- **Reputation Damage**
  While there are various exceptions, it is incumbent on the plaintiff to show that she suffered an appreciable loss because of the defamatory statement. If a professor can't show that her reputation was damaged, then she is likely to not have a case.[21]

One key exception is "defamation per se," where certain defamatory statements are thought to be harmful enough that no need to show reputation loss is needed. Two examples that are relevant here are when a plaintiff is wrongly accused of sexual misconduct or where defamatory statements impute that the plaintiff committed misconduct in his business or profession. For example, a chancellor at a regional state university in Indiana sued an advisory-board member who wrote a letter to the university president, criticizing the chancellor's character. The chancellor argued the letter was defamation per se, but the appellate court disagreed, concluding the controversial statements were not objectively verifiable and were vague enough to not attribute to the chancellor any misconduct.[22] But, in the case mentioned earlier in the chapter, where a professor sued a law student for accusing him of having an affair with the law student's girlfriend (a student of the professor), the court concluded that the false accusation was defamation per se.[23]

THE TAKEAWAY

Defamation occurs when someone makes a false assertion of fact about the plaintiff to a third person, harming the plaintiff's reputation, and causing a quantifiable loss. If the plaintiff is a public figure or a public official, the plaintiff must show that the defendant made the statement with actual malice, meaning that the defendant knew the statement was false or acted recklessly about whether it was false. Otherwise, negligence is the common standard. Some defamatory statements qualify as defamation per se, meaning that no proof of reputation harm needs to be shown.

Slander versus Libel

Historically and going back centuries, slander was spoken defamation, while libel was printed defamation. The reason for this distinction is the belief that printed defamation is more consequential to a plaintiff due to its permanence. Because of that, a plaintiff in a libel case doesn't have to prove the quantifiable harm (often called special damages) required of slander plaintiffs.[24] Libel claims also may be brought based on visual forms of defamation, such as pictures or films. Some legal commentators have argued that the distinction between slander and libel is arcane and legally irrelevant, particularly in the world of social media and text messaging.[25] Regardless, where an instructor or professor is the object of false statements posted on teacher-rating websites or other online media, that would in many jurisdictions be a libel case. While no instructor would have likely sued over high cumulative evaluations of their "hotness," in 2018 RateMyProfessors

.com removed its chili-pepper icon aspect of its teacher evaluation website after faculty complaints that, beyond being stupid, physical attractiveness metrics send wrong messages about gender biases and stereotypes.[26]

THE TAKEAWAY

Slander is spoken defamation and libel is written or other visually presented defamation. Due to the more permanent nature of libel, it historically doesn't require the plaintiff to prove special damages.

Defenses or Immunity to Defamation Liability

You Make the Call

- **The Case of the Fired Professor Who Sued the Students Who He Said Defamed Him**

An assistant professor of education at a public university in Indiana was informed in April of his third tenure-track year that he would not be retained after his fourth year. The reason given was his unsatisfactory teaching performance. One month later, two graduate students who were also graduate assistants in the school of education filed formal complaints with the university's antiharassment/affirmative action office, accusing the professor of sexual harassment. The university procedures for filing a complaint say they "are not those of a court of law," but they include some elements that are similar. Some of those quasijudicial procedures include requiring that a claim be filed within a limited period, requiring that the accused party be notified of the allegations, and allowing the involved parties to file an appeal to the university president after a determination has been made on the allegations, following an investigation of a campus-appointed fact finder. The person appointed to investigate these accusations was the psychology department chair, who interviewed the two graduate students and thirteen other students as well as some of the professor's colleagues. The investigator eventually issued a report concluding that the professor had created a hostile learning environment, most often in class settings, and had sexually harassed one of the graduate students. Because the other student filed her complaint outside the required time frame, no specific harassment conclusion was reached in her case. The report also praised the two students for having the courage to file their complaints. Consequently, the university removed the professor from teaching responsibilities and from his campus office for his upcoming final year. The professor filed several lawsuits in response, including one against the complaining graduate students for defamation, because of what he said were their false and malicious charges. The students sought to have the lawsuit dismissed, arguing that their accusations were absolutely protected against any defamation lawsuit because they, as complainants, were in the same status as witnesses in court who are benefited by this legal privilege for their testimony. The professor argued that there was no defamation-proof, legal privilege for student accusations made in administrative, university investigations.

Is this professor prevented from suing the students for defamation because they made their accusations in an on-campus, quasijudicial setting?

(The answer will be given at the end of the chapter. Consider how the principles in this chapter affect your decision and reasoning.)

There are a multitude of responses a defendant in a defamation suit can make to end the lawsuit early by a dismissal or at trial. Some of the relevant defenses, including those for faculty, are provided below.

- **Internet Service Providers and Section 230 of the Communications Decency Act**
  Before getting to defenses that could apply to those who make statements that are thought to be defamatory, let's get the easy one out of the way: you can't sue a website for defamation that was the conduit for what you believe is libelous. The first case to establish this involved a hoax in which a man was accused on an America Online bulletin board of being involved in the 1994 Oklahoma City bombing. After receiving death threats and needing police protection, he eventually sued America Online for, first, allowing the posting of false information and, then, when informed of the error, not taking down the false information as it promised it would do. But the Fourth Circuit Court of Appeals dismissed his suit because Section 230 of the 1996 Communications Decency Act[27] grants internet service providers (ISP) immunity against liability, in that they are officially not publishers or speakers of that which third parties put on their websites.[28] Pros and cons on this statute's grant of immunity to ISPs against defamation abound, but, unless the statute is amended, it seems to be settled law that ISPs are not defamation defendants.
- **Truth**
  Because defamation concerns how a publicized false statement affected the plaintiff, truth is traditionally an absolute defense against a defamation claim, including if the statement is harmful. That would include faculty or administrators who report or discuss allegations of student misconduct, because, independent of their ultimate accuracy, it is truthful the allegations were in fact made.[29] Because this is the law we're talking about, there is an exception we find in Massachusetts, which has a statute allowing someone to bring

a libel claim over a truthful statement where the statement was made with "actual malice."[30] Because the case law shows the application of that statute to be quite nuanced, if you work at a Massachusetts college or university and find yourself in a prospective libel situation, consult an attorney—which is my continual advice for those reading this book who believes their work situation has reached a legal zone.

- **Opinion and Critique**

  Because an opinion is not provable as either true or false, it generally is outside the scope of defamation. In fact, opinions are generally protected against defamation by the First Amendment.[31] In a case where a cancer researcher at a public university in Ohio sued a biology professor at a public university in Indiana over the professor's statements in a *New York Times* article on the cancer researcher's work, a federal court concluded that the professor's stated belief that the researcher's laboratory was "violating scientific norms" was First Amendment–protected opinion.[32] But the US Supreme Court has held that, where an opinion implies defamatory facts, that is not a protected statement.[33] For example, the statement "in my opinion, professor X sleeps with his female students who want higher grades," is not a wise opinion to make unless there is a nondefamatory basis for the embedded character assassination.

  Criticism is also included in the opinion category. Much of what faculty do involve evaluations, some of which can be harsh or even cold-blooded, and can lead to defamation suits being filed by students or colleagues. As has already been stated in the chapter, courts tend to accept as nondefamatory the strident criticism that (unfortunately?) has been commonly associated with academia. For example, saying that a colleague had a "meltdown" and a "temper tantrum," or that a student's work was "illogical" were found to be opinions that, as a matter of law, couldn't be defamatory.[34] Bear in mind, protection of a professor's or administrator's professional opinion is accepted when the opinion is tethered to sincerity in the underlying calculations generating the opinion. One can't hurl invectives around like a blindfolded dart thrower and then claim the statements were slung while standing in the safe zone.

- **Satire or Parody**

  Who doesn't love dry wit or a smart-alecky joke? Lots of people. Whatever one thinks of it, satire is generally not defamatory, the reason being that satire or parody is not intended to be taken seriously or literally.[35] That doesn't make being the object of satire pleasant or welcome, as was the case when a student newspaper at a private college in New Jersey once created a spoof edition, complete with an advertisements section that had a phone-sex ad with various administrators listed as being available for calls. One of them brought a defamation suit, which was dismissed because the court concluded that the phony ad in a satiric edition of the paper was parody that no reasonable person would take as anything other than a joke (a bad one, the court noted).[36]

- **The First Amendment and "Strategic Lawsuits against Public Participation" Statutes**

  Beyond the First Amendment's protection of opinion, there is another area where the First Amendment provides a defense to defamation. Because a defamation lawsuit and its costs can be used as a cudgel to silence criticism of important matters that affect others, over thirty states and the District of Columbia have passed legislation that provide defamation defendants the opportunity to have those lawsuits dismissed when they are thought to be meritless because they are intended to silence criticism or are an attempt to prevent the exercise of a constitutional right.[37] Often known as anti–strategic lawsuits against public participation (SLAPP) statutes, these state laws—which are not uniform across the country—establish a protection against defamation claims for those who speak out on "matters of a public concern." What is a matter of public concern, also known as a public issue, was discussed in Chapter 3. The genesis of anti-SLAPP laws goes back to the work of two professors,[38] beginning in the 1980s, and the gist is that members of the community should be free to speak out on public issues without having to face reprisal-styled defamation suits.

  Anti-SLAPP laws have been used in defamation cases involving professors, including when professors were the plaintiffs. For example, in a case from a public university in California, a professor sued an associate dean and the university for defamation, stemming from the professor's involvement in reporting students' sexual-harassment allegations about another faculty member and for having allegedly been called "a liar" for saying other students had complained about that faculty member's behavior. The university sought to have the suit dismissed, based on California's anti-SLAPP law, and won. In a lengthy ruling, the court stated that the defendants' alleged defamatory statements were covered by the statute, including that the statements were made in connection to an official university investigation, which conferred a privilege against defamation liability.[39] (Privileges are discussed below.) But the court allowed part of the professor's retaliation suit to continue.

THE TAKEAWAY

There are certain defenses to defamation that are relevant in faculty lawsuits, including that the allegedly defamatory statement was truthful, that it was an opinion rather than an assertion of fact, that it was criticism, and that it was satire or parody and not reasonably intended to be taken literally. Also, statements on issues that affect the public can be protected against defamation suits through anti-SLAPP laws in those states that have such laws.

Privileges against Defamation Liability

A privilege is a defense that speaks to the situation or the status of the defendant more than to the nature of the statement. As discussed in Chapter 5, students sometimes sue faculty for defamation over unsatisfactory reference letters. A defense that faculty can successfully raise is that they have a qualified privilege to write such letters without being liable for defamation. Key factors in deciding if this privilege applies are whether there is a "common interest" between the speaker and the recipient, whether the communication was made in good faith (sincerity), and whether the letter has not been shared with others who have no reasonable need to see it.[40] A qualified privilege against defamation has been successfully used in situations where a department chair was sued over a negative performance evaluation of a tenure-track faculty member,[41] where faculty were sued by a law student over a plagiarism investigation,[42] and where faculty were sued by a PhD student over communications about the student's grades and internship.[43] But, if a plaintiff could show that the defendant's communication was motivated by some ill will or maliciousness against the student (this issue is covered in Chapter 1), that could overcome a professor's qualified privilege against defamation claims.

Occasionally, a faculty or administrator (or student) might seek to be immunized against being sued because of having an absolute privilege against defamation. One way to think about the difference is that a qualified privilege considers the conditions in which the alleged defamatory statement was made, whereas an absolute privilege is limited to certain proceedings or to persons having a protected status. As was discussed in the first chapter, many states have statutes that provide immunity to government employees from tort claims related to an employee's official actions, including those involving the use of discretionary judgment. That is one of the reasons why it is nearly impossible to sue a professor at a state university over a grade—unless there is evidence the faculty acted with maliciousness or ill will. An absolute privilege against defamation has been occasionally provided to faculty and administrators in situations similar to those described for the qualified privilege. For example, absolute immunity applied to administrators at a state university in Indiana who were sued by a former coach because of statements made to the press about her being fired;[44] to faculty who served in public universities in various states and who were sued for defamation over statements made about the behavior or job performance of the plaintiffs, who were also faculty members;[45] and to faculty who served on a tenure review committee at a public university in Pennsylvania who were sued for defamation by a professor whose tenure case they recommended be denied.[46]

Going against the natural meaning of the language "absolute," sometimes an absolute privilege or immunity against defamation won't apply when the state employee is thought to have made an otherwise protected statement with an improper motive or ill will. In one example of this, a court refused to apply absolute immunity against defamation to a professor who served at a state university in Maryland and who was sued by a former student after the professor made false charges that the student had misused funds of a campus pre-law organization from which the student had resigned because he had grown more uncomfortable with how the professor (who was the organization's advisor) acted toward him.[47] Despite the professor being a government employee acting in an official capacity, the court said there was no automatic immunity against defamation due to the issue of her ill will in making the false charges. That case resulted in a jury award of $200,000 to the student,[48] which the judge then greatly reduced on the grounds that the student "virtually suffered no damage" as a result of being defamed.[49]

THE TAKEAWAY

Faculty and administrators might have a qualified privilege against defamation claims, if the communication at issue was one the faculty had a common interest in sharing with the recipient and it was made in good faith. Beyond that, faculty and administrators at state colleges or universities might have an absolute privilege against defamation claims if state law provides immunity to government employees acting in their official capacity, provided the plaintiff cannot show that the defendant acted with ill will or maliciousness.

Privilege or Immunity against Defamation When Making an On-Campus Accusation

Witnesses in court are granted absolute immunity against defamation for whatever they say under oath, regardless of truthfulness or motive. (Of course, lying under oath is not consequence-free and can be the crime of perjury.) Similarly, this type of protection against a defamation suit has also been applied in college and university settings to students that make accusations of sexual misconduct or accusations related to Title IX. Even though, unlike witnesses in court, complainants don't make allegations under oath, some courts view the settings on campuses where complaints are filed as being "quasijudicial" and such complainants as being deserving of the same defamation-proof status.[50] Some courts have applied this absolute privilege in other settings, including to parents whose children attend secondary schools and who have filed complaints of wrongdoing against their children's school administrators or teachers.

Of course, there is a risk that someone in a witness-like setting could make a false accusation maliciously and be completely immunized against a defamation suit. Despite this possibility, courts that apply this privilege do so on the theory that the need for encouraging the reporting of sexual misconduct without fear of retaliation (particularly when an instructor or professor is the one being accused) outweighs the risk that comes with the complete immunity. Additionally, there is a belief that educational institutions can respond in a disciplinary fashion to those who bring false accusations, thus creating a deterrent.

But not all jurisdictions follow this theory. If you recall the case mentioned on prior occasions in the chapter, where the professor at a state university in Texas sued the student who made a false accusation about the professor having an affair with the student's girlfriend, nothing in the majority's decision involved resolving whether the false accusation was privileged against defamation because it was made to the state university's office of equal opportunity services. That is, that was so until a dissenting opinion in the appeal argued that the student's allegations were absolutely immune against a defamation claim because they were made in a quasijudicial setting.[51]

This type of immunity that has sometimes been given to students has been extended by some courts to faculty when faculty were sued for defamation by colleagues about whom grievance-like accusations were made. In one case from a public university in Indiana, the absolute immunity was granted to multiple faculty members who were sued by a colleague after they filed university complaints about his on-campus actions.[52] Years earlier, the same appellate court dealt with a case where a tenured professor was fired for sexually harassing his supervisor (it is possible) and then sued her for defamation over her accusation. In this case, the court acknowledged the existence of the absolute privilege for students but found the qualified privilege sufficient to dismiss this defamation suit.[53]

Does the Quasijudicial Doctrine Apply to a Private College or University?

Because the judiciary is a part of the government, a question arises whether an institutional act at a private college or university can qualify as quasijudicial? In other words, since a private college is not connected to state government, how can its internal investigation mechanisms have a legal or judicial-like status to trigger a witness-like immunity? Despite the distinction, some courts have applied absolute immunity to such situations in private colleges as they do to such situations in public colleges. In a case from a private art institute in Illinois, an appellate court ruled that the absolute privilege against defamation applied when a female student reported to campus police that a male student sexually assaulted her[54] and then restated those charges to college personnel as they conducted their investigation.[55] The court's theory for providing this complete immunity in this situation in a private college in Illinois was that federal law required the college to report crimes committed on campus and that parts of the campus code of conduct were sourced to federal law.

But other states don't automatically grant private colleges the "quasijudicial" status for sexual-misconduct complaints or allegations made in other internal settings. Therefore, absolute immunity against defamation doesn't apply. For example, the Connecticut Supreme Court ruled, in a case involving a private research university, that the complete immunity against defamation did not apply to those making sexual-misconduct allegations because certain essential, judicial-like safeguards for the accused were missing.[56] Put another way, the disciplinary process wasn't found to be quasijudicial. And California and Pennsylvania courts have refused to grant the absolute privilege against defamation to students or employees at private colleges or universities who were sued for defamation after making internal accusations. The reason for refusing to apply the absolute privilege was that nothing in these proceedings touched on what would have qualified as governmental, including that witnesses weren't put under oath and there was no transcript of what was said.[57] Yet, in another case from a private university in Pennsylvania, the absolute privilege was granted to a professor from an out-of-state university who filed a sexual-misconduct allegation against a Pennsylvania professor at his university because the court thought that filing a grievance with the university's Title IX office implicated the absolute privilege against defamation.[58] (As mentioned at the start of this chapter, defamation law has been called incomprehensible.)

THE TAKEAWAY

Some states treat students as being absolutely immune from being sued for defamation when they make official-misconduct or other Title IX–related charges to campus officials, viewing those allegations as having been made in a quasijudicial setting. Beyond that, absolute immunity has been extended in some jurisdictions to college or university employees who make similar accusations. But it is unclear if the quasijudicial immunity applies to formal accusations made at private colleges or universities.

Professors and Administrators as Public Figures for Defamation Purposes

You Make the Call

- **The Case of the Voice Professor's Sour-Notes Lawsuit against a Former Student**

Because what I know about opera I learned from Bugs Bunny cartoons and *Seinfeld*, I'll get right to the facts of the case, which is about an opera singer and voice professor at a public university in Texas who sued her former student over various online postings the student made about her. The student posted anonymously in an online forum for classical singers, stating that the professor "filed lawsuits against each of her former university employers and against [her current employer]"; "loses an average of 3–4 students out of her studio per semester"; "teaches in unhealthy ways [and] causes vocal problems"; and "talks sh*t on singers and faculty in a serious way." The student also posted on RateMyProfessors.com that the professor's teaching methods caused documented vocal injury; that the professor was distracted and not focused during lessons and was often on computers or her phone while a student was singing; that the professor was not organized and was often late to lessons; that the professor demeaned students and was not respected by faculty, peers, or students; and that the professor had been on faculty probation. After discovering who the anonymous poster was, the professor sued the student. The student then sought to have the lawsuit dismissed on the grounds that the professor was a public figure and, therefore, had to show in her lawsuit that the statements made about her (assuming they were false) were made with "actual malice." That means that the defendant made the statements with knowledge that they were false or with reckless disregard about whether they were false. The professor argued that she was not a public figure for defamation purposes and, therefore, her defamation claim was subject to the traditional negligence standard for proving defamation. Related to this issue of being a public figure, the professor maintained her own website that noted her professional accolades, including her Grammy nomination and her public performances at "prestigious institutions and orchestras in the US and abroad." It also discussed her distinguished teaching career and the successes her voice students have experienced in their careers. Her website also had a "Critical Acclaim" page that included excerpts of positive reviews of her performances in national publications. And her university's faculty web page included much of what was on her personal website, including that she "is recognized internationally for her stunning interpretations of repertoire."

Is this professor a public figure for defamation purposes because of her career-related web presence? If so, that would mean that, as a plaintiff bringing a defamation claim, she would be held to the higher negligence standard and would have to show actual malice?

(The answer will be given at the end of the chapter. Consider how the principles in this chapter affect your decision and reasoning.)

If you choose to sue a student or even a colleague for defamation, believing that the personal and financial costs of litigation are worth spending on your reputation, you will have a more difficult time succeeding if you qualify as a public figure.

As stated earlier in the chapter, a plaintiff that is a public figure or public official must show that the defendant's defamation was made with more than negligence and, instead, was made with "actual malice." This means that the defendant made the defamatory statement with knowledge that it was false or with "reckless disregard" of whether it was false.[59] While the US Supreme Court has acknowledged the impossibility of creating an "infallible definition" of reckless disregard for the truth, in that case the court said this standard involves showing that the publisher of the statement "entertained serious doubts" about its truth.[60] And making winning such a case even more difficult, plaintiffs who are public figures must show actual malice by "clear and convincing" evidence,[61] which is a higher standard of proof in a civil case than the traditional "preponderance of the evidence" standard.

A 1964 US Supreme Court case established that public officials must show actual malice in a defamation case. That rule was extended a few years later to public figures who aren't public officials, in a case where an athletic director of a nonpublic organization sued a magazine for accusing him of conspiring to fix a football game with legendary Alabama football coach, Bear Bryant.[62] For those plaintiffs who need to show actual malice, they are either general-purpose or limited-purpose public figures. And as one federal court likened it, being able to characterize a person as a public figure is so nebulous, it is like "nailing a jellyfish to the wall."[63]

THE TAKEAWAY

Actual malice is the higher standard of proof that public officials and public figures need to meet, by clear and convincing evidence, in a defamation case. Meeting this standard requires proving that the defamatory statement was made with knowledge that it was false or with reckless disregard of whether it was true.

General-Purpose Public Figure

A general-purpose public figure is one whose fame or notoriety makes him or her a public figure in all contexts.[64] It is possible that a professor or administrator, particularly those who have national prominence or who have reached a level of celebrity status, could qualify as a general-purpose public figure. Those who aren't famous can still be general-purpose public figures if they are government officials (also known as public officials) with a sufficient leadership responsibility. For example, a former university vice president of external affairs at a public university in Louisiana sued a former professor from that university for libel, alleging the professor had created an anonymous website falsely lambasting the university and its administration for mismanagement and various abuses of power. Part of the court's ruling in this case included a conclusion that the plaintiff, as public official, was required to meet the actual malice standard.[65] Likewise, an assistant dean and faculty member of a state law school in Arkansas who sued a newspaper and others for libel after it published an article that challenged the plaintiff's own academic bona fides was held to the public official defamation standard.[66] (The court also believed the alleged defamation was speech on a matter of public concern, entitling it to some First Amendment protection.)

Professors at state educational institutions who aren't administrators can also qualify as public officials if they have sufficient, bureaucratic decision-making power. For example, after chairing a faculty search committee, a public law-school professor in Illinois filed a defamation suit. Part of the litigation involved the court concluding the plaintiff was (for defamation purposes) a public official, while, in the same defamation case, the assistant professor who was hired (and who also filed a defamation claim) was found not to be a public official because, the court said, he had no decision-making responsibility.[67] Even a college student at a public university who was a member of the student senate was classified as a public official for defamation purposes after suing the student newspaper, which, in an editorial, called him, among other things, "the campus demagogue."[68]

And, with a nod to the inconsistency of this area of defamation law, one can find similarly situated professors who have been declared not to be public figures. In one case from a public university in Louisiana, a math department chair sued two department colleagues over public accusations that the chair had committed payroll fraud, and an associate professor in the same case sued the same colleagues over accusations that the professor committed book-publication deceit. While determining that the plaintiffs didn't qualify as public officials (providing them the lower negligence standard for defamation), the appellate court still concluded that the alleged defamatory statements were just harsh criticism and opinion.[69] And, in a case where a long-standing head coach of a women's basketball team (also a tenured faculty member) at a public university in the District of Columbia sued her employer for defamation after it fired her for what it publicly said was her misuse of public funds, a court of appeals said that she was not a public official or a general-purpose public figure.[70] She exercised no policy-making authority, and her coaching success didn't automatically make her a public figure. Likewise, the administrators she sued were not entitled to any immunity or privilege against defamation.[71] The jury awarded her a six-figure sum.

THE TAKEAWAY

A general-purpose public figure is someone who is either a government official with sufficient authority or someone who has reached a level of fame or notoriety and is a public figure in all contexts. As defamation plaintiffs, general-purpose public figures have to show that the defendant made any defamatory statement with actual malice. Although the law is not consistent across jurisdictions, public-university administrators and faculty with sufficient decision-making authority can qualify as general-purpose public figures.

Limited-Purpose Public Figure

A limited-purpose public figure is a public figure in a limited set of situations, often in those involving a public issue. Suing someone for defamation and becoming well known because of the lawsuit doesn't automatically make the plaintiff a limited-purpose public figure; generally, the public issue or controversy needs to exist before the defamation suit. In the case mentioned earlier in the chapter, where an adjunct professor and director of research at a state hospital sued a US senator for announcing the professor's research as winner of a faux award for wasteful government spending, the US Supreme Court ruled the professor was not a public figure and, therefore, was not required to show actual malice in his defamation claim against the senator.[72] In so doing, the court first declared that the professor had not reached the prominence in society that would make someone a general-purpose public figure. Nor had he—by applying for grants and publishing his research—become a limited-purpose public figure, because he had not inserted himself into the forefront of a controversy in order to help affect its resolution. Furthermore, the court noted, suing for defamation over ridicule of his research didn't bootstrap him into becoming a public figure. And, in what hopefully was an unintentionally unfortunate assessment of the academic profession, the court said that the professor's activities and profile were much like the "countless members of his profession," whose work reaches a "relatively small category of professionals."[73]

Where professors are involved in public-interest matters, or where they make their professional activities a prominent part of their public profile, they can qualify as limited-purpose public figure in cases on those matters. In a Vietnam-era case from Texas where a professor sued a newspaper for publishing a "letter to the editor" that called the professor a traitor and more, due to his public statements on welfare, the professor was found to be a public figure because his anti-war demonstrations had brought him the kind of public attention that generated letters to the editor like the one over which he sued.[74]

In an acrimonious divorce case between two law professors,[75] where the wife wrote a book in which she made various and unsavory allegations about her husband, one issue for the court to resolve in the husband's defamation suit was whether he was a public figure.[76] Being included in his wife's book didn't, on its own, make him a public figure. And, because he was found to be a private figure, he only needed to prove negligent defamation. But the court decided the wife's adultery accusations were nondefamatory opinion, because they were based on rumor and the wife's beliefs, rather than on underlying facts that could be proven false.[77] Finally, remembering again the case of the professor in Texas who was falsely accused of having an affair with one of his students, in that case, the public-figure issue was considered. But, even though the professor was tenured and an interim department chair, the court concluded he was neither a public official nor a public figure due to fame; nor was he a limited-public figure because nothing related to his defamation suit showed that he sought any public interest or comment.[78]

THE TAKEAWAY

Professors and administrators can qualify as limited-purpose public figures. A limited-purpose public figure is one who, as a defamation plaintiff, has attained public-figure status with respect to an underlying public matter or an issue that the suit concerns. As defamation plaintiffs, they would have to show that any defamatory statement was made with actual malice.

Final Takeaways

- Defamation occurs when someone makes a false assertion of fact about the plaintiff to a third person, harming the plaintiff's reputation and causing a quantifiable loss. If the plaintiff is a public figure or a public official, the plaintiff must show that the defendant made the statement with actual malice, meaning that the defendant knew the statement was false or that the defendant acted recklessly about whether it was true. Otherwise, negligence is the standard. Some defamatory statements qualify as defamation per se, meaning that no proof of quantifiable harm needs to be shown.
- Slander is spoken defamation, and libel is written or other visually presented defamation. Due to the more permanent nature of libel, proving libel historically doesn't require the plaintiff to prove special damages.
- There are certain defenses to defamation that are relevant in faculty lawsuits, including that the allegedly defamatory statement was truthful, that it was an opinion rather than an assertion of fact, that it was criticism, and that it was satire or parody and was not reasonably intended to be taken literally. Also, statements on issues that affect the public can be protected by anti-SLAPP legislation in states that have such legislation.
- Faculty who are defamation defendants might have a qualified privilege against being sued, if the communication at issue was one the faculty had a common interest in sharing with the recipient and it was made in good faith.

Beyond that, faculty at state colleges or universities might have an absolute privilege against being sued if state law provides immunity to government employees acting in their official capacity, provided the plaintiff cannot show that the defendant acted with ill will or maliciousness.

- Some states treat students as being immune from being sued for defamation when they make official misconduct or other Title IX–related charges to campus officials, because some courts treat those allegations as having been made in a quasijudicial setting. Beyond that, immunity has been extended in some jurisdictions to college or university employees who make similar accusations. But it is unclear if quasijudicial, absolute immunity applies to accusations made at private colleges or universities.
- Actual malice is the higher standard of proof that plaintiffs who are public officials and public figures need to prove, by clear and convincing evidence, in a defamation case. This standard requires showing that the defamatory statement was made with knowledge that it was false or with reckless disregard of whether it was true.
- A general-purpose public figure is one who is either a government official or one who has reached a level of fame or notoriety and is a public figure in all contexts. As defamation plaintiffs, they would have to show that the defendant made any defamatory statement with actual malice. Although the law is not consistent across jurisdictions, public-university administrators and faculty with sufficient decision-making authority can qualify as general-purpose public figures.
- Professors and administrators can qualify as limited-purpose public figures. A limited-purpose public figure is one who, as a defamation plaintiff, has attained public-figure status with respect to an underlying public matter or an issue that the suit concerns. As defamation plaintiffs, they would have to show that any defamatory statement was made with actual malice.

How Did You Make the Calls?

1 – The Case of the Anthropological Study in Enmity

Here, two anthropology professors' decades-long feud resulted in a defamation lawsuit. According to the court cases, each professor's research focus was on the Huichol Indian community in Mexico. The defendant in this case was the first to observe and study the religious practices of these Indians, beginning in the 1960s. The plaintiff began his research on the Huichols in the late 1970s, whereupon he began to dispute some of the findings of the first professor, including referring to them as inaccurate. Thus began this rancorous beef. As a result and over the years, the defendant called the plaintiff "a lousy anthropologist" in a letter to another anthropologist and explained to a museum curator why the plaintiff was unqualified to do an upcoming project on the Huichol Indians.

The defendant was also alleged to have said he thought the plaintiff was anti-Semitic, and he referred to the plaintiff as "paranoid," "delusional," "beset by devils," "crazy," and "[having] little grasp on reality." He also referred to the plaintiff's work as "pursuing a half-assed fantasy." When the plaintiff wrote a book about his own research on the Huichol Indians, he wrote this about the defendant's research: "I discovered what may be the most complicated and fascinating anthropological hoax of the 20th Century." That prompted the defendant to threaten the publisher with libel if the book was published, which got the book contract cancelled. The plaintiff then found a new publisher and revised what he said, producing what he claimed was now a "libel-proof" manuscript. After the book was published, the plaintiff then sued the defendant for defamation and also tortious interference with a contract, related to the cancellation of the initial book contract. (That part of the lawsuit has not been analyzed because it's unrelated to this chapter.) The defendant argued in response to the defamation claim that nothing he was alleged to have said qualified as defamation.

Are the statements defamatory or, instead, are they something else, such as statements of opinion?

Decision: The New Mexico Supreme Court ruled in favor of the defendant-anthropologist, dismissing the lawsuit with respect to the defamation claims and with respect to the claim that the defendant tortiously interfered with the plaintiff-anthropologist's first book contract.[79] That decision overturned an earlier decision by the New Mexico Court of Appeals, which concluded that at least some of the plaintiff's defamation claims and the tortious-interference-with-a-contract claim should not be dismissed. In short, the New Mexico Supreme Court concluded the various statements and claims the defendant made about the plaintiff weren't, as a matter of law, defamatory. (Even the lower appellate court earlier concluded that the defendant referring to the plaintiff as anti-Semitic wasn't defamatory because it was a subjective opinion.)[80] Summarily, the evidence presented up to that point in the litigation showed that the invectives the defendant spread about the plaintiff had no effect on the recipients' opinions of the plaintiff. The plaintiff didn't suffer a loss to his professional reputation because of what the defendant said about him (regardless of their veracity). In other words, the court's ruling can be summarized as "no harm, no foul." For example, one person in the anthropology community to whom the defendant said that the plaintiff's alma mater had "disowned" him and "were sorry they had ever given him a doctor's degree" didn't see the comments as defamatory. In fact, she said "I would say [some of the statements] are extreme but they are not outside the range of what goes on in academic talk."[81] These kinds of statements might have been defamatory if anyone took them literally, but that's not the case in the academic community, the court noted.

As such, the statements were understood by the recipients to be opinions, and opinions aren't defamatory. Another anthropologist stated in a deposition that what he was told by the defendant about the plaintiff was "typical of what he hears in the anthropological community." The court said that, in a broader sense, the defendant's statements about the plaintiff were commonplace criticism occurring in the academic community, whose members the court stated are able to recognize the "subjective character" of them and to "discount them accordingly."[82]

2 – The Case of the Fired Professor Who Sued the Students Who He Said Defamed Him

In this case, an assistant professor of education at Purdue University Fort Wayne (the university where I work, at that time called Indiana University Purdue University Fort Wayne) was informed in April of his third tenure-track year that he would not be retained after his fourth year. The reason he was given was his unsatisfactory teaching performance. One month later, two graduate students who were also graduate assistants in the school of education filed formal complaints with the university's antiharassment/affirmative action office, accusing the professor of sexual harassment. The procedures for filing a complaint say they "are not those of a court of law," but they include some elements that are similar. Some of those quasijudicial procedures include requiring that claims be filed within a set time period, requiring that the accused party be notified of the allegations, and allowing the parties to file an appeal to the university president after a determination has been made on the allegations, following an investigation of a campus-appointed fact finder. The person appointed to investigate the accusations was the psychology department chair, who interviewed the two graduate students and thirteen other students, as well as some of the professor's colleagues. The investigator eventually issued a report concluding that the professor had created a hostile learning environment, most often in class settings, and had sexually harassed one of the graduate students but that, because the other student filed her complaint outside the required time frame, no specific harassment conclusion was reached in her case. The report also praised the two students for having the courage to file their complaints. As a result, the university removed the professor from teaching responsibilities and from his campus office for his upcoming final year. The professor filed several lawsuits in response, including suing the complaining graduate students for defamation, because of what he said were their false and malicious charges. The students sought to have the lawsuit dismissed, arguing that their accusations were absolutely protected against any defamation lawsuit because they were in the same status as witnesses in court, who are benefited by this legal privilege for their testimony. The professor argued that there was no defamation-proof, legal privilege for student accusations made in administrative investigations.

Is this professor prevented from suing the students for defamation because they made their accusations in an on-campus, quasijudicial setting?

Decision: The Indiana Supreme Court ruled in favor of the students, dismissing the former professor's defamation lawsuit against them.[83] Even though some elements of a judicial proceeding were missing from this type of investigation, including that no witness was put under oath and that the accused person had no right to cross-examination or the gathering of evidence, the court believed this type of "quasijudicial" process warranted completely protecting the students against being sued over the substance of their harassment complaints. Although this is more protection against being sued for defamation than is given to those who file criminal complaints with the police, the court thought an "absolute privilege" (immunity against being sued), as is given to witnesses in court, was necessary because educators are in a position of authority over students. This power imbalance can make fear of being retaliated against an obstacle to filing harassment complaints. And the court thought that a school's power to punish those who file false grievances was a sufficient deterrent to the filing of false charges. Other courts in different states have cited this case approvingly but expressed uncertainty about whether this case's decision applies to student complaints filed in private universities.[84]

3 – The Case of the Voice Professor's Sour-Notes Lawsuit against a Former Student

In this case, an opera singer and voice professor at the University of North Texas sued a former student over various online postings the student made about her. The student, who attempted anonymity, posted on an online forum for classical singers, stating that the professor "filed lawsuits against each of her former university employers and against [her current employer]"; "loses an average of 3–4 students out of her studio per semester"; "teaches in unhealthy ways [and] causes vocal problems"; and "talks sh*t on singers and faculty in a serious way." The student also posted on RateMyProfessors.com, stating that the professor's teaching methods caused documented vocal injury; that the professor was distracted and not focused during lessons and was often on computers or her phone while a student was singing; that the professor was not organized and was often late to lessons; that the professor demeaned students and was not respected by faculty, peers, or students; and that the professor had been on faculty probation. The student sought to have the lawsuit dismissed on the grounds that the professor was a public figure and, therefore, had to show in her lawsuit that the statements made about her (assuming they were false) were made with "actual malice." That means that the defendant made the statements with knowledge that they were false or with reckless disregard about whether they were false. The professor argued that she was not a public figure for defamation purposes and, therefore, the case was subject to the lower, traditional negligence standard for proving defamation. Related to this issue, the professor maintained her own website that noted her professional accolades, including her Grammy nomination and her public performances at "prestigious institutions and orchestras in the US and abroad." It also discussed her distinguished teaching career and the successes her voice students have experienced in their careers. Her website also had a "Critical Acclaim" page that included excerpts of positive reviews of her performances in national publications. And her university's faculty web page incorporated much of what was on her personal website, including that she "is recognized internationally for her stunning interpretations of repertoire."

Is this professor a public figure for defamation purposes because of her career-related web presence, which would mean she is held to the higher negligence standard—actual malice?

Decision: The Texas Court of Appeals affirmed the lower court's decision and dismissed the lawsuit, concluding the professor was a limited-purpose public figure.[85] Because of that, the court found there to be insufficient evidence that the student's postings were made with the required actual malice, which would mean that the student made the statements with knowledge that they were false or with reckless disregard about whether they were false. The court discussed two kinds of public figures: 1) general-purpose public figures, who are those with a significant level of fame or notoriety; and 2) limited-purpose public figures, who are only public figures for a limited range of issues surrounding a particular public controversy. And, here, the court determined the professor to be a limited-purpose public figure because there was a "public controversy" about her status and fitness as a voice teacher, which affected more than her and the student she sued. It affected other potential or current students. Next, the court found that the professor had more than a trivial role in this public controversy because she actively promoted her career—which is benefited by regular media attention—and its accomplishments. And because the professor intertwined her opera renown with her voice-teaching credentials, and because the statements the student posted about her related to her as a voice teacher/professor, the linkage to her being at least a limited-purpose public figure was there, according to the court. As to her argument that she was being punished with public-figure status for promoting her career, the court served her an Abraham Lincoln quote: "[w]hat kills the skunk is the publicity it gives itself."[86]

Notes

1. https://www.insidehighered.com/news/2014/05/23/professor-sues-student-over-his-online-reviews-her-course.

2. https://www.gazettextra.com/archives/case-involving-uw-whitewater-professor-who-sued-former-student-over-online-comments-is-settled/article_143a892e-cbfc-59ed-9291-f24d2682ac8d.html.

3. *Hoskins v. Fuchs*, 517 S.W.3d 834 (Tex. App. 2016).

4. https://www.gazettextra.com/archives/case-involving-uw-whitewater-professor-who-sued-former-student-over-online-comments-is-settled/article_143a892e-cbfc-59ed-9291-f24d2682ac8d.html.

5. https://www.insidehighered.com/news/quick-takes/2023/08/01/notre-dame-professor-sues-student-newspaper.

6. https://www.chronicle.com/article/at-notre-dame-documents-suggest-a-concerted-effort-to-oust-a-professor-over-her-views-on-abortion?emailConfirmed=true&supportSignUp=true&supportForgotPassword=true&email=kauffmak%40pfw.edu&success=true&code=success&bc_nonce=0psqj3rkyymoi94b8n2zah.

7. https://www.businessinsider.com/james-franco-sued-by-nyu-professor-2012-9.

8. https://www.theguardian.com/film/2011/dec/20/james-franco-lawsuit-nyu-professor.

9. https://www.hollywoodreporter.com/business/business-news/james-franco-wins-lawsuit-nyu-443994/.

10. *Capeheart v. Northern Illinois University*, 2010 WL 894052 (N.D. Ill 2010).

11. https://www.insidehighered.com/quicktakes/2014/01/28/northeastern-illinois-settles-professor-defamation-suit#.

12. *Ezrailson v. Rohrich*, 65 S.W.3d 373 (Tex. App. 2001).

13. https://retractionwatch.com/2019/12/02/pitt-researchers-sue-journal-for-defamation-following-retraction/.

14. *Hutchinson v. Proxmire*, 443 U.S. 111 (1979).

15. John Townshend, *A Treatise on the Wrongs Called Slander and Libel and on the Remedy by Civil Action of Those Wrongs* 24 (1868); Diane L. Borden, "Patterns of Harm: An Analysis of Gender and Defamation," *Comm. L. & Pol'y* 2 (1997): 105–6.

16. Lyrissa Barnett Lidsky, "Silencing John Doe: Defamation & Discourse in Cyberspace," *Duke Law Journal* 49, no. 855–946 (2000).

17. *Curtis Publishing Co. v. Butts*, 388 U.S. 130 (1967).

18. *Yeagle v. Collegiate Times*, 497 S.E.2d 136 (Va. 1998).

19. *New York Times Co. v. Sullivan*, 376 U.S. 254 (1964).

20. *Kitco Inc. v. Corporation for General Trade*, 706 N.E.2d 581 (Ind. Ct. App. 1999); *McQueen v. Fayette County School Corp.*, 711 N.E.2d 62 (Ind. Ct. App. 1999).

21. *Fikes v. Furst*, 81 P.3d 545 (N.M. 2003).

22. *Wartell v. Lee*, 47 N.E.3d 381 (Ind. Ct. App. 2015).

23. *Hoskins v. Fuchs*, 517 S.W.3d 834 (Tex. App. 2016).

24. *Gertz v. Robert Welch, Inc.*, 418 U.S. 323 (1974).

25. Leslie Yalof Garfield, "The Death of Slander," *Columbia Journal of Law and the Arts* 35, no. 17 (2011).

26. https://www.insidehighered.com/news/2018/07/02/rate-my-professors-ditches-its-chili-pepper-hotness-quotient.

27. 47 U.S.C.A. § 230 (1996).

28. *Zeran v. America Online, Inc.*, 129 F.3d 327 (4th Cir. 1997).

29. *Averett v. Hardy*, 2020 WL 1033543 (W.D. Ky. 2020).

30. MA ST 231 § 92 (2020).

31. *Croce v. Sanders*, 459 F.Supp.3d 997 (S.D. Ohio 2020).

32. Id.

33. *Milkovich v. Lorain Journal Co.*, 497 U.S. 1 (1990).

34. *Dragulescu v. Virginia Union University*, 223 F.Supp.3d 499 (E.D. Va. 2016); *Seitz-Partridge v. Loyola University of Chicago*, 987 N.E.2d 34 (Ill. App. Ct. 2013).

35. *Hustler Magazine, Inc. v. Falwell*, 485 U.S. 46 (1988).

36. *Walko v. Kean College of New Jersey*, 561 A.2d 680 (N.J. Super. Ct. App. Div. 1988).

37. https://www.rcfp.org/anti-slapp-legal-guide/#:~:text=As%20of%20September%202023%2C%2033,New%20Jersey%2C%20New%20Mexico%2C%20New.

38. G. W. Pring and P. Canan, *SLAPPs: Getting Sued for Speaking Out* (Philadelphia: Temple University Press, 1996).

39. *Laker v. Board of Trustees of California State University*, 244 Cal.Rptr.3d 238 (Cal. Ct. App. 2019).

40. *Olsson v. Indiana University Board of Trustees*, 571 N.E.2d 585 (Ind. Ct. App. 1991).

41. *Mbarika v. Bd. of Supervisors of Louisiana State University*, 992 So.2d 551 (La. Ct. App. 2008).

42. *Beauchene v. Mississippi College*, 986 F.Supp.2d 755 (S.D. Miss. 2013).

43. *Leitner v. Liberty University*, 2020 WL 7128972 (W.D. Va. 2020).

44. *Bull v. Board of Trustees of Ball State University*, 2012 WL 1564061 (S.D. Ind. 2012).

45. *DePree v. Sanders*, 2008 WL 4457796 (S.D. Miss. 2008); *White v. Trew*, 736 S.E.2d 166 (N.C. 2013).

46. *Kull v. Guise*, 81 A.3d 148 (Pa. Commw. Ct. 2013).

47. *Brown v. Brockett*, 2012 WL 1552783 (D. Md. 2012).

48. https://thedailyrecord.com/2013/03/28/jury-awards-200k-to-student-defamed-by-professor/.

49. *Brown v. Brockett*, 2013 WL 8705901 (D. Md. 2012).

50. *Hartman v. Keri*, 883 N.E.2d 774 (Ind. 2008).

51. *Hoskins v. Fuchs*, 517 S.W.3d 834, at 845 (Tex. App. 2016).

52. *Board of Trustees of Purdue University v. Eisenstein*, 87 N.E.3d 481 (Ind. Ct. App. 2017).

53. *Haegert v. McMullan*, 953 N.E.2d 1223 (Ind. Ct. App. 2011).

54. *Razavi v. Walkuski*, 55 N.E.3d 252 (Ill. App. Ct. 2016).

55. *Razavi v. School of the Art Institute of Chicago*, 122 N.E.3d 361 (Ill. App. Ct. 2018).

56. *Khan v. Yale University*, 295 A.3d 855 (Conn. 2023).
57. *Harris v. St. Joseph's University*, 2014 WL 1910242 (E.D. Pa. 2014); *Overall v. University of Pennsylvania*, 412 F.3d 492 (3rd Cir. 2005); *Heineke v. Santa Clara University*, 2017 WL 6026248 (N.D. Cal. 2017).
58. *Fogel v. University of the Arts*, 2019 WL 1384577 (E.D. Pa. 2019).
59. *New York Times Co. v. Sullivan*, 376 U.S. 254 (1964).
60. *St. Amant v. Thompson*, 390 U.S. 727, at 730–31 (1968).
61. *New York Times Co. v. Sullivan*, 376 U.S. 254 (1964).
62. *Curtis Publishing Co. v. Butts*, 388 U.S. 130 (1967).
63. *Rosanova v. Playboy Enterprises, Inc.*, 411 F.Supp. 440, at 443 (S.D. Ga. 1976).
64. *Gertz v. Robert Welch, Inc.*, 418 U.S. 323 (1974).
65. *Baxter v. Doe*, 868 So.2d 958 (2nd Cir. 2004).
66. *Gallman v. Carnes*, 254 Ark. 987 (Ark. 1973).
67. *Grossman v. Smart*, 807 F.Supp. 1404 (C.D. Ill. 1992).
68. *Klahr v. Winterble*, 418 P.2d 404 (Ariz. Ct. App. 1966).
69. *Foote v. Sarafyan*, 432 So.2d 877 (La. Ct. App. 1983).
70. *Moss v. Stockard*, 580 A.2d 1011 (D.C. 1990).
71. Id.
72. *Hutchinson v. Proxmire*, 443 U.S. 111 (1979).
73. Id., at 135.
74. *El Paso Times, Inc. v. Trexler*, 447 S.W.2d 403 (Tex. 1969).
75. https://www.usatoday.com/story/news/nation/2013/08/12/ohio-17-year-divorce-fight/2646423/.
76. *Lassiter v. Lassiter*, 456 F.Supp.2d 876 (E.D. Ky. 2006), affirmed by *Lassiter v. Lassiter*, 280 Fed.Appx. 503 (6th Cir. 2008).
77. Id.
78. *Hoskins v. Fuchs*, 517 S.W.3d 834, at 843 (Tex. App. 2016).
79. *Fikes v. Furst*, 81 P.3d 545 (N.M. 2003).
80. *Fikes v. Furst*, 61 P.3d 855, at 863 (N.M. Ct. App. 2003).
81. *Fikes v. Furst*, 81 P.3d 545, at 550 (N.M. 2003).
82. Id., at 551.
83. *Hartman v. Keri*, 883 N.E.2d 774 (Ind. 2008).
84. *Khan v. Yale University*, 27 F.4th 805 (2nd Cir. 2022).
85. *Lane v. Phares*, 544 S.W.3d 881 (Tex. App. 2018).
86. Id., at 890.

CHAPTER 7

Employment Protection, Tenure Matters, and the Law

You Make the Call

- **The Case of the Handbook Section Switcheroo**

As musician and songwriter Tom Waits wrote, "The large print giveth, and the small print taketh away."[1] And so it was at a public college in Colorado where, within months after the legislature reclassified the college and created a new board of trustees, in 2002, the board revised the faculty handbook, effectively neutering tenure without eliminating it. The former version of the handbook, in existence since 1994, defined the meaning of tenure and said that tenure was granted to reinforce "the concept of academic freedom." It also said that the employment of tenured faculty could only be terminated for cause or due to a reduction in force (RIF). The relevant section in the handbook on grounds for termination included the RIF policy and, in such an event, gave employment priority to tenured faculty over nontenured faculty. It also said that, if tenured faculty were laid off, "every reasonable effort" would be made to relocate them in the college. As well, the 1994 handbook had layers of procedure, including appeals processes, for situations of termination for cause and for RIF situations. But the 2003 handbook eliminated those parts and replaced them with a section giving the president the power to decide which faculty would be laid off in RIF situations, based on various factors, one of which was tenure. That section also said that the "primary consideration shall be the maintenance of a sound and balanced educational program." The new RIF policy also drastically cut back on the procedure to be followed, including appeals processes, for faculty chosen for termination. For example, the 1994 policy provided for judicial review of a final decision, whereas the 2003 policy placed final authority in the president, after consulting with the board—expressly prohibiting any further objection or legal action.

Five tenured faculty members and the Colorado Teachers Federation went to court, seeking an injunction (a court order telling a party to stop or start doing something) and a declaration that the new handbook breached their employment contract and violated their due-process rights. Essentially, the faculty argued that the 1994 employee handbook vested them with tenure rights that couldn't be retroactively and unilaterally altered by the 2003 handbook and its RIF policy. (A "vested" right is one that presently exists and can't be taken away without the owner's consent.) The board responded that the 1994 handbook wasn't immutable and that the board had the legislatively granted authority to revise it in the best interests of the institution and, more specifically, to have financial flexibility to serve the needs of its diverse student body. In other words, the college used a lot of part-time and nontenured faculty, and the board argued that the college needed the power to cancel classes when they weren't financially viable. Terminating the employment of tenured faculty was a cost of doing business, so to speak. Part of the evidence in the litigation included the testimony of a tenure expert who testified that the 2003 handbook revisions violated the history of and the cultural expectations created by tenure, including those created by AAUP policy statements. In response, the board argued that there was no evidence that the tenured faculty expressly relied on the 1994 handbook or that it was made with consideration of the AAUP's statements.

Can this revised faculty handbook unilaterally remove employment protections for tenured faculty in instances of reductions in force?

(The answer will be given at the end of the chapter. Consider how the principles in this chapter affect your decision and reasoning.)

Is academic freedom a reality without tenured faculty? Lofty phrases and high-minded assertions about what academic freedom stands for only have practical effect if one can exercise the principle without needing to regularly go to court to ensure it. While there is no universal agreement on the meaning and application of academic freedom, whatever it is belongs to all faculty. But tenured faculty are those whose status provides them the best chance to practice and defend it. One court put it explicitly:

> The purpose of tenure, as used in the academic community, is the preservation of academic freedom and the correlative protection of economic security for teachers. It insures that a professor will not lose his job for exercising his academic freedom, namely, his rights to teach, to think and to speak in accordance with his conscience in the traditions of the academic community.[2]

Is it merely coincidence that those who most strongly criticize tenure as wasteful or superfluous also advocate for laws that put faculty and librarians at legal risk for actions that were historically safeguarded by academic freedom but are now loosely labeled as offensive or un-American? More than a few states, including Texas, Florida, South Carolina, Iowa, and Ohio, have attempted to eliminate tenure.[3] And, when faculty sue over what they believe to be an infringement or denial of academic freedom, so many of those cases are brought by tenured professors. That would make sense. Nontenured faculty, including the legion of part-time faculty who work so hard for so little, often lack the resources, much less the job security, needed to take on their employer or, in more recent days, their state legislature.

Exceptions can be found to the view that faculty want the tenure system to continue in its historically constructed form. The book, *The Questions of Tenure*,[4] edited by a Harvard scholar of higher education, examines and challenges traditional notions of tenure. There is also the case of an accomplished and distinguished business-school professor at a public university in Texas who repeatedly refused tenure and has argued that tenure is unnecessary for academic freedom.[5] (He won a case against his university on what he thought were academic-freedom violations consisting of retaliation against him because of his anti-tenure stance[6] and has litigated other employment-based claims against his university over what he contends is connected to his anti-tenure views.)[7] As well, one can find some survey evidence showing that more faculty who are under the age of forty believe higher education would be improved by the elimination of tenure than do older faculty.[8]

There is another, uncomfortable aspect to this challenging tenure discussion. Some faculty who have tenure and are part of the multilayers of tenure-recommendation decisions can—and occasionally do—use their influence in ways that can make the tenure review process seem like a derivation of the medieval and early-English Star Chamber courts. While the qualitative aspect of reviewing a tenure case cannot be eliminated, candidates that have no idea if they are meeting or have met the applicable standards along their tenure-track journey are working in a system that allows jealousy or some other irrelevant issue to masquerade as professional judgment. Then there is the possibility that a faculty member seems, on paper, to have met departmental or school standards for promotion and tenure, but a negative decision is reached on vague grounds, like the candidate grades too easily or has not made a significant-enough contribution to his or her discipline.

Boards of trustees, also known as boards of regents or overseers, are generally empowered to grant tenure. Even if a board is considered the rubber stamp for the chancellor or president's decision, the board has the final say. As has been the case in recent high-profile cases, boards of trustees might sit on a tenure case or refuse to grant it even when it has been recommended at every level below.[9] Despite that they collectively possess little direct knowledge about or experience with reviewing a faculty member's professional worthiness, boards hold tenure's "sword of Damocles." In fact, courts have ruled against faculty who sued after being denied tenure even though they were hired with a promise of tenure, concluding that, unless special circumstances exist, only boards of trustees may provide it.[10] And, as discussed in earlier chapters, courts rarely entertain lawsuits involving faculty or students in their roles as faculty or students. In light of the realization that the standards that are used in the judgments that are reached in the tenure process are largely outside the scope of judicial review, deciding if a tenure-denial lawsuit might be worth the financial and career-impacting costs of suing is momentous.

Finally, there is the issue of firing a tenured professor. Despite the folklore and the protestations made by anti-tenure interest groups, tenured professors are not guaranteed their jobs forever. Their employment can—and does—get terminated for reasons that include financial exigency and "adequate" or just cause. But tenured professors, particularly at public institutions, have something the nontenured do not, which is a property right in their employment. What it means to have a property right in one's employment will be discussed later, but, at this point, it can be said that those who have a property right in their employment can only be fired for "just cause," which necessitates that internally accorded or legally granted due-process turnstiles be passed through before one's position or employment is abolished.[11] Unfortunately, there are exceptions. For example, in 2021, Georgia's Board of Regents altered its post-tenure review policies, allowing its public-university administrations to fire tenured employees without faculty input or a hearing,[12] to which the AAUP responded with censure.[13] Recently, tenured professors have been fired without a hearing, and one professor discovered that he had been fired by way of an auto-reply from his own work email account after he emailed it because he had been locked out of a Zoom meeting.[14] Tenured faculty have been disciplined on grounds including that they weren't "collegial."[15] And, as more alumnae and corporate donors behave like activist investors in seeking to influence how colleges and universities operate,[16] and as the proportion of nontenured faculty ever escalates, now constituting 75 percent of faculty,[17] the question can be raised whether tenure will someday be studied as an artifact of history. Until then, it is worthwhile to think about the legal aspects of not having tenure, of it being granted, and of it being stripped.

Because tenure has different and sometimes contrasting meanings throughout the country's private and public colleges and universities—and the country's courts—the amorphousness of tenure can make finding legal clarity perplexing.

A Short History of Tenure

One can find as a driving force in the creation of the AAUP in 1915 a desire to establish grounds for tenure and also grounds for the dismissal of professors.

In fact, the AAUP's "1915 Declaration of Principles on Academic Freedom and Academic Tenure" made the wise comparison of professors to federal judges, who are given lifetime tenure:

> So far as the university teacher's independence of thought and utterance is concerned—though not in other regards—the relationship of professor to trustees may be compared to that between judges of the federal courts and the executive who appoints them. University teachers should be understood to be, with respect to the conclusions reached and expressed by them, no more subject to the control of the trustees, than are judges subject to the control of the president, with respect to their decisions.[18]

The basis for this original linkage of professors to federal judges is independence. If one is beholden to the party that hires or appoints one, then what one researches or teaches is similarly bound. Centuries before the AAUP's birth, Thomas Jefferson created for the University of Virginia, which he founded, a charter that protected its faculty from being easily removed. And, in a letter wherein he wrote about the University of Virginia, Jefferson declared that "tenure is in fact for life."[19] (Jefferson might be unhappy to realize that tenured faculty at the University of Virginia can be fired.)[20]

Independence can even be a commodity in short supply for administrators, as well as faculty, as shown by the case of Brown University President Elisha Andrews, who in 1897 advocated for the free coinage of silver to help farmers and others hurt by deflation. That didn't sit well with his board of trustees, who sought his change of opinion or his resignation.[21] The advocacy of free silver by a Stanford University professor in 1900 was also something that the sole trustee of Stanford University (the widow of founder Leland Stanford) believed warranted ordering termination of the professor's employment. And, despite being a renowned mathematician and chair of the Department of Pure and Applied Mathematics at the University of Texas at Austin, when G. B. Halsted publicly criticized the university's board of regents in 1902 over its hiring of a math professor, Halsted was dismissed.[22]

Spurred on by examples of politically motivated firings of professors and bolstered by the 1925 American Council on Education Conference "Statement on Academic Freedom and Tenure" and the AAUP's "1940 Statement of Principles on Academic Freedom and Tenure,"[23] support for tenure began to take hold. The AAUP 1940 Statement defined tenure as "a means to certain ends; specifically: (1) freedom of teaching and research and of extramural activities, and (2) a sufficient degree of economic security to make the profession attractive to men and women of ability."[24] This impactful statement discussed how tenure standards could be created and how long probationary periods should last, including calling for at least one year's notice for an instructor who would not be retained beyond his or her probationary period. It also included the role of faculty governance as part of a formal process before a tenured professor is fired and the need for a bona fide urgency in order to terminate a tenured professor's position because of a "financial exigency."

While hundreds of educational organizations have endorsed the AAUP's 1940 Statement, the AAUP's role in the tenure process is that it has influenced how tenure-granting institutions adopt policies for their own tenure systems. To be tenured is to have it awarded to you by your college or university, and often those tenure policies bear in varying degrees the imprint of the AAUP.

THE TAKEAWAY

A catalyst for tenure in America was politically motivated firings of professors, which impelled educational leaders and organizations in the early twentieth century to advocate for faculty to have probationary periods of employment, leading to the granting of tenure. The AAUP first analogized professors and their need for tenure to federal judges, whose independence is secured by judicial tenure. The AAUP's "1940 Statement of Principles on Academic Freedom and Tenure" served as the primary advocation for tenure, and it provides a structure for how colleges and universities can establish tenure.

The Tenure Process

There are three classes of faculty in America: tenured; tenure-track; and nontenure-track. The 2021 data from sources aggregated by the AAUP show that only 24 percent of full-time faculty in America are in tenured positions, and 48 percent of faculty teach part-time, which has been a continuing trend and is starker for underrepresented minorities and women.[25] Each college or university that has a tenure system is like a snowflake, in that each system is different in some respect. But generalities can be found. At the outset, bear in mind that tenure is not for nonfaculty employees, regardless of their years of continual employment. In an illustrative case, a psychologist at a state university in Illinois whose position was eliminated sued his employer, alleging he had tenure because he had worked there for over ten years and because his one-year contracts had been altered to be of "continuing appointment." But this psychologist held a nonfaculty position and the court upheld his termination, concluding that tenure is for faculty only because its purpose is to protect academic freedom, and only faculty do the kinds of work that academic freedom is there to protect.[26]

For faculty in a tenure-track system, the period of time before tenure can be granted ranges from three to seven years. This probationary period and its expectations should be established by a department and/or a school document prior to the hiring of the professor, and it should include what efforts are required to be awarded tenure and how those efforts are weighted. If prior publications will count toward a department's tenure-worthy achievements, an assurance should be provided in writing at the time of the hiring and should be verified by someone with sufficient authority, such as a dean, to bind later decision-makers. Otherwise, whatever has been promised is empty.

Excellence in teaching or research is the primary lens through which a tenure-track faculty member's probationary period is viewed, although service can be a considerable variable. Whether it is a minimum number of peer-reviewed publications, the impact those publications have, the number of grants earned, or excellence in teaching, scholarship, and learning, or even some combination of excellence in one area and competence in another, probationary faculty should realize at the outset how they will be judged. Tenure-track faculty should be linked with a faculty mentor who will help the junior faculty member in the substantive and procedural aspects of navigating an arduous process. Moreover, junior faculty should learn during their annual and periodic reviews (such as a third-year review) how their colleagues, department chair, and dean are assessing those efforts. In an ideal world, these written evaluations should note tenure-worthy accomplishments and areas needing polishing or urgent improvement. Failure to provide clarity to a tenure-track faculty member on his or her progress in meeting those written standards is not only unprofessional but also makes the tenure process look like a game of chance, and increases the likelihood of litigation, as will be shown.

Tenure cases are often submitted in the penultimate year of probation, at least where written policy provides a year of employment following a denial of tenure. A tenure case is a large file consisting of narrative and documented portions, and supporting appendixes, showing how the candidate has met the established tenure standards. Part of the tenure process will include external review letters, in which faculty at other institutions, who are of at least the same rank the candidate is seeking, evaluate the candidate's tenure worthiness in light of the documentation provided to them. Often another requirement for tenure, beyond the candidate's track record of achievement, is that the candidate show how he or she, if awarded tenure, would continue to grow as a scholar.

That case is submitted to the candidate's department promotion and tenure committee, which traditionally provides the first layer of multiple levels of review. Along the way, the initial review committee, the department chair, the dean, school-wide tenure committees, university-wide tenure committees, other faculty committees, and administrators in provost or academic-affairs offices will issue to the candidate responsive letters that either recommend the granting or denial of tenure and that explain their reasoning, based on the candidate's tenure case or the recommendation letters that have been forwarded to them, or some combination thereof. Eventually and hopefully, a campus president or chancellor will recommend tenure to the college or university board or a similarly titled governing body, whose decision is conclusive.

Of course, there would be no tenure litigation if everyone who applied for tenure was granted it. While those lawsuits can provide some insights into when and why courts will intervene—going against the judicial history of abstinence in tenure matters—most unsuccessful tenure cases end quietly, notwithstanding a few notable examples of hunger strikes[27] and even an unimaginable case of murder.[28] For those for whom a grant of tenure is not recommended somewhere along this process, opportunities are often afforded for the candidate to write rebuttal letters that become part of the candidate's tenure dossier for later committees and administrators to review. In some institutions, failure to receive a positive departmental recommendation could end the tenure review process at that point. As well, one of the hard truths about the tenure process is that faculty colleagues can recommend a candidate for tenure, even unanimously, but that does not prevent a dean or other administrator from rejecting or denying it. And, when tenure is denied, internal appeal chances can be granted, assuming written policy provides for it.

THE TAKEAWAY

The tenure process is a multilayered review of a tenure-track professor's record of accomplishments during his or her probationary period. Upon submitting the tenure dossier to one's department, various tenure-review committees, deans, other faculty committees, and administrators review the tenure case and issue responsive letters that recommend granting or denying tenure. Those letters, along with the tenure case, are submitted through higher levels of review, unless institutional policy dictates that failure to achieve a committee's majority recommendation or failure to receive an administrator's recommendation ends the process. If the needed positive evaluations have been made, a recommendation for tenure is generally placed in the hands of the institution's governing board, whose decision is conclusive.

PROMOTION VERSUS TENURE

Promotion results in a change of title and, hopefully, a compensation increase. Tenure results in a change of status. Unlike a peanut-butter cup, it is possible to have one flavor without the other: one could be promoted in rank and not have tenure. For example, clinical professors might have opportunities to seek promotion and they might have multiyear, rather than year-to-year, contracts, but they do not acquire tenure because of a promotion.

A professor with tenure might be promoted again by applying for and receiving a full professorship, after already having been awarded the rank of tenured associate professor. But, without tenure, promotion does not ensure independence or job security, especially at religious colleges or universities, because those institutions have a First Amendment prerogative to hire and fire within the constraints of their theology or creed. That is, unless a court were to conclude that the faculty member does not fall within what is known as the "ministerial exception" to applicable employment-discrimination laws.[29] This means that, if an employee at a religious college or university has job aspects that involve spiritual leadership, or spiritual encouragement or guidance activities, they can be considered ministers, who, legally speaking, are religious employees whose work status starts and ends with their employer. In a case on point, a tenured social-work professor at a Christian liberal-arts college in Massachusetts was denied a promotion to full professor, and she sued, alleging she was being retaliated against for opposing the college's LGBTQ+ policies, which she had called discriminatory. In the lawsuit and appeal, the key issue was whether she qualified as a "minister," which would have meant her discrimination claim would have given way to the college's religious-freedom claim. Notably, over the objection of the college's faculty, the college's lawyer had inserted into the faculty handbook a sentence that referred to all faculty as "ministers." Nevertheless, the Massachusetts Supreme Court concluded that the ministerial exception didn't apply to the professor because she was not ordained, did not teach religious courses, and had no role on campus that would fall within an accepted meaning of "minister."[30]

THE TAKEAWAY

Promoted professors who are nontenured still lack the independence and job security that are afforded tenured professors; this is especially true for faculty who work at religious educational institutions and whose work qualifies them for the "ministerial exception."

POST-TENURE REVIEW

Post-tenure review is when a college or university implements a system for conducting some form of periodic evaluation of tenured faculty, or where states or state boards of regents require such evaluation by their universities. More than a few states, including Arkansas, California, Florida, Indiana, Texas, Minnesota, and Virginia, have done so. What its purpose is can be difficult to say. Some argue it treats tenured faculty like they are going up for tenure again and creates a structure for universities to fire them, even though tenured professors already can be fired for extreme misconduct or other forms of cause. Others argue that post-tenure review is the saw for the "Deadwood"[31]—those who have distinctive job security but do nothing in return, as the saying goes. Others argue that it provides a means to regularly evaluate the efforts and progress of those who have tenure. Recently, as demonstrated by Indiana's "intellectual diversity" legislation, discussed in Chapter 3, which is concerning for academic freedom, post-tenure review is also sometimes premised on the need to assess whether tenured faculty are possibly teaching in ways that the majority in the legislature thinks they should not. Decades ago, the AAUP expressed caution about post-tenure review and how it might impact academic freedom,[32] and its website contains more information on the subject, notably its view that post-tenure review creates conditions for violating the due-process rights of tenured faculty.

With post-tenure review, it is not unreasonable to assert that the employment of tenured faculty is subject to termination, coterminous with that of other full-time faculty, regardless of the job security that one associates with tenure. Whereas a productivity report or similar self-evaluation is often linked to merit raises, a post-tenure review can take on the feel of a traditional job evaluation, where one is numerically ranked in categories of performance or classified as satisfactory or unsatisfactory. Critically, implementation of post-tenure review policies can serve as the triggering event for instituting a termination investigation, where a tenured professor has been found lacking in the review. Why? Because post-tenure review mechanisms create specific conditions for which tenured faculty can be fired, whereas, without post-tenure review, those same faculty are subject to termination only in less defined and more extreme circumstances that place more emphasis on due-process rights.

Post-tenure reviews established by state action have been challenged on the grounds that they retroactively and unconstitutionally change the terms of employment for then-tenured faculty. But post-tenure review has been judicially upheld on grounds that it is simply a procedural change (not a substantive change) to the tenure system.[33] Legal cases involving faculty fired after post-tenure review show appellate courts have needed to resolve whether employment contracts have been breached, whether the firings (at public institutions) have been constitutional, whether due-process requirements have been violated, and even whether such firings might be retaliatory. For example, in a strange case involving a tenured professor at a public university in Nevada who was fired after two consecutive negative post-tenure reviews, he and his employer reached a settlement providing him nontenured employment. After the university breached that settlement, the professor sued, and, during the trial, the university agreed that it would return the professor to a tenured status (and give him back pay) if the jury ruled in his favor, which it did. Then—six years after the initial post-tenure review firing—the university resurrected the initial post-tenure review evaluations so it could fire him a second time. The professor won a second jury trial, and the decision was upheld on the grounds that, among other things, the university breached its contractual duty of "good faith" to the professor.[34]

As uncomfortable as it may be to realize, post-tenure review can provide the justifiable cover that administrators need to instigate the kind of "just cause" or "serious misconduct" firing anchor points that otherwise might seem too unwieldly to use to begin a termination process. In a case from a public university in Kansas, a tenured professor was given a performance evaluation score of less than 2, which was officially unsatisfactory. But his colleagues' evaluation of him was lower than his chair's. The next year, the evaluation numbers were even lower, and, in a post-tenure review, multiple areas of inadequacy were documented, resulting in termination of the professor's employment. In the resulting lawsuit and appeal, the court ruled in favor of the university, noting there was substantial evidence supporting the decision to fire the professor under the professional-incompetence policy that was applied. That policy was tied to university metrics already in place for tenured faculty who met the label of "chronic low achievement." Furthermore, various department colleagues and a faculty panel that reviewed the termination decision agreed that those chronic low-achievement metrics were met.[35]

Collective bargaining rights can affect performance reviews of tenured faculty. Where tenured faculty have employment rights that are collectively bargained for and where the contract language does not empower faculty administrators, such as a dean, to order tenured faculty to engage in remedial actions because of a periodic performance review, then disciplining or firing an underperforming professor for failure to follow the mandate can be an action courts will reverse.[36]

THE TAKEAWAY

Post-tenure review is a structure, whereby tenured faculty undergo periodic performance evaluations, including of their scholarly activities and teaching, the outcome of which ultimately can lead to termination decisions for unsatisfactory performance. If your college or university has a post-tenure review policy, read it carefully to see what inflection points are embedded that allow for or trigger a termination process. Likewise, do the same thing if you work at a public institution and your state has post-tenure review legislation or regulations. Finally, if your college or university is in the process of initiating a post-tenure review policy, consider how your participation could help ensure fair-mindedness in the details.

The Legal Rights of Part-Time Faculty to Their Employment

Having worked as a part-time faculty member myself, teaching anything that was available, from criminal law to introduction to American government to even introduction to college writing, it pains me to say that adjunct faculty are essentially at-will employees. Even though there are adjunct instructors who work full-time in professions adjacent to the courses they teach, thousands of so-called part-time faculty teach more than what would be a full-load of courses, and many of them still work in other parts of the gig economy.

At-will employment can exist in all areas of employment, including in academia. At-will employment is more like an employment setting, rather than an employment relationship, because either party is free to leave the other for any reason: good, bad, or no reason at all. For example, if I'm an at-will employee and my employer doesn't like that I wear a lot of my favorite color, blue, my employer can show me the door. (Montana is commonly thought to be the only state without at-will employment, which means that, after a probationary period has ended, Montana employees who aren't in specified-term employment contracts generally need to be fired for cause.)[37] An at-will employee working under a part-time teaching contract is generally not protected from either termination during the semester or a contract nonrenewal. In a case from a public university in Mississippi, a part-time music instructor was told he would not be retained after the conclusion of the current semester wherein he made some controversial comments to a student that the university thought violated its antidiscrimination policy. The instructor believed these statements were protected by the First Amendment and sued the university for, practically speaking, being fired, since university policy allowed him to contest the accusation made against him. In dismissing the instructor's lawsuit, the federal district court noted that just because the college's handbook allowed faculty to file an appeal after being accused of discrimination didn't overcome the basic truth that the instructor, who was clearly an at-will employee, could be terminated or nonrenewed for any legal reason, including "no reason at all."[38]

There are exclusions from at-will employment, starting with the constitutional kind. Clearly, an adjunct instructor cannot be fired for racial or other reasons that violate the US Constitution or statutory law that covers protected classes; such law includes Title VII of the 1964 Civil Rights Act. Some states have additional categories of protected classes. So, if I was employed in Michigan and was fired because I'm not tall, I might have a case because height is a protected status there.[39] Then, there are exceptions to the general rule on at-will employment. Various employment laws can protect an at-will employee from being fired for specifically stated reasons. For example, many states protect all employees from being fired for missing work due to jury-duty service. There are also public-policy exceptions, which might include protecting an at-will employee who has been fired for filing a worker's compensation claim or testifying at an unemployment-compensation hearing.

And, wherever the contours of academic freedom legally extend, they would protect part-time faculty. If a college policy statement clearly endorses academic freedom for faculty, then one could argue that a contractual exception to at-will employment has been created. A part-time instructor at a public college or university would have a valid claim if the instructor was fired for reasons that courts say are in the constitutional zone of academic freedom. For example, recall that in Chapter 3, a part-time instructor at a community college in Kentucky filed a suit after he was fired over what was labeled an offensive word-association exercise he conducted in an interpersonal communication class. Thankfully, the Sixth Circuit Court of Appeals concluded that the college violated First Amendment rights by way of impinging on his academic freedom in class.[40]

THE TAKEAWAY

Part-time faculty are at-will employees, which means they can be dismissed for any reason not covered by an at-will exclusion, such as those protections provided by antidiscrimination laws, including statutes that protect employees against retaliatory firings in certain instances. Likewise, the legal protections of academic freedom apply to part-time faculty.

The Legal Rights of Nontenured, Full-Time Faculty to Their Employment

Although it may seem counterintuitive, much of what has been said about part-time faculty and their lack of job protection also applies to full-time faculty that are not tenured, including tenure-track faculty. In fact, in a case from South Carolina involving a suit brought by a tenured professor who was fired, that state's supreme court referred to full-time faculty who lack tenure as "at-will" cmployccs.[41] Onc might think that would not bc thc casc for a profcssor who has signed a contract with a stated length of term, such as a one-year contract that is expected to be renewed annually. But other courts have likened nontenured full-time faculty with such annual contracts to at-will employees.[42]

NONTENURED FACULTY HAVE NO PROPERTY INTEREST IN THEIR EMPLOYMENT

Even though it is normal to plan one's life based on an expectation of continued employment, a unilateral expectation is not the same as having a "property interest" in that employment. The US Supreme Court has spoken to what it means to be a tenure-track professor at a public institution and, in a 1972 case where a first-year assistant professor was told he would not be back for his second year, stated there is no property interest protected by the Fourteenth Amendment in a nontenured position.[43] In this case, *Board of Regents of State Colleges v. Roth*, even though the professor was not told why he was not being retained for a second year, the court said that, since he was not being accused of any wrongdoing that might seriously damage his reputation or opportunity to be rehired, he had no due-process right to a hearing.

So, for those that work at public institutions, the key difference between having a property interest and simply having an expectation interest in one's employment is that those with a property interest (protected by the Fourteenth Amendment's due-process clause) must be fired "for cause."[44] Tenured faculty at private colleges or universities might also reasonably believe they have a property interest in their employment, but, if they have any such interest, it would be created by contract, assuming the institution's tenure statements on job security are strong and certain enough to have legal effect.

Pedagogical differences do not favor instructors over their chairs or departments at public or private institutions, and such differences are generally outside the scope of academic freedom. This is because colleges and their departments have their own right of academic freedom. Courts have found that pedagogical choices and teaching styles are ultimately not in the hands of nontenured faculty, who, when these conflicts appear, can be fired in short shrift.[45]

Tenure-track faculty are still probationary faculty and have no legally protected right to continued employment. And so they will lose the argument in a tenure-denial case that they were denied procedural rights that amount to a violation of their due-process rights when, for example, they are given an informal hearing instead of a formal hearing.[46] Full-time faculty who are not in a tenure track should realize they have less of an expectation in continued employment, even if their contracts are multiyear. This is so because even faculty who are in a tenure track can be fired simply because they are thought not to be a "good fit" in their department or with tenured faculty.[47] That does not mean, for example, that a clinical professor in a three-year contract could not win a breach-of-contract case if she were fired in violation of the contract's terms, but it would be rare that those terms, themselves, would only allow the professor to be fired for cause to the same degree that a tenured professor could be fired for cause. For example, having a multiyear faculty contract at a public or private institution might provide that a faculty member is entitled to a stated term of employment following a decision not to renew the faculty member's contract. But often in employment contracts for nontenured faculty, the decision to fire or nonrenew is in the hands of one person, such as a department chair or dean, or one committee, providing much less opportunity for even a cursory appeal of that judgment.

ACADEMIC FREEDOM AS A PROTECTION AGAINST BEING DISMISSED?

The same day the US Supreme Court ruled against the tenure-track professor in *Board of Regents of State Colleges v. Roth*, the court also ruled in favor of a nontenured professor who sued after his yearly contract was not renewed. Here, in *Perry v. Sindermann*,[48] the court concluded the professor was entitled to a trial to present his evidence that he was fired in violation of his First Amendment rights. The distinction between the two cases is that, in the *Perry* case, the professor's claim that he was fired because he—as the head of a state teacher's rights organization—had publicly criticized the college's administration did implicate a protected right of freedom of speech. And a violation of that right would overcome his lack of a property interest in his job. Of interest in the case was the professor's claim that he had a de facto (in effect) form of tenure. Here, the professor argued that he was tenured because of his length of employment and because the college's faculty handbook, while expressly stating there was no tenure, still curiously said that faculty should feel that they have "permanent tenure" as long as their teaching was satisfactory, they had a cooperative attitude, and they were happy in their employment.[49] While not concluding that the professor had what might be thought of as implied tenure, the court said that if it existed, the professor was also entitled to a hearing at his college on the circumstances of his firing. There will be more on handbooks and tenure expectations later in the chapter.

It is one thing to say that a full-time instructor or professor without tenure can't be fired in violation of his or her academic freedom, but it is quite another to say what activities are fire-proof because they are inside the academic-freedom sphere. In a case from Texas involving a nontenured professor at a public university who was fired, a key issue was whether the professor was fired for refusing to give a student a course grade of a B, as allegedly ordered by the department head. To the federal district court, this order violated the professor's academic freedom, but, to the Fifth Circuit Court of Appeals, it did not.[50] In fact, the court ended its opinion by referencing the US Supreme Court case of *Perry v. Sindermann*, discussed earlier, in saying that, outside of being fired for exercising a constitutionally protected right, a "nontenured professor may be fired for any reason or for no reason at all."[51] But, in another case with a similar fact pattern, a different federal court concluded that forcing a tenure-track professor to change a grade (provided it otherwise meets administrative standards on grading) and not renewing the professor's employment contract for refusing the order is an academic-freedom violation.[52]

THE TAKEAWAY

Full-time faculty at public colleges or universities who are not tenured do not have a property interest in their employment, whereas tenured faculty do. That means nonrenewal of their employment contracts is generally not a litigation-worthy event, provided the procedural boxes have been ticked. If those faculty are accused of wrongdoing and that is the reason for which they are being fired or their contracts are not being renewed, they are entitled to some due process, allowing them to present a rebuttal to the charges. And, if nontenured faculty at public institutions can show they were fired in violation of antidiscrimination laws or a constitutionally protected right, including due-process rights, they would be able to sue.

NONTENURED FACULTY AT PRIVATE COLLEGES AND UNIVERSITIES AND EXPECTATIONS OF CONTINUED EMPLOYMENT

As far back as the 1990s, the AAUP expressed concern about the status of nontenured faculty at private educational institutions, including their lack of opportunity to be considered for positions that convert to tenure-track positions.[53] From a legal perspective, it still bears repeating that faculty at private colleges and universities do not stand in the shade created by the constitutional aspects of academic freedom or due process. For those faculty, academic freedom and the right to have a terminal employment decision reviewed exist in the nuances of contract law—including any AAUP statements on those matters that have been included in employment contracts. In 1982, the US Supreme Court confirmed this principle in a case where faculty whose employment at a private school had been terminated alleged that the firings violated their Fourteenth Amendment due-process rights. But the court said, 1) the school was a private actor and, therefore, not obligated to provide due process; and 2) just because a private school receives federal funding does not mean the school is equivalent to a state actor.[54] Even the National Collegiate Athletic Association (NCAA) was declared a private actor and, therefore, not subject to liability for any Fourteenth Amendment violations in a 1988 US Supreme Court case involving a famous college basketball coach whom the NCAA had investigated for years.[55]

Exceptions that mitigate the harshness of contract law can be found, and antidiscrimination law is one of them. While the Bill of Rights generally doesn't apply to private colleges and universities, federal and state antidiscrimination statutes generally do. Consequently, a nontenured professor at a private college, just like his public-college counterpart, would have grounds to sue if he could establish that he was fired in violation of antidiscrimination law. A case from Oregon is illustrative. There, an unmarried exercise-science professor at a Christian college got pregnant. The college asked her to marry the future father or to stop living with him. She was fired after refusing either of those options, and then she sued the college for discrimination on the basis of sex and pregnancy. The college responded that it had a religious-freedom right to expect its employees to live within its biblical precepts on sexuality and marriage. Despite that defense, the federal district court allowed the discrimination lawsuit to go forward, concluding that the ministerial exception didn't apply to her because—even though she was a professing Christian—she taught a secular subject, she didn't hold herself out as a minister, and she performed no traditionally religious functions at work.[56] And, in a case involving a tenure-track professor at a New York Ivy League university who was fired and who then filed suit, a lower court ruled that he had no Fourteenth Amendment (constitutional) right to due process related to his firing because the university was not a state actor; however, a higher court ruled that he did have a Title VII (legislative) right to allege his firing was the result of gender discrimination.[57]

COLLECTIVE BARGAINING LIMITATIONS FOR FACULTY AT PRIVATE COLLEGES AND UNIVERSITIES

The right to collectively bargain is initially granted in the National Labor Relations Act,[58] but it only applies to private-sector employers. Public-institution faculty may collectively bargain where their states' laws allow it, as do the laws of over thirty states. Where faculty have collective bargaining rights, their employment contracts clearly alter at-will employment presumptions and can give faculty procedural protections concerning decisions to fire and any internal appeals rights. But state laws determine how far collective bargaining rights extend beyond pay, including whether the right to strike is included, for example. The AAUP has many resources on collective bargaining, including on intellectual-property information for faculty unions.[59]

While the National Labor Relations Board (NLRB) ruled in the 1970s that private-college faculty could collectively bargain, in 1980 the US Supreme Court nearly eliminated that allowance in *NLRB v. Yeshiva University*.[60] There, the court ruled that the full-time faculty at this private, religious university could not collectively bargain, despite the specific grant by the NLRB, because they were, in fact, managerial employees. How such a conclusion could be possible was that the court reasoned that those faculty (primarily but not exclusively the tenured faculty) having authority over the curriculum and a persuasive influence over other related matters (including tenure, termination, and sabbatical decisions) were—for labor-law purposes—managers. And managers are exempt from collective bargaining rights. But even the court's 5–4 majority acknowledge in its last footnote that it was not saying how far its decision extended beyond the affected Yeshiva faculty. The court even said it wasn't expressing an opinion on whether its decision created a collective-bargaining dividing line between nontenured and tenured faculty.[61] A strenuous dissent made the point that the faculty in question were exercising "professional" and academic discretion in making those various decisions that the court majority labeled managerial and that those faculty lacked the requisite institutional role that managers have. Nevertheless, full-time faculty and, especially, tenured-faculty at private colleges are rowing upstream when attempting to collectively bargain.

THE TAKEAWAY

Full-time faculty at private colleges and universities do not have the employment-related constitutional protections that faculty at public institutions have. But antidiscrimination legislation can protect those faculty who have been wrongfully fired. Such protection extends to faculty at religious institutions if those faculty are not covered by the "ministerial exception." And, due to US Supreme Court case law, collective bargaining rights for private-institution faculty are limited.

HANDBOOKS AND THEIR EFFECT ON EMPLOYMENT CONTRACTS

As discussed in Chapter 2, which is on syllabi and legal issues, a contract is more than just *an agreement*. A contract is a binding exchange between parties, the result of offer and acceptance. Some contracts are oral and some are in writing, and some, such as real estate contracts, are required to be in writing and signed in order to be enforceable. And certain documents can be incorporated into an existing contract and be made part of the contract, which brings us to faculty handbooks or policy statements.

Whether one is teaching on a semester-by-semester basis or has tenure, the starting point for a faculty member's contractual relationship with her employer should start with a signed document. Then, there are other documents, online or otherwise, that colleges or departments expect faculty to review and agree to follow in exchange for their compensation. For example, an academic-affairs regulation prohibiting faculty from giving exams during a semester's penultimate week ("dead week") is enforceable and is not an academic-freedom violation. Often, these documents are incorporated by reference, meaning that the author of the anchor document alerts the reader to other, existing documents that are made a part of the contract. For example, language in a contract might say, "This Notice of Appointment is subject to and incorporates the provisions of *X*'s Policy Manual and the University's Faculty Handbook." And, on many campuses, the faculty handbook is the North Star. Generally, policy manuals and handbooks contain rules of behavior that are mandatory for faculty. But, to discern if a handbook's affirmations or protective statements about faculty employment rights or protections are contractually binding on a college or university, one must look at the handbook's language itself.

A Handbook May Explicitly Declare It Is Not Making Binding Promises

When a handbook states it is granting no contract rights, then . . . it grants no contract rights. That may seem like the paving of a one-way street (follow these handbook rules or else!), but a court is very unlikely to find that a handbook has made binding promises to faculty when it includes such discounting language. In a calamitous case involving a female tenured medical-school professor at a public university in Indiana who was fired for multiple failures to meet the university's post-tenure research expectations, her lawsuit alleged she was targeted by her department chair and her dean, who had opposed her tenure appointment—which she was awarded after she filed a post-denial grievance. Part of her argument, which was based on gender discrimination and retaliation, rested on what seemed to be supporting statements about tenure made in the university's academic handbook. But the federal appellate court noted, in dismissing her suit, that the preamble to the handbook expressly stated that it (the handbook) was creating neither a contract nor any contractual rights.[62]

Other courts within and outside of Indiana have noted in suits brought by tenured and nontenured faculty that, where a handbook states that it is not creating any express or implied contract rights or rights to continued employment, or even where a handbook refers to itself as a "general guide," the handbook's content is not contractually binding on the employer.[63] In fact, a federal appellate court in a related case said that, where universities have a tenure system, then a handbook generally doesn't create a contractually binding expectation of continued employment for those that aren't tenured.[64]

THE TAKEAWAY

Read your faculty handbook to see if it has preamble language disavowing that the handbook is creating contract rights. If so, that likely will be conclusive, and a court would find that the handbook does not create binding expectations concerning continued employment. Even statements that refer to a handbook as a general guide can result in the handbook being found to lack contractual enforceability.

A Handbook Grants Contract Rights Where It Is Clear that It Does or Other Employment Documents Confirm It

A contract that is the result of one side, in effect, telling the other side to take it or leave it, is known as an "adhesion contract." Think of any online "terms of service," where you either agree to them and click "yes," or you no longer have access to the services. Adhesion contracts are disfavored in the law but are not automatically unenforceable. Because most faculty have no power to negotiate in the creation or revision of faculty policy manuals or handbooks that apply to all faculty, courts have the power to strictly enforce them against the educational institution, because the institutions drafted the terms. In one such case at a public college in Alaska, certain nontenured faculty sued after being dismissed, alleging a violation of their contracts, as supplemented by policy statements. Here, the university lost the argument that it had validly (but unilaterally) altered the handbook's termination policy. In so deciding, the court stated that it was strictly enforcing the employment contract and related documents against the university because of the unequal bargaining power between the administration and faculty. Therefore, the handbook couldn't one-sidedly take away a right that had already been granted.[65]

Courts have found that a faculty handbook can create enforceable rights where it affirms that, or where its language allows for that reasonable inference. In order for a handbook to rise to the level of contract worthiness, it must be specific enough to meet the contract-law requirements in the employee's jurisdiction and the employee needs to continue working at the institution long enough to show that the employee is performing his or her side of the exchange.[66] An example of this is found in a case from a junior college in Texas that had no formal tenure system and that fired a professor. But the professor succeeded in showing that she was denied due process because the college handbook had a section labeled "Tenure," which discussed how faculty were to be annually reviewed and, ultimately, discharged, and it wasn't followed in her situation.[67] In another case from an Ivy League university in Connecticut, a professor who was denied tenure filed a breach-of-contract suit. That lawsuit survived the university's motion to dismiss it because the court concluded that the handbook policies on tenure were clear and contractually binding and because the conflict-of-interest section arguably appeared to have been violated by two professors on a tenure committee who voted against recommending tenure who should have abstained.[68]

The employment contract, itself, can use language that contractually links it to a handbook. In a case involving a private college in Texas, where a professor was denied tenure and lost his legal fight, the appellate court still acknowledged that the language of the professor's employment contract referenced the handbook (where the tenure standards were located), making the handbook binding on both parties.[69]

It is also possible that a faculty handbook can impliedly be made part of an employment contract when it is reasonable to conclude the former is intended to be bound to the latter. In a law-school case from the District of Columbia involving a professor who was denied tenure and whose lawsuit was based on racial discrimination, part of the legal claim rested on the failure of the law school to annually review the professor, as was supposed to be done according to the faculty handbook. This, the professor said, was a breach of an implied contractual obligation. A lower court agreed[70] (allowing the suit to go forward), and a higher court also agreed (allowing the suit to go forward again).[71] And, in a similar case, nontenured faculty who were dismissed from a private university in the District of Columbia filed a lawsuit, alleging that the university handbook required providing faculty with an advance notice date for nonrenewal and that they were wrongly terminated after that year's nonrenewal deadline. The university argued that the handbook, itself, wasn't granting any contract rights, but the court found it more important that the handbook repeatedly stated it would be the university's practice to provide written notice of nonrenewal to faculty on one-year contracts, and it listed those dates. This specific language, along with the fact that the university had in the past adhered to its written affirmation, created a legal obligation to honor the handbook, especially when the faculty were fired after the deadline for alleged misconduct and were not provided a hearing—also required in the handbook.[72]

THE TAKEAWAY

A faculty handbook can create contractually enforceable protections for faculty when its language is affirming enough that it is reasonable for faculty to rely on those promises, particularly where the administration has historically adhered to them.

Handbook Statements Applying to Tenured Faculty

Another wrinkle to the handbook discussion relates to tenured faculty. Tenure creates a special legal status, and the employment rights of tenured faculty are "vested." A vested right is one that exists presently and unconditionally and that generally may not be unilaterally diminished or eliminated. (Think of the importance of when a right to a pension vests, where such rights exist.) That is why nontenured faculty are sometimes referred to as "contingent" faculty.

When a handbook discusses rights that tenured faculty have to their employment, including layers of review for termination for cause or in cases of financial emergencies, courts tend to view the making of material changes to such policies, whether by a board of trustees or administrators, as pulling the rug out from under tenured faculty.[73] (In fact, nontenured faculty have been treated as if they also had vested rights in situations where binding handbook statements on nonrenewal or employment reductions were not followed.)[74] Job security is one of the essential elements of tenure, and handbooks that don't discount their contractual enforceability cannot be disregarded or overruled by administrative fiat.[75]

A 2024 case involving a private medical school in Massachusetts is instructive. Policy changes at this medical school stated that faculty failing to secure grants that covered 50 percent of their salary and lab expenses would be subject to significant reductions in salary and laboratory space—and their employment would be reduced from full- to part-time status. Certain faculty who were already tenured sued, alleging that the new policy violated the existing faculty handbook statements on economic security and academic freedom for tenured faculty. The first court dismissed the professors' lawsuit, but the Massachusetts Supreme Court reversed most of that decision.[76] Critical to this case, all parties in the suit agreed that the pre-existing faculty handbook and other policy statements pertaining to tenured faculty, including on economic security and academic freedom, were part of their employment contracts and tethered to the letters they received when they were awarded tenure. While noting that the college's academic freedom and tenure policy was essentially the same as the AAUP's "1940 Statement of Principles on Academic Freedom and Tenure," the court concluded that tenure would have no value if those statements lacked enforceability. It, therefore, sent the case back to determine if the new income-reduction policy violated the tenured professors' reasonable expectation of economic security. But the court ruled that reductions in laboratory space did not violate the meaning of academic freedom, in light of how academic freedom was defined in the tenure documents.[77]

That does not mean that all handbook terminology pertaining to tenured faculty will be interpreted to the degree desired. In a case at a private medical school in New York, faculty were subject to their compensation being reduced or increased because a new policy linked the salaries of research faculty to their success in being awarded grants. Tenured professors whose salaries had substantially shrunken over a few years sued, alleging that the policy could not be applied to them because the tenure statements in the faculty handbook referred to the "economic security" granted to tenured faculty, which was a borrowed AAUP phrase. Not so fast, the court opined, concluding that the "economic security" policy statement was only introductory in nature and could not gather under its wings of meaning what the tenured faculty purported. Furthermore, as these salary reductions were not for "disciplinary" purposes (remember, one could get grant-based salary increases), no related procedural review was warranted.[78]

THE TAKEAWAY

Changes that are made to policies in college or university handbooks, insofar as they adversely affect the status of tenured faculty, implicate their vested rights; generally, such changes affecting those who were tenured before the policy change cannot be made unilaterally.

Tenure Rejections and Legal Recourse

You Make the Call

- **The Case of the Division Chair's Tenure-Conclusive, One-Time Teaching Review**

At a private university in New York, a tenure-track professor of instrumental music found himself in a "do as I say, not as I do" loop, when his division chair recommended that he not be granted tenure because the chair was dissatisfied with the professor's teaching. At this university, whether to grant tenure is decided in the faculty member's sixth year, and the section of the faculty handbook on the tenure process states "proven teaching performance" is the primary condition for the grant of tenure. Other listed factors for consideration included scholarly activity, advising of students, and participation in campus activities. Tenure-track faculty are to be annually reviewed by their division chair, and the criteria for the annual review are the same as for deciding whether to grant tenure. The handbook also states that chairs shall, through class visitations, stay up-to-date on the teaching capabilities of tenure-track faculty. But, after five years in the tenure-track system, this faculty member's chair had never reviewed or observed his teaching, despite conducting annual evaluations of the professor. The chair did conduct one teaching evaluation in the professor's sixth year. The handbook requires the division chair to provide a written evaluation to the promotion and tenure committee in the tenure-decision year. In this tenure denial case, the chair's recommendation was based on student evaluations of the professor's teaching, the comments of colleagues, and the one teaching evaluation that the chair conducted. The chair's evaluation was positive in certain areas, but the negative recommendation was based on the professor's teaching weaknesses. The promotion and tenure committee (which included the dean) also recommended denying tenure, based on lack of teaching abilities, and that decision was upheld by the provost. After losing his administrative appeals, the professor sought a review by the faculty council. It concluded that the professor had procedural grounds for his appeal because the chair had only reviewed his teaching one time (despite the chair expressing concern over his teaching), and that was in the tenure-decision year. Moreover, the chair didn't review the music classes that comprised two thirds of the professor's teaching load. The faculty council also concluded that the professor was denied access to certain parts of his employment file. The promotion and tenure committee rejected the faculty council's recommendation, leading to the professor's lawsuit, seeking a judicial annulment of the decision to deny him tenure and also alleging breach of contract.

Did the chair (and other decision-makers) act arbitrarily and capriciously in denying tenure to a professor, based on one teaching evaluation, where teaching performance is the primary consideration?

(The answer will be given at the end of the chapter. Consider how the principles in this chapter affect your decision and reasoning.)

For those who have been denied tenure, the defenestration of one's career comes by way of paragraphs on letterhead. The decision to then hire an attorney is a heavy one, requiring answers to a number of related questions, including whether to spend money that should be saved for when you are unemployed and whether to search for a new academic position while you are suing your former employer.

In my case, I hired an attorney but never needed to deploy him because the highest academic officer at my university stood up for me. My then–department committee's majority strongly recommended against my tenure case, which was based on teaching excellence and research competence, while a minority of the committee strenuously defended my tenure case. My then–department chair issued a letter, recommending in no uncertain terms that I not be tenured. And my business school's promotion and tenure committee issued a majority recommendation against my tenure, while the only minority member of that committee wrote a welcome dissent. Throughout, I wrote my own rebuttal to each negative letter, thanks to the support of extraordinary friends. My dean supported my tenure case, as did the university promotion and tenure committee. By the time my tenure dossier and all the documents got to the university's vice chancellor of academic affairs (the provost) and it was his turn to consider my tenure application, he wrote a letter unequivocally recommending that I be tenured. In discussing those three negative tenure recommendations, he stated that they were so arbitrary, inconsistent, and combative that he was disregarding them. His manifest support for my tenure case helped to ensure that it would earn the chancellor's recommendation and ultimately be approved by the board of trustees. At the same time, in endorsing my tenure application when he had nothing to gain by doing so, he—as chief academic officer—supplied what would have been my strongest evidence had I not been tenured and had then filed a lawsuit against *his* employer.

While you might ultimately decide against bringing a tenure-denial lawsuit, that conclusion should be made after consulting an attorney who can advise you on the law of tenure in your state or federal jurisdiction and evaluate whether you have reasonable grounds to legally contest the decision. If you do meet with a lawyer, the lawyer is likely to tell you that rare is the judge who will intervene in a lawsuit based on the denial of tenure, because those lawsuits often get dismissed. A primary reason why dismissals are likely is because the judiciary is averse to get involved with what has for decades been considered the province of the academic community. (This legal stance of nonintervention extends beyond when students sue professors over grades or allege they are victims of academic malpractice, as was covered in Chapter 1 and Chapter 2.) Courts know where in the hymnal the correct stanzas are found, and they go something like this:

> Achieving tenure . . . is a multistep process fraught with nuanced and highly contextualized value judgments.[79]

> Which side is right in this scholarly debate is an academic issue that should not be decided by the courts.[80]

> Deference should be accorded to a university's discretion in making tenure decisions, and judicial review is circumscribed to whether the university failed to substantially comply with its internal rules and whether its decision was arbitrary or capricious or made in bad faith.[81]

Generally, a successful lawsuit is one with sufficient evidence to establish that the tenure denial was the result of one of the following: 1) arbitrary and capricious decision-making; 2) a material violation of the tenure policies (which is like breach of contract); or 3) discrimination of the kind protected by civil-rights law. In my view, a settlement in a tenure-denial lawsuit counts as a success and might be achieved if the college or university is unable to get the case dismissed, necessitating the administration to weigh the prospects of the case going to trial.

Soberingly, winning a tenure-denial lawsuit does not mean that one will be awarded tenure. So, in those rare instances where a professor wins a tenure-denial lawsuit and then wins on appeal (or where a university gets the suit dismissed and the professor wins on appeal), the likely result will be that the college or university is ordered to conduct a brand new ("de novo") review of the tenure case, sending the matter back to the original decision-makers.[82] Even where a professor wins a tenure-denial case that is based on breach of contract, the remedy could include monetary damages, but it will not include being awarded the precluded position (which in contract law is a type of equitable remedy known as "specific performance").[83] While a court has the power to order someone to be returned to a tenured position that was wrongly snatched from them, that does not mean a judge will award someone a new position, much less a job that comes with a legal interest in continued employment. Winning the right to a brand-new tenure review may seem like a pyrrhic victory, but a second bite at the apple could lead to a new result. And, yes, it does give the same tenure evaluators their own second chance at reaching the same decision while following the tenure-review process more circumspectly or reframing their earlier, negative recommendations.

THE TAKEAWAY

Courts rarely overturn a tenure-denial decision because of the longstanding legal tradition of nonintervention in matters that are considered to belong to the academic community. However, a tenure-denial lawsuit is viable where evidence demonstrates that the decision was arbitrary or capricious, where the tenure-review process was not followed, or where a tenure candidate was subject to illegal discrimination. But winning a tenure-denial lawsuit means getting a new tenure application review, not being granted court-awarded tenure.

AN ARBITRARY AND CAPRICIOUS TENURE REVIEW

Chapter 1 discussed how professors of all ranks are protected against liability for their grading decisions if those decisions are not considered arbitrary and capricious. (Remember also from Chapter 1, the phrase "arbitrary or capricious" is sometime used instead of "arbitrary and capricious.") Likewise, courts also use the alternative term, acting with "bad faith," which means acting with a malignant or dishonest purpose. That same doctrine applies to lawsuits over tenure denials. One could say that a tenure review is the most extreme form of subjective grading. Consequently, courts are loath to get substantively involved in colleges evaluating their faculty's academic work for the same reasons they want to stay out of grade disputes—even though the stakes are clearly higher. This threshold is not whether a court would disagree with the decisions of those empowered to review tenure dossiers. In fact, a judge's personal opinion on the bona fides of a tenure case is irrelevant. Rather, this standard means that courts ask if the decisions reached can be thought of as rational. So, a professor who litigates her tenure denial faces an uphill battle: from the beginning she has to demonstrate that what happened to her was more than subject to disagreement or susceptible to being considered inaccurate. Instead, the tenure-review process has to smell of absurdity or some dark-hearted motive that shows the deck was stacked against the candidate in indefensible ways.

The subjective nature of tenure evaluation is not eliminated just because of stated publication requirements or metrics that apportion journal quality or citation indexes. One might hit the mark, therefore believing that one landed on the right side of publish or perish, only to find out that one committee (or even, in one case, one external reviewer out of six)[84] thought that the candidate's publications lacked the quality or the disciplinary-specific focus needed for a positive tenure recommendation. Or, one might have won teaching awards or created new and popular classes, only to learn that one's teaching lacked depth or that one's student evaluations weren't high enough. In a case from a private university in New York that is illuminative on the subjectivity of the decision-making in this area, a dance and theater professor in a tenure system where teaching excellence was the primary consideration was denied tenure because his provost concluded—after others issued positive recommendations—that the professor did not work with colleagues in a "sufficiently collegial and collaborative manner." That professor's tenure-denial lawsuit was dismissed.[85] That is not the lone example where courts said "no, thank you" to a request to intervene in a tenure-denial lawsuit where a lack of collegiality was the concluding factor. It might be surprising to learn that more than a few universities make collegiality an expected condition of continued employment, including, at some institutions, a condition of tenure.[86] The AAUP disagrees with this approach.[87] One concerning point about the issue of collegiality (which should never be in short supply) is whether charges or even threats of lack of collegiality stifle what would otherwise be protected, university-criticism speech.[88]

In the following cases, courts have applied the "arbitrary and capricious" or the "bad faith" standard in tenure-denial suits and ruled in favor of the colleges or universities, finding that it was not arbitrary or capricious or in bad faith to deny tenure:

- even though a majority of the original committee recommended granting tenure and even though a faculty grievance committee recommended reconsideration of the application after the dean rejected tenure, based on insufficient publications;[89]
- when, after the original review of the applicant was thought to be tainted by an unproven allegation of sexual misconduct, the tenure-review committee then recommended granting tenure, but the dean still affirmed his original tenure-denial decision;[90] and
- when, after receiving a unanimously positive department recommendation, a positive chair recommendation, and a positive school recommendation, where higher committees and administrators recommended against granting tenure and where the chancellor and president denied tenure on the grounds of poor production of published research.[91]

Similarly, a court concluded that it was not bad faith for a university president to deny tenure where a professor sought tenure a year early and where there were split decisions on her case throughout the decision-making process. Part of the reasons for recommending against granting tenure included inadequate scholarship and lack of collegiality. At trial, the jury awarded the professor $450,000, but she lost it all on appeal because the court said that the judiciary shouldn't second-guess these academic judgment calls.[92] In another tenure-denial case from the 1970s involving a public university, a federal court said that, as far as federal courts are concerned, a state (the board of trustees) can deny tenure for no reason, for any reason, including even a reason based on erroneous facts, provided that the reason doesn't violate the US Constitution.[93] (This view is unlikely to withstand an analysis under the widely accepted arbitrary and capricious standard that came into its own years later.)

In light of the difficulty of showing arbitrariness, capriciousness, or bad faith, instances where professors have overcome that hurdle are considerably fewer than instances where they have not. But that standard can be met where a professor is denied tenure based on a structure or on variables that differ from what the professor was given and under which he worked for tenure, or where those involved in the tenure review had a conflict of interest.[94] Such sleight of hand would make the tenure review arbitrary, and intentionally doing the tenure review in this way would satisfy the capriciousness and bad-faith standards.

A noteworthy example of this occurred at a private college in Connecticut, where a chemistry professor was denied tenure on the grounds of insufficient publications. The college's tenure policy explicitly said a tenure denial was to be based on the candidate's failure to achieve the improvements specified in the candidate's last reappointment letter. But, in that professor's most significant letter, she was told to continue her original research in her lab. The letter also was notably vague on ways in which she should improve her tenure case. So, denying her tenure because her publications list was slim, which was not addressed in her last reappointment letter, and not pointing to any failure to improve of hers, when in fact she did exactly what she was encouraged to continue doing, showed arbitrariness.[95] Due to other evidence of arbitrariness and the jury's belief that the professor was also discriminated against based on her sex, it awarded her over $12 million, which the trial judge reduced by $9 million. On appeal, the discrimination verdict was overturned, but the monetary damages related to the arbitrary tenure denial—which the court referred to as negligent misrepresentation (a form of fraud)—were affirmed.[96]

THE TAKEAWAY

To win a tenure-denial lawsuit, or at least to prevent it from being dismissed, on the grounds that the tenure review process was arbitrary and capricious, or was conducted in bad faith, requires more than showing the process or decision-making is subject to disagreement. One must show that the decision-making process lacked rationality or that it was tainted by the involvement of decision-makers who had a conflict of interest.

BREACH OF CONTRACT FOR FAILURE TO FOLLOW THE TENURE POLICIES

The terms "arbitrary and capricious" and "bad faith" originate in tort law, where standards of negligence and recklessness or intentionally harmful conduct are applied. But, in tenure-denial case law, it is not uncommon for courts to apply the arbitrary and capricious standard in cases that are based on breach of contract. The reason for this is that an arbitrary deviation from an established tenure standard can be a breach of contract, too. For instance, if you hire me to deliver a package for you and, while driving my car, I run off the road while texting, destroying your cargo, I have breached my contract with you due to my negligence. In similar fashion, a college or university's failure to follow tenure policy in ways that courts consider arbitrary, or going off script and judging a tenure applicant on inappropriate standards, can be thought of as a tortious performance of a contract. For example, in the case cited in the prior paragraph, where a jury awarded a professor millions of dollars due to an arbitrary application of her college's tenure policy, the appellate court referred to those actions as a "breach of contract."[97]

But just because there has been an arbitrary and capricious denial of tenure does not automatically equate to a breach of contract, where, for example, the tenure policy comes from a handbook that is not thought to be specific enough to be contractually enforceable, or where the handbook itself doesn't qualify as contractually binding.[98] So, if a court (or a jury) finds a denial of tenure to be arbitrary and capricious but not to be a breach of contract, then the only recourse is a new review of that tenure case and not an award of monetary damages.

Where there has been a breach of contract in a tenure denial, the monetary damages relate to what the professor lost due to the breach of contract. In a long and winding case from a public university in Ohio, a pathology professor was denied tenure and her internal appeals went to two faculty committees, both of which concluded that the review process was unfair, including that it applied an unapproved tenure standard, disregarding the applicable standard, to her case. Per university policy, those findings and recommendations required the university to conduct a new and impartial tenure evaluation. Instead, according to the first court involved in the litigation, the provost reissued the tenure denial, which was a breach of contract.[99] That university's tenure policy stated that a professor who is denied tenure is entitled to an additional year of employment. But, because there was not a new and impartial review of the professor's tenure case (as a result of the initial tenure review that constituted a breach of contract) for almost five years, a second court ruled that the professor had a legal right to continued employment until the year after the university conducted a valid (and still negative) second tenure review.[100] So, even though she had found other employment after her first tenure denial, the professor still was entitled to monetary damages for those years between the wrongful termination that breached her employment contract and the court-required, second tenure review and denial.

Breach of contract for failure to follow the tenure policies occurred at a private women's liberal-arts college in New York, where an art-history professor was denied tenure despite having the unanimous support of the two faculty committees. But the interim dean opposed her tenure on grounds that included declining enrollment in art-history classes, and the board of trustees made its tenure denial decision in response to the dean's negative recommendation. However, the tenure policy required the college president to have an "active role" in the tenure process, especially when the administration disagreed with the faculty's recommendations, and that never happened. Furthermore—and equally importantly—declining enrollment was not an acceptable reason to deny tenure when the tenure policy did not allow for that variable. In fact, the applicable tenure policy established that "eligibility" for a tenure-track position was made at the time of the appointment, not at the time of the tenure decision.[101] Declining enrollment could have been a consideration when deciding against creating a tenure-track position, but not in denying tenure. After the court ordered a de novo review of the professor's tenure case, the litigation ended with a settlement for an undisclosed amount.[102] But, in a nearly identical case from a private college in the same state, a court concluded that low enrollment could be a reason to deny tenure when the faculty handbook (which was made part of the employment contract) made enrollment an allowable factor for tenure consideration.[103]

The tenure-review process does not have to be perfect, and it is unlikely that a nonmaterial deviation from faculty employment policy will result in the administration being required to take a tenure-review mulligan.[104] (In contract law, a "material breach" of a contract is when one party in the contract fails to perform that which is essential to the agreement or does something that substantially defeats the purpose of the contract.)[105] The question is whether there has been "substantial compliance" with the policy. Of course, what constitutes substantial compliance is not answered with a formula or an equation. In a case from a private university in the District of Columbia, a theater-arts professor who sued after being denied tenure won her claim of breach of contract—to the tune of hundreds of thousands of dollars. The key issue for the university's appeal was if there was sufficient evidence for the jury to conclude that the university's failure to provide the professor with biennial evaluations—as required by the handbook's tenure policy—was a substantial factor in her tenure denial. The court said yes and, in affirming the breach-of-contract verdict, the court noted that, had the biennial evaluations been done, the professor would have known how to differently approach her scholarly work and her eventual tenure application.[106] Hence, this was a material breach of the tenure policy.

THE TAKEAWAY

Winning a tenure-denial case, or at least preventing it from being dismissed, based on breach of contract requires showing that contractually enforceable tenure-review policies were not followed in a material way, including arbitrarily and capriciously. That can include evaluating a tenure case based on the wrong standards.

CIVIL-RIGHTS OR CIVIL-LIBERTIES VIOLATIONS AND TENURE DENIALS

It is beyond the scope and page count of this chapter to explain in detail how to establish illegal discrimination or how to prove that a governmental restriction of a freedom constitutes an infringement of one's civil liberties. However, Chapter 3 discussed how academic freedom intertwines with First Amendment notions and case law. And remember, the US Constitution's protections, as contained in the Bill of Rights, do not protect faculty at private colleges and universities, but civil-rights legislation can—unless a constitutional protection would shield a college or university from liability. For example, and as stated earlier in the chapter, an otherwise discriminatory firing of a professor at a religious college might be permissible because of the First Amendment–protected ministerial exception.

Tenure Denial and Illegal Discrimination

As the case law shows, it is no small task to establish that one has been rejected for tenure because of an illegally discriminatory reason. As mentioned earlier in this chapter, the female professor who was initially awarded a $12 million dollar verdict for her wrongful tenure denial and who won her appeal on the breach-of-contract claim nevertheless lost the part of the appeal on her sex-discrimination claim, because the court said that the evidence was insufficient.[107] As one federal court forthrightly stated, the structure of the tenure process is an "additional obstacle" to a successful discrimination claim, requiring "compelling evidence" that "'clear discrimination' pervasively infected the final tenure decision."[108] That is no walk in the park. Denying tenure to a candidate who is a woman or who is part of another protected class is not, on its own, proof of discrimination. What needs to be shown is that the stated reason for denying tenure is a "pretext" for the impermissible reason.[109] That might bring to mind again the arbitrary and capricious standard, in that, if the reasons given for denying tenure appear to pass the rationality muster, it is nearly impossible to then show that a discriminatory motivation affected the rejection.

In a case from a public university in Indiana, a case that is indicative of this difficulty, a professor in the school of education was denied tenure and sued, alleging intentional racial discrimination. Of his six external review letters, all but one was positive, and that sixth letter qualified its support by declaring that the professor's research was "not clearly excellent." The professor's department and its chair each recommended granting tenure, but the school of education and every other committee or evaluator did not, concluding that the professor's research was not excellent, as required, and his teaching was unsatisfactory. In upholding the dismissal of his lawsuit, the appellate court noted that the professor's argument that he was worthy of tenure was irrelevant because the court had no role in second-guessing the judgment of tenure experts.[110] And that no other Black male had been tenured in the school of education was "beside the point" to the issue of whether he was denied tenure based on his race.[111] As well, the court noted that the professor was hired through a minority-recruitment initiative.

And, in a remarkable case from a regional public university in Wisconsin, a female zoological professor who was the first woman in thirty-five years to be hired into a tenure-track position like that one, and who then became the first person in a tenure-track position ever to be denied tenure by her department, sued for sex discrimination. At the time of her tenure denial, only six of the 323 tenured science-related faculty were women. The professor had evidence showing a male colleague in her department whose tenure case was similar to hers (although she had published more articles in prestigious journals than he had) had been awarded tenure in the same year. Despite the starkness of these facts, the appellate court still upheld the dismissal of her lawsuit. It concluded that *being qualified for tenure*, which the professor was, didn't equate to *being worthy of tenure* and that the stated reason for denying her tenure—that her work showed less promise—wasn't a discriminatory pretext.[112] But the dissenting judge was having none of that. In discussing the tenure review of what he considered to be two marginal candidates, that judge concluded that the female professor, as a path breaker in an environment with so few women, had to perform better than a male in order to succeed, which he thought violated Title VII.[113]

Despite the difficulty in establishing a "prima facie" (on first impression) case of a discriminatory tenure denial, a lawsuit may continue when it can be shown. One federal court noted in a tenure-denial lawsuit based on sex discrimination that, despite the historical regard given to academic judgments like tenure, judicial deference should not give way to "judicial abdication" of a court's responsibility to provide a forum for discrimination cases involving institutions of higher learning.[114] In a law-school case from the District of Columbia, a female professor was able to make out that prima facie case because (as alleged in her lawsuit), even though she was denied tenure for failing to publish the required number of law-review articles, around the same time a white male colleague who had published less than she was awarded tenure.[115] (Some years later, she was named associate dean for DEI at that law school.)[116]

Establishing that a member of a tenure committee displayed discriminatory bias toward the candidate does not guarantee victory, however. At a public university in Indiana, a tenure denial for a female nuclear-engineering professor led to litigation that focused on whether a named, distinguished full professor of nuclear engineering, who is Asian and who was accused of racial animus toward non-Asians and female professors, controlled the initial tenure committee, which voted 6–2 against recommending tenure. Despite the female professor's prodigious publication record and her other awards, the nub of her tenure consideration was if she lacked the required independence in research and publication, because much of her scholarly work was conducted with her mentor, who was also in the same department and who was a named, distinguished full professor in his own right. The assistant professor asserted a theory of liability known as the "Cat's Paw" (owing its name to a Renaissance-era French fable, *The Monkey and the Cat*), whereby an employee or supervisor having discriminatory intent but lacking decision-making power exerts influence over a decision-maker that causes an adverse employee outcome to the plaintiff.[117] Various members of the faculty, including a tenured, female professor (who was denied tenure in nuclear engineering but was granted tenure in materials engineering), went on the record to state they heard the Asian professor disparage women, say the assistant professor would "never get tenure," call whites "stupid, lazy Americans," and even disparage the then-dean, a white woman, because of her gender, once referring to her as "stupid."[118] The full professor repeatedly denied making all those statements or attempting to influence the tenure voting process. (Animosity was so intense in this department that the assistant professor's mentor, in an unrelated matter, sued the Asian professor for defamation, resulting in a settlement.)[119] The assistant professor's lawsuit survived the university's attempt to have it dismissed, and a trial was eventually held. But, even though the jury concluded that the Asian professor harbored racial hostility that led to discrimination against the assistant professor, she lost the case because the jury also found that the university, through its administrative personnel, didn't reject her tenure case for discriminatory reasons.[120]

Tenure Denial and Violations of Free-Speech Rights

To make a legitimate claim that one's exercise of free-speech rights was the reason for an adverse employment action requires showing that, 1) the employee works at a public college or university; 2) the employee spoke on a matter of public concern; 3) the employee spoke as a private citizen (rather than as a public employee); 4) the protected speech was a motivating factor in the adverse employment action; and 5) the employer would not have taken the adverse employment action except for the protected speech.[121] Some of these concepts, including what speech qualifies as a matter of public concern and when a public-college faculty member is speaking as a citizen rather than as an employee, were tackled in Chapter 3, which is on academic freedom. For example, criticizing one's public employer due to personal dissatisfaction with how one is treated at work is usually not the kind of speech that is a matter of public concern.[122] By way of contrast, in a case where the contract of a nontenured professor at a public university in New Mexico was not renewed on the grounds that he was making insufficient progress toward his doctorate and that his teaching was lacking, the professor won his lawsuit on First Amendment grounds. Here, the trial judge, sitting as the fact finder in place of a jury, was convinced that it was the professor's public criticism of his university's administration that was the real and unlawful reason for letting him go. That decision was upheld on appeal, including the award of monetary damages for emotional distress, tied to his inability to find another full-time teaching job and his eventual divorce—affected by the financial distress of being terminated for exercising his First Amendment rights.[123]

A tenure-denial lawsuit might be linked to allegations of retaliation against the candidate for engaging in what is known as a "protected activity." In an instructive case from an Ivy League university in Connecticut, a professor who was denied tenure filed a federal lawsuit, alleging numerous instances of wrongful conduct. She claimed she was denied tenure for speaking out against the tenure process in which she was engaged and for criticizing the way her department was run. The court dismissed the claim, concluding that this kind of speech didn't implicate a protected activity.[124] On a related matter and around the same time, she took part in a sexual-harassment investigation against members of her department, including the chair, whom the professor also accused of harassment. Her conduct in that matter was found to be a protected activity within the ambit of Title VII, yet her claim of being denied tenure as retaliation for her Title VII activity was also dismissed because the court concluded that there was a sufficient, nonretaliatory reason to deny her tenure.[125] But . . . her claim of breach of contract was allowed to go forward due to the tenure policy's conflict-of-interest provision and because some of the members who voted against her tenure case were the objects of her Title VII complaints.[126]

Can the forum for, rather than the content of, academic publications be the subject of a First Amendment claim? That question was answered yes by a federal judge in charge of certain litigation that the judge thought was the first case of its kind. In the case, an electrical-engineering professor of Indian national origin at a regional campus of a public university in Pennsylvania alleged that, due to discrimination, he was denied a promotion to full professor, but also that his dean (who also was the chancellor) retaliated against him by discounting for his promotion application all the professor's open-access publications, which were many. To the university, the choice of where to publish neither implicated the First Amendment nor was a matter of "public concern." But the court disagreed, ruling that the lawsuit could continue, concluding that widespread access to academic scholarship was a matter of public concern that involved academic freedom and, therefore, First Amendment consideration.[127]

THE TAKEAWAY

Winning a tenure-denial case, or at least preventing it from being dismissed, based on a violation of civil rights or civil liberties, requires showing that the stated reason for denying tenure to the candidate was really a pretext for an unlawful reason, such as discrimination or retaliation for engaging in a protected activity.

Firing a Tenured Professor

You Make the Call

- **The Case of the Terminally Tardy Tenured Professor**

Whether it's famous football coaches who say arriving on time is lateness ("Lombardi time"), or Shakespeare, who wrote "Better three hours too soon than a minute too late,"[128] or professors who heavily penalize students for lethargy in attendance or submissions, it seems timeliness might be more next to godliness than cleanliness.[129] But can tardiness get you fired if you're a tenured professor? After over a decade in the African American and African studies department at a state university in Minnesota, a tenured professor's colleagues, who assessed the tenured professor's performance in conjunction with the university's peer review policy, expressed enough dissatisfaction with the professor's performance that the dean initiated termination proceedings. According to the university policy, termination of a tenured faculty member is appropriate for causes "which seriously interfere with the person's capacity competently to perform his duties, or with his usefulness to the University." After an eight-day hearing, a faculty panel recommended that the professor's employment be terminated for cause. The gravamen of the charges and evidence presented was that the professor rarely showed up to class on time and, when he wasn't tardy, he wasn't there. He had a 35 percent absentee rate. He didn't keep his office hours, sporadically attended faculty meetings, and left meetings early. In one of his classes, only six of twenty-two students received a grade, and many students were none too pleased that a teaching assistant did much of the teaching. That may have been a blessing in disguise because other evidence showed that the professor was often ill-prepared for class, taught in a disorganized way, and failed to acquaint students with the course requirements. Colleagues testified that he had been cavalier about meeting his responsibilities for quite some time, and they thought the source of what might now be called quiet quitting was his extensive consulting activities. Ultimately, all the administrative boxes were checked and the tenured professor was fired, whereupon he filed a lawsuit against the university (including his dean), seeking reinstatement to his faculty position, alleging racial discrimination and that his due-process rights were violated.

Based on the tenure policy regarding removal for cause, does the evidence presented warrant the firing of a tenured professor? (No evidence was presented here on his racial-discrimination claim. So, please focus on the facts provided.)

(The answer will be given at the end of the chapter. Consider how the principles in this chapter affect your decision and reasoning.)

As of this writing, no tenured faculty member at Harvard University—America's oldest college—has been stripped of tenure.[130] That is quite a history, considering John W. Webster, a tenured chemistry and medical-school professor was hanged in 1850 for murdering George Parkman, another Harvard Medical School professor, over a loan Webster hadn't paid back to Parkman. While Webster took his tenure to the grave,[131] at many other institutions something less than a criminal homicide can be the catalyst for tenure removal or even termination.

Despite the mislabeling by tenure opponents, tenure is not a "job for life" or a permanent position. Independent of post-tenure review mechanisms, tenured professors are still subject to losing their appointments. While being awarded tenure does create a vested interest in one's position, which has aspects of an indefinite commitment, tenured faculty are subject to dismissal for what is often called "just" or "adequate" cause. If there really are deadwood faculty, as the tenure aspersion conjures, it is not their tenured status that allows them to coast on the basis of prior achievements. It is their inert departments and administrators who allow it.

The most common categories of that which qualifies as adequate or just cause are the following: 1) serious misconduct; 2) incompetence; and 3) financial exigency (emergency). Occasionally, a tenure policy might obliquely refer to that which "impairs one's usefulness" to one's college or university. For example, insubordination or actions toward colleagues that are disruptive to a college's operation can springboard into termination efforts.[132] But in light of the purpose of tenure—the preservation of academic freedom and economic security[133]—and in light of the distinct legal status tenure creates, dismissal of a tenured professor is supposed to occur after higher procedural protections have been followed than would be required for nontenured faculty. Those protections vary based on the jurisdiction and whether the professor works for a public institution (where constitutional notions of due process apply in addition to any contractual promises) or for a private one (where those protections start and end with applicable tenure policies).

When courts are faced with lawsuits brought to challenge the dismissal of a tenured faculty member, they generally take a hands-off approach to the substantive reasons for termination and consider only if the decision was arbitrary or not supported by "substantial evidence," which a US Supreme Court case defined as "relevant evidence as a reasonable mind might accept as adequate to support a conclusion."[134] But whether the required procedure was followed prior to termination is much more subject to judicial review.

Before going into the legal analysis on dismissing tenured faculty, it should be stated that moving a tenured professor out of his department, including because of interpersonal conflict, is not an action that affects the professor's tenure status—unless enforceable policy says otherwise. Therefore, it is unwise to sue over that kind of personnel decision, claiming one's tenure rights have been improperly abrogated. In a case on point from a public university in Alabama, where the court noted that the mechanical-engineering department "had been subject to factionalism and in-fighting" for over a decade,[135] the administration finally transferred certain tenured members of that department to other engineering departments. No affected faculty member lost any pay or rank. In affirming the university's right to separate the tenured faculty, the federal court of appeals said no liberty interest or property interest protected by the Fourteenth Amendment's Due Process Clause was implicated.[136]

SERIOUS MISCONDUCT

Unless a tenure policy defines or provides examples of what constitutes "serious misconduct," an accusation of such behavior is necessarily guided by ad hoc considerations at the institutional level and by judicial analysis in any future litigation. Take, for example, the case discussed in Chapter 3, which is on academic freedom, where the employment of a tenured professor of education at a state university in Louisiana was terminated for various coarse statements she made in class and at student-teaching evaluations. She considered her in-class statements about sex to be something less than a violation of the university's sexual-harassment policy; nonetheless, students filed complaints in which they accused her of sexual harassment. And, even though a faculty committee appointed to investigate the matter recommended that she be censured for creating what it found to be a hostile learning environment, the administration chose instead to seek termination of her employment. Throughout her appeals, all courts concluded her firing was within legal, including procedural, bounds.[137]

Academic fraud certainly qualifies as the kind of serious misconduct for which a university could seek to revoke one's tenured status or to terminate one's employment. In 2023, over ten thousand academic research journal articles were retracted.[138] While the lion's share of those retractions was sourced to journals run by one publishing company, the specter of research and publication misconduct couldn't come at a more inopportune time for an already beleaguered academia. And, as has been well noted, former presidents of Stanford and Harvard were entangled in research[139] or plagiarism[140] scandals, and a widely read, tenured Harvard Business School professor has faced multiple accusations of research misconduct or plagiarism.[141] In the following cases, courts sided with colleges or universities (including on due-process issues where the faculty worked at public institutions) that suspended or terminated the employment of tenured professors after concluding that they committed discipline-worthy misconduct:

- An English professor at a public university was suspended without pay for five days and was put on probation after he sent emails to students regarding his dissatisfaction about having to teach face-to-face classes (a COVID-19 issue). In his emails to students, he shared parts of the discordant email exchanges between his chair and him on the matter. As well, the professor was accused of failing to attend a mandatory department meeting and failure to follow a supervisor's directive—all in violation of university policy.[142]

- The employment of a criminal-justice professor at a public university was terminated after, among other things, an investigation showed that she secretly recorded confidential faculty meetings of tenured faculty and posted the recordings and transcripts on an anticorruption website that she and her husband had created. A faculty committee unanimously recommended dismissal before the chancellor did.[143]
- The employment of an engineering professor at a public university was terminated for various internal and public criticisms of the administration, including statements he made at a faculty meeting. He also was accused of creating a toxic atmosphere. A university grievance committee recommended that he be reinstated to his position, but he was fired. The court said that the professor's speech, which was criticism of management, was outside that which is protected by academic freedom.[144]
- An English professor at a private religious college was fired over an incident in which he got an ambulance for a student-athlete in his class whom the professor realized had a recent head injury. The administration concluded that the professor's help to the student somehow violated its rules on dealing with athlete injuries. Consequently, a grievance was filed against the professor, which became so rancorous that even more employment violations were assessed as a result. After the professor posted on social media his negative thoughts about the college, the die was cast, and he was fired. A jury awarded the professor $600,000 for being wrongfully fired, which the trial judge ruled was legally incorrect, setting the verdict aside. The professor then lost on appeal, wherein the court upheld the firing, saying that there was no breach of contract in his termination and that a contract would be the only source of employment rights afforded to a professor at a private institution.[145]
- A journalism professor at a state university was fired after refusing to resign, following an investigation that concluded with an accusation that he gamed the system and violated university policy in how he profited from sales of a textbook that he had authored and that was required in his classes. A faculty committee investigating the matter recommended that the professor not be fired. In affirming the dismissal of the professor's suit against the university, the court noted that he was given the due process that his status as a public-university tenured professor required. It also ruled against his First Amendment argument that his speech (meaning, his defense) in reaction to being accused of financial misbehavior was a matter of public concern.[146]
- A criminal-law professor at a private law school was fired after refusing to teach constitutional law instead of criminal law, but she was not accorded a faculty vote on the firing, as required by employee policy. A federal judge ordered the law school to comply with its own policy and a faculty conference was convened, and it concurred with the original decision to fire her. On appeal, the terminated professor lost the argument that the school's tenure

statements ensured her more process than she was given. The court not only said that the professor only had tenure process rights that were found in her employment contract but also said that the law school's handbook policies on tenure were written in a way that these policies only granted tenured faculty one-year employment contracts. The handbook did not, by its language, promise continued employment.[147] (One wonders if the other tenured faculty realized what it meant to be tenured at that law school before this case.)

As was stated earlier in the chapter on tenure-denial litigation, there are more cases where suspended or fired tenured professors lose their lawsuits (including having them dismissed) than cases where they win them. That could be because the initial decisions to sanction or terminate were not unreasonable or because many tenured faculty lack the kinds of employment protections that anti-tenure proponents claim keep tenured faculty forever ensconced. But, in a case where a tenured professor of accounting at a public university in Ohio won his lawsuit after being suspended without pay for making a horribly uncouth joke in class, it was the university's tenure policy that saved the day for him. After chastising a student who arrived for his class fifteen minutes before it ended, the professor remarked that he should shoot all his students with his AK-47. Some students in the class felt threatened and alerted the administration about what was said. After being suspended without pay for the remainder of the semester for violating the university's antiviolence policy (and after a faculty panel concluded that the professor should not have been suspended), the professor sued, and he was awarded backpay for being wrongly treated for what the court called a one-time lapse in judgment. The university appealed and there the court upheld the professor's legal victory, noting that the university violated its charter on tenure rights and disciplinary processes by suspending him without pay. That charter stated, among other things, that, even if a tenured professor was fired for adequate cause, the professor was still to be paid for an additional academic year.[148]

A male photography professor at a private university in Pennsylvania was fired after being accused of sexual harassment by a female professor at another college who contacted the male professor's university to say that, twenty-one months earlier, he, uninvited, kissed her when they greeted each other at a conference. A day after the first complaint was filed, another woman accused the professor of giving her his hotel key, instead of his business card, when they were at a conference in the same month as the incident that formed the basis for the first accusation occurred. The professor denied the accusations but was fired without a hearing. He sued his former university, his female supervisor, and the accusing professor for defamation. And he also alleged a Title IX violation consisting of anti-male bias in the sexual-harassment investigation. His lawsuit survived an attempt to have it dismissed.[149]

There are occasions where courts express respect for the rights a tenured faculty acquires but still rule against a dismissed professor. In one case, a tenured journalism professor at a private college in Illinois was fired after being found to have plagiarized substantial portions of a textbook while writing his own textbook. While the professor denied that the plagiarism was intentional, the professor's employment was nonetheless terminated after he refused to resign. The professor sued the college and key administrators for, among other things, breach of contract. While rejecting the college's argument that its tenure policy was not subject to judicial review, the court still found that the decision to terminate the professor's employment rather than to impose a smaller sanction (as the tenure policy encouraged in "ordinary circumstances") was still within the bounds of the policy's language.

THE TAKEAWAY

A tenured professor may be suspended or fired for serious misconduct, provided the enforceable tenure-policy language has been followed, including rights for faculty committees to be involved or the rights of the professor to internally appeal the decision. While a court has limited discretion to intervene, it still could declare that a sanction was arbitrary or that a public-university professor's property rights in tenure were taken without the needed due-process protection.

INCOMPETENCE

Because tenure comes with an expectation of continued employment, for a tenured professor to be dismissed for adequate cause on the grounds of incompetence, the underlying transgression is likely that which could also fairly be categorized as serious misconduct. That Venn diagram would have considerable overlap. Incompetence might also be categorized in tenure policies, particularly in a post-tenure review system. There, findings of incompetence could be based on repeated failures to meet publication or grant funding standards or even unsatisfactory performance in attaining teaching evaluation benchmarks.

Being fired for incompetence still requires that the tenured professor be accorded the procedural protections required in contractually binding tenure policy and—in the case of a tenured professor at a public institution, where tenure is a property interest—sufficient due-process protections. In the following cases, professors who were fired for incompetence issues lost their legal battles.

- A medical-school professor at a state university failed to meet annual performance requirements in research (which included securing grants) for three successive years. A faculty committee was convened, and it suggested no discipline or remedial action because of the professor's service and outstanding teaching performance, which included earning a prestigious, national teaching award. Three more successive years of unsatisfactory research led to her dismissal on the grounds of serious misconduct, rather than incompetence. The professor alleged that her research deficiencies were caused by her chair's attempts at sabotaging her work; this allegation was part of a sex-discrimination claim she made in response. Her case was dismissed on all grounds, including breach of contract related to her tenure status.[150]

- A physics professor at a public university was reprimanded for plagiarism, and the next year he was charged with incompetence related to his teaching after students filed a complaint about his teaching, which included accusations of harassment. A faculty committee concurred with the accusations, and a second faculty committee appointed for the dismissal proceedings concluded dismissal was warranted on the grounds of incompetent teaching, which the committee thought impaired his usefulness to the university. All administrators recommended the professor's dismissal, and all courts involved thought there was "substantial evidence" of incompetence, supporting the termination decision.[151]
- A commercial-arts professor at a public college disclosed confidential information about a student in front of a class and made a required apology that was considered inappropriate, leading to her dismissal for cause (which was defined in the tenure policy). During the investigation, additional charges of teaching incompetence were raised, including what was called an inappropriate pattern of behavior while assisting students and an accusation that she ended a course one month prior to the semester's conclusion. Two faculty committees recommended that she not be fired, one of which concluded that the "clear and convincing evidence" standard hadn't been met. The administration disagreed with those recommendations, concluded that the faculty committees disregarded key evidence, and she was dismissed. On appeal, the court ruled that just because faculty committees and administrators placed differing weights on the evidence collected didn't show unreasonableness in the decision to fire the professor.[152]
- An engineering professor at a public university received three consecutive years of unsatisfactory performance reviews in a post-tenure review system where two consecutive years constituted incompetence worthy of discipline, including discharge. His teaching was rated poorly, as was his service; he was considered so disruptive in working with colleagues that they believed the effective operation of the department was impaired. Upon being fired, he sought a faculty committee review, which disagreed with the conclusion that he was an incompetent teacher but concluded, based on a tight majority vote, that he was incompetent in service. On appeal from his dismissal, the court

concluded there was substantial evidence showing his behavior (and lack of collegiality) constituted incompetence.[153]

THE TAKEAWAY

A tenured professor may be suspended or fired for incompetence, provided the enforceable tenure-policy language has been followed, including rights for faculty committees to be involved or the rights of the professor to internally appeal the decision. Findings of incompetence could be based on repeated failures to meet publication or grant funding standards or even unsatisfactory performance in maintaining teaching evaluation benchmarks. While courts have limited discretion to intervene, they still could declare that a sanction was arbitrary or that a public-university professor's property rights in tenure were taken without the needed due-process protection.

FINANCIAL EXIGENCY

The demographics are not favorable: the college-age population is shrinking,[154] and college enrollment has been declining since 2010.[155] With enrollment decreases come budget shortfalls. Whether in a household or in an organization, there are two responses to a cash crunch: raise revenue or cut expenses. Many colleges and universities have been dealing with these problems by creating new programs and degrees that draw more students, but cutting faculty is always an unfortunate option. These RIFs (reductions in force) can affect tenured faculty as well, despite the economic security advantage tenure provides. But tenured faculty whose employment has been terminated due to a financial exigency are not without legal recourse. In those instances, the chance of success depends first on the institution's tenure policy, which establishes what tenure provides with respect to economic security. If there is no enforceable language that protects tenured faculty over other faculty or that describes how a RIF decision is justly to be made, another legal tactic would be to argue that the administration failed to demonstrate the existence of the kind of financial emergency that would permit tenured faculty to be dismissed.

A case from the 1970s illustrates the competition between the interests of a college in dire financial straits and those of tenured faculty with protected employment status. A public college in New Jersey had experienced years of declining enrollment. Consequently, the board of trustees, in conjunction with the college president, terminated the employment of thirteen tenured faculty (on one day's notice), due to financial exigency, and then announced that all remaining faculty, including remaining tenured faculty, would be working on one-year contracts. The college then hired twelve new faculty members for the upcoming academic year but said that those hirings were in response to attrition and that the new faculty members were not replacements for the fired tenured faculty. The thirteen fired tenured faculty, represented by their collective bargaining–qualified AAUP chapter, sued to get their job backs, which is a contract remedy known as "specific performance." For the court involved in the suit, the starting point was the tenure policy, which said in part, "Termination of continuous appointment because of financial exigency . . . must be demonstrably bona fide." The policy also said that new faculty couldn't be hired when there was a tenured faculty reduction, except in "extraordinary circumstances." In deciding in favor of the tenured faculty, the court noted that the college owned a large golf club that it could sell without affecting the college's operations and whose sale would greatly mitigate the financial distress that precipitated the RIF. Ultimately, the court concluded there had been no showing to the faculty that their terminations were without an alternative, and that the administration was really trying to eliminate tenure altogether. The court ordered the professors to be returned to their former positions.[156]

But, even at a public college, where due-process requirements protect tenured faculty, in the setting of RIF, the employment of a tenured faculty member can be terminated and the employment of a nontenured faculty member continued if the tenure policy doesn't elaborate on who must draw the short straw. At a public college in Colorado, a tenured professor was dismissed due to financial emergency while a nontenured department colleague was retained because the department chair thought that keeping the nontenured professor provided more curriculum flexibility. There was no dispute about the bona fide emergency or the due process afforded the professor, and the tenure policy was silent about RIF protections for tenured faculty. Despite the tenured professor's claim that there was an implied protection, the appellate court upheld her dismissal, concluding there was substantial evidence that the decision was made in good faith and was not arbitrary.[157]

You may have read this before, but tenured faculty at private colleges and universities don't have the constitution-sourced job protections that public-university faculty have, and that includes protection from termination due to low enrollment, financial exigency, or even an institutional restructuring. Consequently, legal review of tenure revocations or dismissals of tenured professors because of financial exigency are limited to whether an enforceable contract promise existed and, if so, whether it protected tenured faculty in ways that were ignored, or whether any internal review process for the decision was not substantially followed.[158] In a case from a private liberal-arts college in New York, where most of the music department's programs were eliminated due to low enrollment, tenured members of the faculty were dismissed. The dismissed tenured faculty sued, and the first court annulled their terminations. But the appellate court reversed the first court, concluding that there was nothing "arbitrary and capricious" in the college's actions.[159] Furthermore, there was no breach of contract because the key policy provision at issue only required that the college "*should consider* [emphasis added] . . . all reasonable alternatives" before eliminating tenured faculty.[160] "Should consider" is a modal verb that is nearly impossible to defeat in court.

Despite the wide berth granted to private colleges and universities in how they conduct their student and faculty affairs, they don't act freely of consequences. Recall the mention earlier in this chapter of the tenured professor at a private university who learned he was fired after his own work email's auto-reply alerted him he was no longer employed. While the university's given reason for his termination was "for serious breaches of the individual's duty to the institution,"[161] the professor believed he was fired in retaliation for his accusations that the president and the board had abused their power in handling sexual-misconduct allegations made against several board members. The professor, who is Jewish, also alleged he was a victim of religious harassment.[162] Two years later, the college settled the matter by agreeing to pay the professor more than one million dollars.[163]

THE TAKEAWAY

A tenured professor may be fired because of a financial exigency, including declining enrollment or an institutional restructuring. While a court has limited discretion to intervene, it still could find that contractually enforceable policies on RIFs for tenured faculty were disregarded or that a public-university professor's property rights in tenure were taken without the needed due-process protection.

Final Takeaways

- A catalyst for tenure in America was political firings of professors, which impelled educational leaders and organizations in the early twentieth century to advocate for probationary periods of faculty employment leading to tenure. The AAUP first analogized professors and their need for tenure to federal judges, whose independence is secured by judicial tenure. The AAUP's "1940 Statement of Principles on Academic Freedom and Tenure" served as the primary advocation for tenure, and it provides a structure for how colleges and universities can establish tenure.

- The tenure process is a multilayered review of a tenure-track professor's record of accomplishments during their professor's probationary period. Upon submitting the tenure dossier to the department, various tenure review committees, other faculty committees, and administrators review the tenure case and issue responsive letters that recommend in favor of or against granting tenure. Those letters, along with the tenure case, are submitted through higher levels of review, unless institutional policy dictates that the failure to achieve a committee's majority recommendation or the failure to receive an administrator's recommendation ends the process. If the needed positive evaluations have been made, a recommendation for tenure is generally placed in the hands of the institution's governing board, whose decision is conclusive.
- A promoted professor who is nontenured still lacks the independence and job security that is endowed to a tenured professor; this is especially true for faculty who work at religious educational institutions and qualify for the "ministerial exception."
- Post-tenure review is a structure, whereby tenured faculty undergo periodic performance evaluations, including of their scholarly activities and teaching, the outcome of which ultimately can lead to termination decisions for unsatisfactory performance. If your college or university has a post-tenure policy, read it carefully to see what inflection points are embedded that allow for or trigger a termination process. Likewise, do the same thing if you work at a public institution and your state has post-tenure review legislation or regulations. Finally, if your college or university is in the process of initiating a post-tenure review policy, consider how your participation could help ensure fair-mindedness in the details.
- Part-time faculty are at-will employees, which means they can be dismissed for any reason not covered by an at-will exclusion, such as those protections provided by antidiscrimination laws, including statutes that protect employees against retaliatory firings in certain instances. Likewise, the legal protections of academic freedom apply to part-time faculty.
- Full-time faculty at public colleges or universities who are not tenured do not have a property interest in their employment, whereas tenured faculty do. That means nonrenewal of their employment contracts is generally not a litigation-worthy event, provided the procedural boxes have been ticked. If those faculty are accused of wrongdoing, and that is the reason for being fired or nonrenewed, they are entitled to some due process, allowing them to present a rebuttal to the charges. And, if nontenured faculty at public institutions can show they were fired in violation of antidiscrimination laws or a constitutionally protected right, including due-process rights, they would be able to sue.
- Full-time faculty at private colleges and universities do not have the employment-related constitutional protections that faculty at public institutions have. But antidiscrimination legislation can protect those faculty who have

been wrongfully fired, including faculty at religious institutions if those faculty are not covered by the "ministerial exception." Due to US Supreme Court case law, collective bargaining rights for private institution faculty are severely limited.

- Read your faculty handbook to see if it has preamble language disavowing that the handbook is creating contract rights. If so, that language likely would be found by a court to be conclusive and the handbook would be found not to create binding expectations concerning continued employment. Even statements that refer to a handbook as a general guide can result in the handbook being found to lack contractual enforceability.
- A faculty handbook can create contractually enforceable protections for faculty when its language is affirming enough that it is reasonable for faculty to rely on those promises, particularly where the administration has historically adhered to them.
- Changes to policies in faculty handbooks that adversely affect the status of tenured faculty implicate their vested rights, and such policies generally cannot be unilaterally altered insofar as they apply to those who were tenured before the policy change.
- Courts rarely overturn a tenure-denial decision because of the longstanding legal tradition of nonintervention in matters that are considered to belong to the academic community. However, a lawsuit based on the denial of tenure is viable where evidence demonstrates that the decision was arbitrary or capricious, where the tenure review process was not followed, or where a tenure candidate was subject to illegal discrimination. But winning a tenure-denial lawsuit means getting a new tenure application review, not being granted court-awarded tenure.
- To win a tenure-denial lawsuit, or at least to prevent it from being dismissed, on the legal grounds that the tenure-review process was arbitrary and capricious or was conducted in bad faith requires more than showing the process or decision-making was subject to disagreement. One must show that the decision-making process lacked rationality or that it was tainted by the involvement of decision-makers who had a conflict of interest.
- Winning a tenure-denial case based on breach of contract, or at least preventing it from being dismissed, requires showing that contractually enforceable tenure-review policies were not followed in a material way, including arbitrarily and capriciously. That can include evaluating a tenure case based on the wrong standards.
- Winning a tenure-denial case based on a violation of civil rights or civil liberties, or at least preventing it from being dismissed, requires showing that the stated reason for denying tenure to the candidate was really a pretext for an unlawful reason, such as discrimination or retaliation for engaging in a protected activity.

- A tenured professor may be suspended or fired for serious misconduct, provided the enforceable tenure-policy language has been followed, including rights for faculty committees to be involved or the rights of the professor to internally appeal the decision. While a court has limited discretion to intervene, it still could declare that a sanction was arbitrary or that a public-university professor's property rights in tenure were taken without the needed due-process protection.
- A tenured professor may be suspended or fired for incompetence, provided the enforceable tenure-policy language has been followed, including rights for faculty committees to be involved or the rights of the professor to internally appeal the decision. Findings of incompetence could be based on repeated failures to meet publication or grant funding standards or even unsatisfactory performance in maintaining teaching benchmarks. While a court has limited discretion to intervene, it still could declare that a sanction was arbitrary or that a public-university professor's property rights in tenure were taken without the needed due-process protection.
- A tenured professor may be fired because of financial exigency, including declining enrollment or an institutional restructuring. While a court has limited discretion to intervene, it still could find that contractually enforceable policies on RIFs for tenured faculty were disregarded or that a public-university professor's property rights in tenure were taken without the needed due-process protection.

How Did You Make the Calls?

1 – The Case of the Handbook Section Switcheroo

In this case, after the Colorado legislature reclassified the Metropolitan State College of Denver (now called Metropolitan State University of Denver) and created a new board of trustees in 2002, within months the board revised the faculty handbook, effectively neutering tenure without eliminating it. The former version of the faculty handbook, in existence since 1994, defined the meaning of tenure and said that tenure was granted to reinforce "the concept of academic freedom." It also said that the employment of tenured faculty could only be terminated for cause or due to a RIF. The relevant section in the handbook, on grounds for termination, included the RIF policy, and it gave priority to tenured faculty over nontenured faculty. It also said that, if tenured faculty were laid off, "every reasonable effort" would be made to relocate them in the college. As well, the 1994 handbook had layers of procedure and an appeal process for situations of termination for cause or in a RIF situation. The 2003 handbook eliminated those parts and replaced them with a section giving the president the power to decide which faculty members' employment would be terminated in an RIF, based on various factors that included tenure. That section also said that the "primary consideration shall be the maintenance of a sound and balanced educational program." The new RIF policy also drastically cut back on the procedure to be followed, including appeals, when faculty are chosen for termination. Five tenured faculty members and the Colorado Teachers Federation brought a suit, seeking an injunction (a court order telling a party to stop or start doing something) and a declaration that the new handbook breached their employment contract and violated their due-process rights. Essentially, the faculty argued that the 1994 employee handbook vested them with tenure rights that couldn't be retroactively and unilaterally altered by the 2003 handbook and its RIF policy. (A vested right is one that presently exists and can't be taken away without the owner's consent.) The board responded that it had the legislatively granted authority to revise the 1994 handbook in the best interests of the university, including its having financial flexibility to serve the needs of its diverse student body. Part of the evidence in the litigation included the testimony of a tenure expert who testified that the 2003 handbook revisions violated the history of and the cultural expectations created by tenure, including those created by AAUP policy statements. In response, the board argued there was no evidence that the tenured faculty expressly relied on the 1994 handbook or that it was made with consideration of the AAUP's statements.

Can this revised faculty handbook unilaterally remove employment protections for tenured faculty in instances of reductions in force?

Decision: After going through multiple rounds of litigation, the Colorado District Court ultimately concluded that tenured faculty were in possession of vested rights to priority employment status in the 1994 faculty handbook, and that the 2003 handbook changes violated Colorado's constitution, which prohibited governmental actors from retroactively changing contractual obligations.[164] Two years earlier, the Colorado Court of Appeals decided that the faculty's procedural rights were violated by the 2003 handbook changes concerning appealing a RIF decision because under the new policy, the college president was given authority to initiate faculty reductions, while at the same time also possessed the final authority in a very limited internal appeal about whether those decisions were correct.[165]

That court then sent the case back to the trial court to determine if the 1994 handbook granted vested rights to tenured faculty over RIF-related and other terminations. In analyzing whether tenured faculty had vested rights to being prioritized over nontenured faculty in a RIF, the court conducted a balancing test, weighing the public interest in academic freedom against the public interest in flexibility in staffing decisions. Finding that the scales weighed in favor of academic freedom, which is the purpose of tenure, the court noted that the 1994 handbook represented the reasonable expectations of tenured faculty. The court found support for its conclusion in the acknowledged tradition and custom of tenure in America, which creates a special category of faculty whose employment status is prioritized over that of nontenured faculty. That tradition had been attested to by the faculty-plaintiffs' tenure expert. Consequently, those who were tenured before 2003 had vested rights that couldn't be retroactively impaired.

2 – The Case of the Division Chair's Tenure-Conclusive, One-Time Teaching Review

At Alfred University in New York, a tenure-track professor of instrumental music found himself in a "do as I say, not as I do" loop, when his division chair recommended that he not be granted tenure because the chair expressed discontent with the professor's teaching. But, after five years in the tenure-track system, his chair had never reviewed or observed his teaching, despite conducting annual evaluations of the professor. The chair did conduct one teaching evaluation in the professor's sixth year, the year in which the professor's tenure status was to be decided. The faculty handbook on the tenure process stated "proven teaching performance" is the primary condition for granting tenure. Other listed factors for consideration include scholarly activity, advising of students, and participation in campus activities. Tenure-track faculty are to be annually reviewed by their division chair, and the criteria for annual reviews are the same as for granting or denying tenure. The handbook also states that chairs shall, through class visitations, stay up-to-date on the teaching capabilities of tenure-track faculty. In the year when a decision about a professor's tenure status is to be made, the handbook requires the division chair to provide a written evaluation to the promotion and tenure committee. In this case, the chair's recommendation was based on student evaluations of the professor's teaching, the comments of colleagues, and the one teaching evaluation that the chair conducted. The chair's evaluation was positive in certain areas, but the negative recommendation was based on the professor's teaching weaknesses. The promotion and tenure committee (which included the dean) also recommended against granting tenure, based on lack of teaching abilities, and that decision was upheld by the provost. After losing his administrative appeals, the professor sought a review by the faculty council. It concluded that the professor had procedural grounds for his appeal because the chair had only reviewed his teaching one time, and that was in the year during which the tenure decision was to be made. Moreover, the chair didn't review the music teaching that comprised two thirds of the professor's teaching load. It also concluded that the professor was denied access to certain parts of his employment file. The promotion and tenure committee rejected the faculty council's recommendation, leading to the professor's lawsuit, alleging breach of contract and seeking a judicial annulment of the tenure denial.

Did the chair (and other decision-makers) act arbitrarily and capriciously in denying tenure to a professor, based on one teaching evaluation, where teaching performance was the primary consideration?

Decision: The New York Supreme Court, Alleghany County (this is a trial court, despite its name), ruled that Alfred University violated its tenure policy in an arbitrary and capricious manner. The court nullified the decision to deny the professor tenure and ordered the university to conduct a de novo tenure review.[166] At the outset, the court acknowledged that courts should use the greatest caution and restraint in entering into areas as sensitive as academic appointments and tenure controversies. Nevertheless, the court believed it was appropriate here because Alfred University didn't comply with its own rules, as stated in the handbook, on how to fairly evaluate a candidate for tenure. Because the handbook calls for "classroom visitations" (plural) of faculty in a setting where teaching is the primary consideration for tenure, the chair's inaction over the years in conducting the needed evaluations and then basing his negative decision on one class visit was arbitrary and capricious.[167] But—and this is a significant point—it ruled that the university did not commit breach of contract in refusing to award tenure to the professor, meaning that he wasn't granted any damages (money) for the mistreatment.

3 – The Case of the Terminally Tardy Tenured Professor

In this case, a tenured professor in the African American and African studies department at the University of Minnesota was fired for cause. This professor's colleagues, who assessed the tenured professor's performance in conjunction with the university's tenure policy, expressed enough dissatisfaction with the professor's performance that the dean initiated termination proceedings. Per the university policy, termination of a tenured faculty member's employment is appropriate for causes "which seriously interfere with the person's capacity competently to perform his duties, or with his usefulness to the University." After an eight-day hearing, a faculty panel recommended the professor be terminated. The gravamen of the charges and evidence presented was that the professor rarely showed up to class on time, and, when he wasn't tardy, he wasn't there, sporting a 35 percent absentee rate. He didn't keep his office hours, sporadically attended faculty meetings, and left meetings early. In one of his classes, only six of twenty-two students received a grade, and many students were none too pleased that a teaching assistant did much of the teaching. Other evidence presented showed that the professor was often ill-prepared for class, taught in a disorganized way, and failed to acquaint students with the course requirements. Colleagues testified that he had been cavalier about meeting his responsibilities for quite some time and that they believed that the cause of his behavior was his extensive consulting activities. Ultimately, all the administrative boxes were checked, and the tenured professor was fired, whereupon he filed a lawsuit seeking reinstatement to his faculty position, alleging racial discrimination and that his due-process rights were violated.

Based on the tenure policy regarding removal for cause, does the evidence presented warrant the firing of a tenured professor?

Decision: After a trial held without a jury (a "bench trial"), a federal district court judge ruled in favor of the university on all counts.[168] As to the racial-discrimination claim, the court found it to be "wholly unsupported," noting that Black members of the department voted to remove him. The court ruled that the evidence presented of the professor's poor attention to his teaching responsibilities and of his lack of timeliness sufficiently showed that the university faculty panel and the decision-makers all acted permissibly. Even though the professor argued at trial that the evidence presented against him at the university level was mostly hearsay (an out-of-court statement used as evidence to prove a fact), the judge noted the rules of the university's senate judiciary committee allowed hearsay to be presented. Furthermore, other evidence presented corroborated whatever may have been hearsay. Despite the professor accusing the dean of treating him unfairly, the judge had as evidence the statement of the initial faculty panel, which said the dean might have been accused of administrative negligence if he hadn't taken action against the professor. The extent to which the university followed its policy on conducting a formal hearing, as well as having various forms of review, showed there was no violation of the professor's due-process rights. According to the court, the record clearly showed the tenured professor was fired "not because of his race, but because he wasn't doing his duty."[169]

Notes

1. Tom Waits, "Step Right Up," *Small Change*, Asylum Records, 1976.

2. *Rehor v. Case Western Reserve University*, 331 N.E.2d 416 (Ohio 1975).

3. Alcino Donadel, "Tenure Takedown: What Schools—and States—Have Recently Turned against It?" *University Business*, May 1, 2023, available at *https://*universitybusiness.com/tenure-takedown-what-schools-and-states-have-recently-gone-against-it/.

4. R. P. Chait, ed., *The Questions of Tenure* (Cambridge, MA: Harvard University Press, 2002), https://doi.org/10.2307/j.ctvk12qgg.

5. Jim Wetherbe, "Does Tenure Protect Academic Freedom—or Academic Mediocrity?" *The Federalist*, May 5, 2023, available at https://thefederalist.com/2023/05/05/does-tenure-protect-academic-freedom-or-academic-mediocrity/.

6. https://www.kcbd.com/story/29129239/ttu-professor-wins-retaliation-case-against-university/.

7. *Wetherbe v. Texas Tech University System*, 699 Fed.Appx. 297 (5th Cir. 2017).

8. R. Chait, "The Future of Academic Tenure," *AGB Priorities*, 3 (spring 1995): 6.

9. Josh Moody, "New College Board Denies Tenure for 5 Professors," *Inside Higher Ed*, April 27, 2023, available at https://www.insidehighered.com/news/governance/trustees-regents/2023/04/27/new-college-board-denies-tenure-5-professors.

10. *Johns Hopkins University v. Ritter*, 689 A.2d 91 (Md. Ct. Spec. App. 1997); *Cohen v. Board of Trustees of the University of Medicine and Dentistry of New Jersey*, 867 F.2d 1455 (3rd Cir. 1989).

11. *Fong v. Purdue University*, 692 F. Supp. 930 (N.D. Ind. 1988).

12. https://www.nytimes.com/2021/10/13/us/georgia-university-system-tenure.html.

13. https://www.aaup.org/news/aaup-censures-university-system-georgia.

14. https://www.chronicle.com/article/everybody-is-a-target-right-now.

15. *Porter v. Board of Trustees of North Carolina State University*, 72 F.4th 573 (4th Cir. 2023); https://www.thefire.org/news/hit-academic-freedom-fourth-circuit-holds-public-universities-can-punish-faculty-lack.

16. https://www.theguardian.com/education/2024/jan/03/bill-ackman-billionaire-attacks-claudine-gay-harvard-twitter-x; https://fortune.com/2023/12/04/harvard-whistleblower-lawsuit-disinfo-team-mark-zuckerberg-donation/.

17. https://www.insidehighered.com/news/2018/10/12/about-three-quarters-all-faculty-positions-are-tenure-track-according-new-aaup.

18. https://lipa.access.preservica.com/uncategorized/IO_521ad3ae-8eb9-4e4d-a8e3-c8e0f9123f5c/.

19. https://founders.archives.gov/documents/Jefferson/03-13-02-0311.

20. https://provost.virginia.edu/academic-policies/disciplinary-suspension-termination.

21. https://www.hetwebsite.net/het/profiles/andrews.htm#:~:text=The%20Brown%20trustees%20complained%20that,Brown%20to%20reject%20his%20resignation; John Parker, *R. L. Moore: Mathematician and Teacher* (Washington, DC: Mathematical Association of America, 2005).

22. https://archive.org/details/rlmoorémathemati0000park.

23. https://www.aaup.org/report/1940-statement-principles-academic-freedom-and-tenure.

24. Id.

25. https://www.aaup.org/article/data-snapshot-tenure-and-contingency-us-higher-education#.ZCxtQnbMI2w.

26. *Grimes v. Eastern Illinois University*, 710 F.2d 386 (7th Cir 1983).

27. https://www.washingtonpost.com/news/grade-point/wp/2016/09/01/this-college-professor-was-denied-tenure-his-response-a-hunger-strike/; https://www.science.org/content/article/mit-professor-ends-hunger-strike.

28. https://www.nbcnews.com/news/us-news/after-5-years-alabama-university-killer-apologizes-first-time-n447481.

29. *Hosanna-Tabor Evangelical Lutheran Church and School v. E.E.O.C.*, 565 U.S. 171 (2012).

30. *DeWeese-Boyd v. Gordon College*, 163 N.E.3d 1000 (Mass. 2021).

31. https://www.int-res.com/articles/esep2015/15/e015p087.pdf.

32. https://www.aaup.org/report/post-tenure-review-aaup-response.

33. *Johnson v. Colorado State Board of Agriculture*, 15 P.3d 309 (Colo. App. 2000).

34. *State of Nevada, University and Community College System v. Sutton*, 103 P.3d 8 (Nev. 2004).

35. *Wiest v. State*, 78 P.3d 498 (Kan. Ct. App. 2003).

36. *Moosa v. State Personnel Board*, 102 Cal.App.4th 1379 (Cal. Ct. App. 2002).

37. Mont. Code Ann. § 39-2-904 (2023).

38. *Nichols v. University of Southern Mississippi*, 669 F.Supp.2d 684, at 694 (S.D Miss. 2009).

39. MCL 37.2202 (2024).

40. *Hardy v. Jefferson Community College*, 260 F.3d 671(6th Cir. 2001).

41. *Crenshaw v. Erskine College*, 850 S.E.2d 1 (S.C. 2020).

42. *Schovanec v. Assadi-Porter*, 2018 WL 1404494 (Tex. App. 2018); *Stanton v. Tulane University of Louisiana*, 777 So.2d 1242 (4th Cir. 2001).

43. *Board of Regents of State Colleges v. Roth*, 408 U.S. 564 (1972).

44. *Beitzell v. Jeffrey*, 643 F.2d 870 (1st Cir. 1981).

45. *Parate v. Isibor*, 868 F.2d 821 (6th Cir. 1989); *Hetrick v. Martin*, 480 F.2d 705 (6th Cir. 1973); *McElearney v. University of Illinois at Chicago Circle Campus*, 612 F.2d 285 (7th Cir. 1979).

46. *Goodisman v. Lytle*, 724 F.2d 818 (9th Cir. 1984).

47. *Lashley v. Spartanburg Methodist College*, 66 F.4th 168 (4th Cir. 2023).

48. 408 U.S. 593 (1972).

49. Id., at 2699.

50. *Hillis v. Stephen F. Austin University*, 665 F.2d 547 (5th Cir. 1982).

51. Id., at 553.

52. *Parate v. Isibor*, 868 F.2d 821 (6th Cir. 1989).

53. https://www.aaup.org/report/status-non-tenure-track-faculty.

54. *Rendell-Baker v. Kohn*, 457 U.S. 830 (1982).

55. *NCAA v. Tarkanian*, 488 U.S. 179 (1988).

56. *Richardson v. Northwest Christian University*, 242 F.Supp.3d 1132 (D. Or. 2017).

57. *Vengalattore v. Cornell University*, 2020 WL 2104706 (N.D.N.Y. 2020); *Vengalattore v. Cornell University*, 36 F.4th 87 (2nd Cir. 2022).

58. 29 U.S.C. §§ 151–169 (1947).

59. https://www.aaup.org/issues/collective-bargaining/resources-collective-bargaining.

60. 444 U.S. 672 (1980).

61. Id., at 690.

62. *Packer v. Trustees of Indiana University*, 800 F.3d 843 (7th Cir. 2015).

63. *Board of Trustees of Purdue University v. Eisenstein*, 87 N.E.3d 481(Ind. Ct. App. 2017); *Stanton v. Tulane University of Louisiana*, 777 So.2d 1242 (4th Cir. 2001); *Klin-*

gler v. University of Southern Mississippi, 612 Fed.Appx. 222 (5th Cir. 2015); *Martin v. State University of New York*, 704 F.Supp.2d 202 (E.D.N.Y. 2010).

64. *Spular v. Pickar*, 958 F.2d 103 (5th Cir. 1992).

65. *Zuelsdorf v. University of Alaska, Fairbanks*, 794 P.2d 932 (Alaska 1990).

66. *Taggart v. Drake University*, 549 N.W.2d 796 (Iowa 1996).

67. *Zimmerer v. Spencer*, 485 F.2d 176 (5th Cir.), abrogated on other grounds by *Carey v. Piphus*, 435 U.S. 247 (1978).

68. *Byrne v. Yale University*, 450 F.Supp.3d 105 (D. Conn. 2020).

69. *Halper v. University of the Incarnate Word*, 90 S.W.3d 842 (Tex. App. 2002).

70. *Mawakana v. Board of Trustees of the University of the District of Columbia*, 113 F.Supp.3d 340 (D.D.C. 2015).

71. *Mawakana v. Board of Trustees of the University of the District of Columbia*, 926 F.3d 859 (D.C. Cir. 2019).

72. *Greene v. Howard University*, 412 F.2d 1128 (D.C. Cir. 1969).

73. *Saxe v. State Board of Trustees of Metropolitan State College of Denver*, 2009 WL 3485976 (D. Col. 2009).

74. Id.; *Zuelsdorf v. University of Alaska, Fairbanks*, 794 P.2d 932 (Alaska 1990).

75. *Wilson v. Clark Atlanta University*, 794 S.E.2d 422 (Ga. Ct. App. 2016).

76. *Wartis v. Trustees of Tufts College*, 228 N.E.3d 1163 (Mass. 2024).

77. Id.

78. *Monaco v. New York University*, 204 A.D.3d 51 (N.Y. App. Div. 2022).

79. *Haynes v. Indiana University*, 902 F.3d 724 (7th Cir. 2018).

80. *Loebl v. New York University*, 255 A.D.2d 257 (N.Y. App. Div. 1998).

81. *Vengalattore v. Cornell University*, 161 A.D.3d 1350 (N.Y. App. Div. 2018).

82. *Lill v. The Ohio State University*, 132 N.E.3d 149 (Ohio Ct. App. 2019).

83. *University of Baltimore v. Iz*, 716 A.2d 1107 (Md. App. Ct. 1998).

84. *Haynes v. Indiana University*, 902 F.3d 724 (7th Cir. 2018).

85. *Bresnick v. Manhattanville College*, 864 F.Supp. 327 (S.D.N.Y. 1994).

86. D. D. Dawson, E. Morales, E. C. McKiernan, L. A. Schimanski, M. T. Niles, and J. P. Alperin, "The Role of Collegiality in Academic Review, Promotion, and Tenure," *PloS One* 17, no. 4 (April 6, 2022), e0265506, https://doi.org/10.1371/journal.pone.0265506.

87. https://www.aaup.org/report/collegiality-criterion-faculty-evaluation.

88. *Porter v. Board of Trustees of North Carolina State University*, 72 F.4th 573 (4th Cir. 2023).

89. *Loebl v. New York University*, 255 A.D.2d 257 (N.Y. App. Div. 1998).

90. *Vengalattore v. Cornell University*, 161 A.D.3d 1350 (N.Y. App. Div. 2018).

91. *Chu v. Jones*, 151 A.D.3d 1341 (N.Y. App. Div. 2017).

92. *University of Baltimore v. Iz*, 716 A.2d 1107 (Md. App. Ct. 1998).

93. *Megill v. Board of Regents of the State of Florida*, 541 F.2d 1073 (5th Cir. 1976).

94. *Sackman v. Alfred University*, 717 N.Y.S.2d 461 (2000).

95. *Craine v. Trinity College*, 791 A.2d 518 (Conn. 2002).

96. Id.

97. Id., at 538.

98. *Sackman v. Alfred University*, 717 N.Y.S.2d 461 (2000).
99. *Lill v. The Ohio State University*, 2016-Ohio-5502, Case No. 2015-00387 (July 12, 2016).
100. *Lill v. The Ohio State University*, 132 N.E.3d 149 (Ohio Ct. App. 2019).
101. *Bennett v. Wells College*, 219 A.D.2d 352 (N.Y. App. Div. 1996).
102. https://www.newspapers.com/article/the-ithaca-journal-diane-in-bonnie-benne/16992253/.
103. *Roklina v. Skidmore College*, 268 A.D.2d 765 (N.Y. App. Div. 2000).
104. *Beville v. University of South Dakota/South Dakota Board of Regents*, 420 N.W.2d 9 (S.D. 1988); *Stensrud v. Mayville State College*, 368 N.W.2d 519 (N.D. 1985).
105. *Teuscher v. CCB-NWB. LLC*, 437 F.Supp.3d 849 (E.D. Wash. 2020).
106. *Howard University v. Roberts-Williams*, 37 A.3d 896 (D.C. Cir. 2012).
107. *Craine v. Trinity College*, 791 A.2d 518, at 540 (Conn. 2002).
108. *Haynes v. Indiana University*, 902 F.3d 724, at 734 (7th Cir. 2018).
109. *Harel v. Rutgers, State University*, 5 F.Supp.2d 246 (D.N.J. 1998).
110. *Haynes v. Indiana University*, 902 F.3d 724 (7th Cir. 2018).
111. Id., at 735.
112. *Namenwirth v. Board of Regents of University Wisconsin System*, 769 F.2d 1235 (7th Cir. 1985).
113. Id., at 1251.
114. *Sweeny v. Board of Trustees of Keene State College*, 569 F.2d 169 (1st Cir. 1980).
115. *Brown v. Sessoms*, 774 F.3d 1016 (D.C. Cir. 2014).
116. https://law.udc.edu/?s=stephanie+brown.
117. *Staub v. Proctor Hospital*, 562 U.S. 411 (2011).
118. *Sizyuk v. Purdue University*, 656 F.Supp.3d 796, at 809 (N.D. Ind. 2023).
119. https://www.purdueexponent.org/city_state/article_410ba2d8-b704-11ee-907c-ab51aced881c.html.
120. https://www.purdueexponent.org/campus/article_2c2ee61e-bd20-11ee-ba6b-e7deeb847999.html.
121. *Sadid v. Vailas*, 936 F.Supp.2d 1207 (D. Idaho 2013).
122. *Connick v. Myers*, 461 U.S. 138 (1983).
123. *Jacobs v. Meister*, 775 P.2d 254 (N.M. Ct. App. 1989).
124. *Byrne v. Yale University, Inc.*, 450 F.Supp.3d 105 (D. Conn. 2020).
125. Id., at 121.
126. Id., at 125.
127. *Nelatury v. Pennsylvania State University*, 633 F.Supp.3d 716 (W.D. Pa. 2022).
128. William Shakespeare, *The Merry Wives of Windsor* (1602).
129. https://www.christianity.com/wiki/christian-life/what-does-it-mean-cleanliness-is-next-to-godliness.html.
130. https://poetsandquants.com/2023/08/29/if-harvard-succeeds-in-revoking-francesca-ginos-tenure-it-would-be-history-making/?pq-category=business-school-news.
131. J. Fishman, "Tenure and Its Discontents: The Worst Form of Employment Relationship Save All Others," *Pace Law Review* 21, no. 1 (2000), https://digitalcommons.pace.edu/cgi/viewcontent.cgi?article=1250&context=plrE.; J. Kahn Jr., *Harvard: Through Change and through Storm* (New York: W. W. Norton & Company,1968).

132. *Phillips v. State Bd. of Regents of State University and Community College System of State of Tenn.*, 863 S.W.2d 45 (Tenn. 1993).

133. *Rehor v. Case Western Reserve University*, 331 N.E.2d 416 (Ohio 1975).

134. *Consolidated Edison Co. v. NLRB*, 305 U.S. 197, 229 (1938).

135. *Maples v. Martin*, 858 F.2d 1546 (11th Cir. 1988).

136. Id.

137. *Buchannan v. Alexander*, 919 F.3d 847 (5th Cir. 2019).

138. R. Van Noorden, "More than 10,000 Research Papers Were Retracted in 2023—A New Record," *Nature* 624, no. 7992 (December 2023): 479–81, doi: 10.1038/d41586-023-03974-8. PMID: 38087103.

139. https://www.npr.org/2023/07/19/1188828810/stanford-university-president-resigns#:~:text=Marc%20Tessier%2DLavigne%2C%20who%20has,taken%20from%20other%20research%20papers.

140. https://www.washingtonpost.com/education/2023/12/21/harvard-president-plagiarism-allegations/.

141. https://www.thecrimson.com/article/2024/4/11/harvard-business-gino-plagarism-allegations/.

142. *Burt v. Fuchs*, 2023 WL 4103942 (N.D. Fla. 2023).

143. *Burton v. Board of Regents of University of Wisconsin System*, 2021 WI App 74 (Wis. Ct. App. 2021).

144. *Saidid v. Vailas*, 936 F.Supp.2d 1207 (D. Idaho 2013).

145. *Crenshaw v. Erskine College*, 850 S.E.2d 1 (S.C. 2020).

146. *Ryan v. Blackwell*, 979 F.3d 519 (6th Cir. 2020).

147. *Branham v. Thomas M. Cooley Law School*, 689 F.3d 558 (6th Cir. 2012).

148. *Eckel v. Bowling Greene State University*, 974 N.E.2d 754 (Ohio Ct. App. 2012).

149. *Fogel v. University of the Arts*, 2019 WL 1384577 (E.D. Pa. March 27, 2019).

150. *Packer v. Trustees of Indiana University*, 800 F.3d 843 (7th Cir. 2015).

151. *Agarwal v. Regents of University of Minnesota*, 788 F.2d 504 (8th Cir. 1986).

152. *Peterson v. North Dakota University System*, 678 N.W.2d 163 (N.D. 2004).

153. *Bernold v. Board of Governors of University of North Carolina*, 683 S.E.2d 428 (N.C. Ct. App. (2009).

154. https://www.axios.com/2023/01/08/public-school-enrollment-decline.

155. https://nces.ed.gov/programs/digest/d22/tables/dt22_303.70.asp.

156. *American Association of University Professors, Bloomfield College Chapter v. Bloomfield College*, 322 A.2d 846 (N.J. Ch. Div. 1974).

157. *Brenna v. Southern Colorado State College*, 589 F.2d 475 (10th Cir. 1978).

158. *Hansbrough v. College of Sant Rose*, 209 A.D.3d 1168 (N.Y. App. Div. 2022).

159. Id.

160. Id., at 1171.

161. https://www.opb.org/article/2023/02/06/linfield-university-agrees-pay-fired-professor-one-million-whistelblower-settlement/.

162. https://www.chronicle.com/article/everybody-is-a-target-right-now.

163. https://www.opb.org/article/2023/02/06/linfield-university-agrees-pay-fired-professor-one-million-whistelblower-settlement/.

164. *Saxe v. State Board of Trustees of Metropolitan State College of Denver*, 2009 WL 3485976 (D. Col. 2009).

165. *Saxe v. State Board of Trustees of Metropolitan State College of Denver*, 179 P.3d 67 (Colo. App. 2007).

166. *Sackman v. Alfred University*, 717 N.Y.S.2d 461 (2000).

167. Id., at 465.

168. *King v. University of Minnesota*, 587 F. Supp. 902 (D. Minn. 1984).

169. Id., at 906.

Index

Author Biography

Kent Kauffman is an associate professor of business law in the Doermer School of Business at Purdue University Fort Wayne, where he primarily teaches business law and ethics at the undergraduate and graduate levels. He also serves as the faculty liaison for the master of business administration programs in the Doermer School of Business. He has a BA from Temple University and a JD from The Penn State University–Dickinson School of Law, and holds an Indiana law license.

In addition to having published articles in peer-reviewed journals, Kauffman is the author of *Legal Ethics* (through the third edition); is a coauthor of *Legal Terminology*; and is a contributing author for two other buisness law texts. He also is the author of the *Movie Guide for Legal Studies*, a pedagogical book for legal professors who want to utilize film scenes in their teaching or assignments. He is the recipient of multiple publication awards, including a Midwest Academy of Legal Studies in Business "Distinguished Paper Award" and a Textbook and Academic Authors Association "McGuffey Longevity Award" for *Legal Terminology*.

Kauffman is a Purdue member of Indiana University's selective, scholarly teaching community, the Faculty Academy on Excellence in Teaching (FACET). He is a proponent of and an active contributor to his campus's Center for the Enhancement of Learning and Teaching (CELT), has served CELT as an advisory board member and a teaching fellow, and has conducted multiple workshops for faculty. He has won multiple awards for his teaching, including his online teaching, at the undergraduate and graduate levels.

www.ingramcontent.com/pod-product-compliance
Ingram Content Group UK Ltd.
Pitfield, Milton Keynes, MK11 3LW, UK
UKHW021904150926
475560UK00004B/335

9 781538 197288